LAUGHING AT
NOTHING

LAUGHING AT NOTHING

Humor as a Response to Nihilism

JOHN MARMYSZ

STATE UNIVERSITY OF NEW YORK PRESS

Published by
STATE UNIVERSITY OF NEW YORK PRESS, ALBANY

© 2003 State University of New York

For information, contact State University of New York Press,
Albany, NY   www.sunypress.edu

Production, Laurie Searl
Marketing, Jennifer Giovani

Library of Congress Cataloging-in-Publication Data

Marmysz, John, 1964–
    Laughing at nothing : humor as a response to nihilism / by John Marmysz.
      p. cm.
    Includes bibliographical references and index.
    ISBN 0-7914-5839-3 (alk. paper) — ISBN 0-7914-5840-7 (pbk. : alk. paper)
    1. Nihilism (Philosophy) 2. Comic, The. I. Title.
  B828.3.M265 2003
  149'.8—dc21

                                                                    2003042561

                    10 9 8 7 6 5 4 3 2 1

Contents

ACKNOWLEDGMENTS

This work began as a doctoral dissertation written under the guidance of Professors Pablo De Greiff, Carolyn Korsmeyer, Mariam Thalos, and Henry Sussman at the University at Buffalo. Their encouragement, thoughtful comments, and enthusiasm were indispensable in allowing this book to take its present form.

I am indebted to Frances Marmysz and Juneko Robinson for their encouragement and companionship during the time that I was engaged in researching, writing, and polishing this work. They struggled along with me day after day and helped me get through some rough periods. Thanks to them I avoided becoming overwhelmed by nihilistic despair. I could not have done without their insights and willingness to listen.

Kent Daniels and Juneko Robinson provided me with helpful comments and suggestions on various drafts and also took the time to explore and discuss many of the themes and issues that are dealt with in this book. I thank both of them, as well as Dario Goykovich, for the opportunity they gave me to talk about nihilism and the nature of humor during long hikes through the hills and forests of northern California. There is much more to be said, and I hope that we can continue our hiking and philosophizing sometime in the near future.

Portions of chapters 2, 6, and 5 were presented at the ninth, twelfth, and thirteenth annual Philosophy, Interpretation and Culture Conferences held at SUNY Binghamton in 1999, 2002, and 2003 respectively. Portions of chapter 7 were presented at the Rocky Mountain Division meeting of the American Society for Aesthetics in 1999, held at St. John's College in Santa Fe, New Mexico. Part of chapter 7 appeared in *Consciousness, Literature and the Arts*, Volume 2, Number 8, December 2001. I give thanks to all of those who offered their comments and criticisms concerning these early versions of my work.

Finally, I would like to give thanks to my cats, Zeta and Dot. Their unconcern with this whole project is somehow comforting.

THE PROBLEM OF NIHILISM

> For the wise man as of the fool there is no enduring remembrance,
> seeing that in the days to come all will have been long forgotten.
> How the wise man dies just like the fool! So I hated life, because
> what was done under the sun was grievous to me; for all is vanity
> and a striving after wind.
>
> —Ecclesiastes 2:18

The problem of nihilism, as this passage from the Old Testament suggests, is nothing new. It is, in fact, a perennial concern and a source of anxiety that has had an influence upon human life and thought throughout history. A phenomenon that has affected both individuals and whole cultures, nihilism has been likened to a "malaise," a "cancer," and a "sickness," while also having been called a "divine way of thinking," and an inspiration to artists and scholars. Nihilism has been deemed both a "disease" and a "cure"; something to be feared as well as welcomed. In short, it is a phenomenon that has been considered both an evil and a good.

However, by far the most common and widely accepted understanding of nihilism today places it in the category of things to be avoided and shunned. The term has come to be used as a popular expression of ridicule or insult, though it is, even in scholarly literature, often utilized without much precision. These days, the term *nihilism* is regularly deployed as a weapon, calculated to dismiss an opponent's "overly negative" or "pessimistic" line of reasoning. Tellingly, despite the many accusations of nihilism, very few of those so charged have been eager to accept the label. The energy directed against dispelling allegations of nihilism testifies to the disturbing power of the word, yet rarely have either the attacks or their rebuttals been informed by an adept understanding of the history or philosophical ideas that accompany the word and the concepts to which it is attached. One purpose of this book is to explore and clarify these meanings.

As traditionally constituted, the problem of nihilism exhibits itself in a tendency toward despair that accompanies philosophical reflection on the discrepancy between realistically attainable accomplishment and the superlative standards that humans formulate for themselves. Simply put, the problem of nihilism asks, "Why should I strive for knowledge when certainty is never attained? How can I avoid despair when the greatest excellence eludes me? Why should I struggle to do good when in the end I, and everyone who remembers me, will die?" All human effort, nihilism incessantly torments us, is a "striving after wind." Because of the emphasis that nihilism places upon the hopelessness and vanity of life's struggles, it has often been assumed that it always necessarily leads to an attitude dominated by despair. This is untrue. A second goal of this book is to demonstrate that nihilism is compatible with, and indeed preferably accompanied by, a more well-balanced attitude that includes a sense of humor.

The two major foci of this investigation, then, are to explore the complexities and ambiguities that are involved in the concept of nihilism, ultimately with the aim of formulating a clear and philosophically adequate definition of the term; and to demonstrate that the phenomenon of nihilism may be responded to with an attitude of good humor.

The opening four chapters of this investigation pursue the first goal. Chapters 1 through 3 offer a selective historical survey of philosophers, literary figures, and political movements that have explicitly dealt with the problem of nihilism. This beginning step toward scrutinizing the phenomenon proceeds by simply presenting the problem and describing the manner in which it has been confronted in the past. I focus in these sections not necessarily upon those who have analyzed and offered scholarly studies of nihilism, but on those who have wrestled with the problem existentially, expressing their struggles passionately in their works and actions. In this manner I illustrate how the concept has evolved over time, taking on the associations that help to explain why today the term *nihilism* contains so many difficult ambiguities.

During the course of the fourth chapter I isolate the fundamental issues that are important to the problem as considered in the previous chapters and propose a richer, more complete and clear definition of nihilism than has been previously offered. Nihilism, I find, is a philosophy that rests upon three basic assumptions: (1) Humans are alienated from such perfections as absolute Being, Truth, Goodness, Justice, Beauty, etc.; (2) This circumstance of alienation is other than it ought to be; (3) There is nothing that humans can do to change this circumstance. The premises of this philosophy imply a circumstance that I call "nihilistic incongruity." Nihilistic incongruity is an incongruity between actual human capacities and the ideal standards against which those capacities are judged. In the course of clarifying this point, I contrast certain non-nihilistic thinkers with the more fully nihilistic thinkers from the first three chapters. A common misunderstanding is thus cleared up, and we discover that while many different kinds of thinkers deal with nihilistic issues, this does not mean that they themselves are nihilists.

Chapters 5 through 7 pursue this study's second focus. Having already formulated a working definition of nihilism, in these chapters I show that the phenomenon as defined does not necessarily lead to unmitigated despair. My strategy for doing so is to demonstrate that the incongruity implied by nihilism might be viewed from a perspective such that it appears to serve a constructive and useful, rather than a simply negative and destructive, purpose for nihilists. Interpreted in this manner, nihilistic incongruity is transformed into an unthreatening kind of incongruity that is compatible with an attitude of good humor.

In chapter 5, I pursue an inquiry into the experience underlying the nihilist's adherence to the premises of nihilism. What I find is that the acceptance of these assumptions derives from a sort of sublime admiration for the "highest" of ideals. This insight provides us with a point of leverage with which to separate nihilism from its association with absolute negativity and despair. The experience of nihilistic incongruity, it turns out, is not the result of a wholesale rejection of value, but of a deep, almost religious sense of respect for that which is of superlative value. In light of this ideal standard, everything that actually exists may, from one perspective, appear substandard and relatively worthless. However, as I show in chapter 6, from another perspective, this same admiration for the superlative may also confer degrees of value upon things that exist in the actual world. Our accomplishments in this world, though they are all ultimately worthless failures according to the nihilist, are judged to be so in relation to an ideal and absolute standard. Insofar as the failures of this world serve to make us mindful of our objects of highest aspiration, however, they might be thought of as possessing a degree of instrumental value. They serve to reveal something of the absolute, if only in a negative fashion. Failure, thus, might act to attune and bind nihilists into a relationship with their most supreme objects of value. In striving for the unattainable superlative and constantly failing to achieve it, nihilists might not only find an inexhaustible source of inspiration for purposeful, unending activity, but they also might succeed in cementing a relationship between themselves and that which is most valuable to them.

The seventh and final chapter examines the relationship between incongruity and humor. Not all incongruities are occasions for negative emotional reactions, and the potential usefulness of nihilistic incongruity makes it a possible candidate for a more positive psychological reception than is generally recognized. Incongruity theories of laughter and humor suggest that amusement is a natural and appropriate response to those kinds of incongruities that are understood to be unthreatening. When viewed from the perspective of usefulness, thus, nihilism may potentially be greeted with good humor.

The final chapter of this project navigates its way through the phenomena associated with laughter and humor in an attempt to isolate and identify the conditions underlying the humorous attitude. My claim is that the humorous attitude involves an ability to create and adopt novel and unexpected perspectives from which the otherwise painful, frustrating, and threatening incongruities of life may be revealed as potential objects of merriment. Humor is not simply an emotional response. Rather, it is an ability, talent, or capacity for interpreting life's incongruities in a manner that brings pleasure rather than pain to the humorist. It differs from the easy pleasures involved in enjoying a joke or a comedy in that humor takes work. The humorist has developed the capability to step outside of a rigidly self-centered and self-interested viewpoint in order to imagine the ways in which seemingly isolated and unrelated phenomena might be connected in previously unanticipated ways. This ability is associated with feelings of competency, mastery, and superiority.

In adopting a humorous attitude, an individual breaks the boundaries of those background expectations that normally constrain the way we think about a subject when we are serious. In so doing, expectations are shattered, yet they are shattered in such a manner that we are given access into a new way of regarding the world. With humor, though we abandon the usual way of looking at things, we still have an avenue of retreat open to us, and as we withdraw in this direction, we demonstrate to ourselves and others that we are strong enough and clever enough to find alternatives to our run-of-the-mill viewpoints. We exercise a degree of psychological mastery and creativity in building bridges that link the usual and the mundane with the unusual and surprising. When ready-made systems of thought are unable to account for something, it is at that point that a shift of our own perspective becomes necessary. A humorous attitude encourages us to practice becoming adept with such shifts. The development of this kind of flexibility allows us to make some sense, even if it is a comic sort of sense, out of incongruities that might otherwise remain painfully baffling, frustrating, and disillusioning.

Approaching the experience of nihilism with a humorous attitude does not serve to eliminate or do away with the nihilist's suffering, but it helps to make sense of that suffering, allowing the nihilist to endure the unavoidable frustrations of life. The authentic nihilist, as we will see, always speaks from the perspective of fatalism. Existence necessarily offers much failure and frustration. The nihilist's highest hopes are doomed to failure. Yet fatalism is not the same as determinism.[1] Though we are fated to fall short of our highest goals, this does not determine what we should do or how we should choose to live our lives. The nihilist, in claiming that our fate is unfair, unwanted, and unfavorable nevertheless need not take this as a signal that it is necessary to collapse in despair or to abdicate a passionate adherence to the highest and most unattainable ends. Rather, with humor this individual might understand life, and all of the failures that we endure during its course, as part of a comic drama that is amusing in its ultimate absurdity.

Though many individuals have speculated on the physical and psychological benefits of laughter and humor, no one has attempted systematically to apply these speculations to nihilism, the greatest spiritual concern of modern times. This book attempts to carry past discussion a step farther in this direction and to draw some previously unnoticed, and perhaps unanticipated, connections. By emphasizing those aspects of humor that are uplifting and regenerative, I shall demonstrate its power to confront and to transform the experience of nihilistic incongruity into an occasion for the pursuit of unending activity, progress, and the improvement of the human soul.

With this study I offer more than just a novel synthesis and interpretation of past thought on the topic of nihilism. I also offer a unique and sympathetic confrontation with a troubling and pervasive philosophical syndrome. While my own belief is that there is no "solution" to the problem of nihilism, I do hope to suggest a means of utilizing the despair and anxiety that is associated with the problem as a spur toward liveliness, activity, and the celebration of life. This study is, thus, not simply an abstract, academic exercise. It also aspires to offer practical suggestions for the those who are engaged in the battle with meaninglessness.

Before undertaking the substance of this investigation, I would like briefly to discuss some contemporary scholarly treatments of nihilism in order to highlight a current controversy in the field. This controversy concerns the question of whether or not the problem of nihilism is unique to a specific time in the history of the West. The literature tends to be divided into two camps. The first views nihilism as a phenomenon unique to European culture in the modern age. The other camp, in contrast, sees in nihilism a chronic danger for all humans regardless of place or time. A brief assessment of the strengths and shortcomings of these accounts will offer an appropriate introduction to some of the issues that we will be encountering and will serve to situate this book within the current debate.

Originally published in 1960, Johan Goudsblom's *Nihilism and Culture* represents one attempt to analyze nihilism as a cultural problem stemming from the West's tacit acceptance and adherence to the Socratic "truth imperative."[2] Though Goudsblom consciously seeks to avoid reducing "nihilism to a trivial abstraction,"[3] he nevertheless does focus predominately on the epistemological elements of nihilism as they are interpreted and experienced through Western culture. As a result, he tends to underemphasize nihilism's ontological, existential, ethical, and political themes, and to overemphasize nihilism as a distinctively European phenomenon.

According to Goudsblom, we can think of any culture in terms of a complicated set of "options" and "commands"[4] that shape human behavior and allow for the expression of human nature. The options and commands that a culture makes available not only define the culture itself, but shape the society and psychologies of the individuals within that culture. Goudsblom uses the example of wearing clothes to illustrate his point. The particular clothes that individuals wear in the West are largely a matter of personal choice or taste. The fashion that one follows is, thus, an option that allows for personal, individual expression, in turn contributing to the overall flavor and texture of society, which in turn influences others in their optional choices. However, it is not an option for Westerners to go around unclothed in public. There is a cultural command demanding that people wear garments of some type. Those who break such cultural commands are punished, formally or informally, and excluded from interaction with others. Cultural commands cut to the core of what defines a civilization. They are the soil that allows for human cultivation.

One of the fundamental commands that lies at the heart of Western culture, writes Goudsblom, is the "truth imperative." This imperative command can be traced all the way back to the beginning of Greek philosophy. It is operative in the efforts of the Presocratics and their attempts to find the true nature of Being behind the appearances of the world, but, according to Goudsblom, "Socrates is the first to give the truth imperative explicit expression."[5] This imperative touches upon an element that already was present in Greek culture, and it was for this reason that Socrates was, first, able to formulate the imperative and, second, able to find students receptive to his teachings. The truth imperative commands that the truth is the highest and most worthy of all pursuits. It belittles and criticizes anything that falls short of absolute certainty, demanding irrefutability as the criterion of knowledge. In accordance with this imperative, Socrates used logic and argument to expose the inconsistencies and vanity of those who pretended to wisdom, while at the same time admitting that the only thing he knew was that he knew nothing. The standards set by the truth imperative were so high that if followed faithfully, all beliefs and assertions were exposed as inadequate.

The influence of Socrates, according to Goudsblom, has been powerful in Western culture, but the ultimate implications of the truth imperative did not become fully apparent until the nineteenth and twentieth centuries with the emergence of greater democratization and individual freedom to think and formulate beliefs. This change in European society has led to the multiplication of faiths, opinions, and philosophies. The availability of these claimants to the "truth" has produced a bewildering situation. With so many beliefs to choose from, and so many arguments and counterarguments poking holes in them from all sides, modern humans are exposed in full force to the problem of nihilism. Nothing seems true, since everything is up for dispute. All beliefs are devalued when, in accord with the Socratic truth imperative, individuals uncover the contradictions and inconsistencies in and between the myriad competing systems of belief that are up for grabs. No ideas remain sacred. The solution to this situation, Goudsblom tells us, is to recognize that the truth should not be pursued at the expense of all other social and cultural commands. Sometimes the truth must be mediated by other group considerations for the sake of societal confidence and cohesion. Nihilism can be cured, then, by resisting the urge to regard the truth imperative as supreme.

Goudsblom's treatment gives a clear, sociological account of nihilism. However, the tradeoff for this clarity is an oversimplification of the subject matter. Goudsblom emphasizes nihilism as a problem of epistemology at the expense of its ontological, existential, ethical, and political themes. In fact, he classifies all but the epistemological manifestations of nihilism as "spurious" forms of the problem. "A full range of possibilities extends, then, from the most 'authentic' forms of nihilism which arise from the dilemmas of the truth imperative on the one hand to, on the other, the more 'spurious' forms assumed by the problematic when it has been assimilated into the personality as a ready-made cultural element."[6] As a consequence of his too narrow focus on the truth imperative as the core of nihilism, Goudsblom neglects to provide an adequate account of nihilism in general, but especially of those threads of nihilism that participate most heavily in the ontological and existential manifestations of the phenomenon. By his own admission, he treats nihilism solely as an "intellectual problem" and so leaves out of his account any discussion of "political terrorism and hooliganism."[7] But such an omission ignores an important and historically influential part of the phenomenon.

Furthermore, overemphasis on Greek origins tends to highlight nihilism as a distinctively European occurrence that, again, ignores important aspects of the phenomenon. "Something has changed in European culture,"[8] Goudsblom tells us, and it is due to this critical change, he thinks, that nihilism has emerged. Nihilism, he suggests, is a crisis specific to nineteenth- and twentieth-century Western European culture. However, as we will see, the eighteenth-century Germans and the nineteenth-century Russians also wrestled with nihilism. In addition, Asian thinkers have long grappled with similar issues in their religions and philosophies, and as the quote at the beginning of this introduction suggests, nihilistic worries are present even in the Old Testament. The issues and themes characterizing nihilism are not, in fact, unique to twentieth-century Europe, but are concerns cutting across geographical regions and historical periods. Focusing on the truth imperative and its formulation by Socrates tends to distort our view of the issues by limiting our field of vision to only those traditions that participate in the Greek legacy.

Goudsblom is not alone in his view of nihilism as an occurrence unique to the West. Michael Allen Gillespie also finds the roots of nihilism in the Western tradition, though he sees the problem stemming from around the late medieval and early modern period, really gaining steam with Descartes' notion of the absolute will and Fichte's extreme subjectivism. In contrast to Nietzsche, Gillespie argues that it was not the death of God, but the birth of an inscrutable and all-powerful God, leading to the emphasis of will over reason, that defines the nihilistic impulse. "The history of nihilism is the history of the development of this notion of will."[9] Unlike Goudsblom, Gillespie has a place for the movements of political nihilism in this tradition. However, like Goudsblom he overemphasizes one strand of nihilism while suppressing the significance of the others. Active, existential themes dominate Gillespie's treatment, and so nihilism is represented as a "Promethean" movement, in reference to the Greek Titan who stole fire from the gods. Again, a narrow focus on one theme in Western thought produces a clear, yet overly simplified view of the phenomenon.

In contrast to those like Goudsblom and Gillespie who present nihilism as a modern, Western occurrence, many other writers see something more universal and chronic at work. Stanley Rosen, for instance, writes, "Nihilism is a permanent danger to the human condition. . . ."[10] He sees in the phenomenon a tendency that is not unique to modern Europeans, but one that characterizes all rational, human creatures. This tendency is the desire for "complete speech." Humans, by their very natures, want to know "why" things are the way that they are. They ask questions and look for solutions to problems and puzzles. When confronted with contradictory and partial accounts of the world, the natural, human response is to try to reconcile them or look for criteria by which to dismiss the false ones. Humans are speaking animals, or, in other words, rational animals. But this rationality is inextricably bonded with desire, and so humans both need and desire justification for the way things appear to be. They try to make sense of the world, demanding explanations that satisfy their curiosities. More than this, they desire complete, fully certain, and justified explanations.[11]

The reason why humans demand justification is because they are separated from the world around them. "Men speak because they are partially detached from things and try to overcome this disjunction with a bridge of language."[12] Language and rationality are tools used to try and come into contact with and understand a world from which we are alienated. To be reunited with the ultimate, to experience reality as it is "in itself," is the supreme human goal. However, this is impossible. The nature of language and rationality is that it needs distance in order to perform its function. Bridges only work when straddling a gap, and the bridge that is language requires separation so that it may engage in "discrimination, restraints, or evaluations."[13] So, humans as a whole find themselves in a paradoxical situation. They desire a completeness in understanding that, if attained, would eradicate their very natures as reasoning animals.

Rosen draws a connection with politics and ethics. Conservative and radical political movements are both attempts to dissolve the human paradox of desire and understanding. On the one hand, conservatives try to separate philosophy from the public sphere, relegating the desire for ultimate answers and perfect understanding to the private domain of prayer and religion. Radicals, on the other hand, encourage the multiplication of philosophies in the public sphere, believing that the satisfaction of free expression will replace the desire for ultimate answers. Neither of these responses, however, is adequate according to Rosen: "[E]verything I have said is intended to show that there cannot be any final solutions to man's problems, that man is a problem (or paradox), however little this may appeal to common sense, and that to 'solve' the problem would be to dissolve man."[14] Humankind is separated from the world by language, and it is the impossible struggle to overcome language that defines the species. Action directed toward closer and closer approximations of ultimate and complete reality is a Sisyphian struggle. It is never ending, yet at each moment it is a fulfillment of human nature.

As with Albert Camus, Rosen conceives of nihilism as the desire for peace and the end of life's struggles; the end of speech. He points to the philosophies of Ludwig Wittgenstein and Martin Heidegger as two very influential nihilistic systems that, in refusing to speak rationally about foundations, reduce speech to silence. The alternative, he claims, is a return to the thoughts of Plato and Aristotle, and the Greek notion of an interrelationship between Truth and Goodness in Wisdom. Our incomplete understanding of the world only makes sense as incomplete if we have a shared notion of completeness as the criterion against which to judge all philosophical approximations. But this means that we already, at some level, have an intuition into the ultimate. This intuition is our common, shared, traditional Wisdom. Humans periodically forget this intuitive Truth, and it is then that there is a descent into nihilism, irrationality, and fragmentation. The opposite of nihilism is genuine philosophy, and philosophy may only be intelligibly pursued in the light of Wisdom, which is the nexus of Truth and Goodness. The appeals of ordinary language philosophy or Heidegger's radical historicity are aimed toward dismantling the notion of transcendent forms of Truth and Goodness, and so they also dismantle the notion of Wisdom, which in turn makes genuine philosophy impossible. There are just some things, these nihilists claim, that you can't talk about.

Rosen's account does justice to the many themes that permeate the concept of nihilism, although his solution to the problem seems hopelessly Platonic. Like Nietzsche, he looks for a subjective standpoint from which to reconcile the individual with the ultimate, but unlike Nietzsche, he seems to suggest that it is an intuition into the forms of intelligibility that will provide humans with this standpoint. It is not enough to love wisdom. Rosen wants us to believe, in addition, that we already possess wisdom. We just forget this from time to time, and it is then that nihilism rears its head. Nihilism is a constant threat to rational beings, but it may be surmounted during our most lucid moments of rationality.

Rosen is one among a whole host of contemporary authors who, contrary to Goudsblom and Gillespie, see in nihilism a perpetual threat to human well-being. "It is false, or certainly inadequate, to say that nihilism is a contingent historical event."[15] Nihilism is, on this view, one of the many dangers inherent in being human. It arises out of either human nature or the human condition. Keji Nishitani, Martin E. Marty, Michael Novak, and Cornel West all consider the problem of nihilism to be a lurking danger that breeds negativity because it threatens the human desire for certainty, meaning, hope, connectedness, and potency.[16] Though I think that these commentators have hit upon an important point in stressing the chronic nature of nihilism's dangers, I also think that they underplay the constructive and positive role of nihilism in both individual and collective human history.

Karen Carr, who seems to think of nihilism as a distinctively modern problem and not as a universal menace, comes close to recognizing the potentially positive role of nihilism's negativity. However, she still considers nihilism as "something from which we must escape."[17] Carr never produces a very satisfying definition of nihilism, though she does attempt to delineate five different themes that are often times "layered" together in the problem. "Epistemological nihilism" denies the possibility of knowledge, "alethiological nihilism" denies the reality of truth, "metaphysical nihilism" denies the world's existence, "ethical nihilism" denies the reality of moral value, and "existential nihilism" is a feeling of emptiness.[18] Carr claims that the most common sense of the term is this last one.

Carr thinks that postmodernism has succeeded in "banalizing" nihilism to the point where the themes that characterize the phenomenon are no longer regarded as a threat, but are rather greeted with "a yawn."[19] This situation, which she sees especially in the work of Richard Rorty, robs nihilism of its transformative power. Postmodernists are resigned to nihilism, and so have no motivation to create new values, truths, and meanings. She worries that this development will produce stagnation and a "reification" of the current attitude of historicism and relativism. Instead of vital and dynamic intellectual activity, "the banalization of nihilism" leads, ironically, to absolutism. It does so, according to Carr, because with the belief that all justification is in vain, the nihilist loses the desire and the need to search for absolute standards of behavior. All determinations of morality and truth reduce to matters of personal taste and community norms. Because there is no higher authority to which an appeal can be made on these issues, there is no motivation for individuals to try and responsibly seek social change through reasoned discourse and political activism. In the words of Rosen, nihilism reduces speech to silence.

My agreement extends farther than my disagreement with Carr, and I intend to develop some of the themes that she only touches upon in her book. With her, I emphasize the transformative power of nihilism, but against her I argue that the escape from nihilism is not such a self-evidently good thing. Nihilism does not ultimately have to lead to absolutism, despair, or destruction. Instead, the unpleasantness of nihilism is a potentially useful spur toward unending change, progress, and spiritual development. Against Goudsblom, Gillespie, and Carr, I claim that the symptoms of nihilism reach far beyond the modern, European experience. Nihilism, and here I agree with Rosen, constitutes a predicament lying at the very heart of the human condition. The entire fabric of human existence is woven through with a particular pattern of ontological, epistemological, existential, ethical, and political nihilistic threads. Exploring and giving voice to the form of this design is the task to be undertaken in what follows.

Perhaps the most serious shortcoming of recent scholarly treatments of nihilism is that they fail adequately to define nihilism and so they throw about the term as though any vaguely "negative" philosophy falls into this category. Too often scholars proceed to draw conclusions about nihilism itself on the basis of philosophies that are, in fact, very poor models. This has only contributed to further confusion and ambiguity. In order to truly understand the concepts behind the word, it will be necessary to embark upon our own investigation into the background of the usage of the term *nihilism*. Once we have explored the thought and intentions of those who have explicitly grappled with, and thus given shape to, the problem, we will be in a position to offer a more precise definition than has previously been attempted. Once this is accomplished it will become clear that an attitude of good humor is not as incompatible with nihilism as we have been led to believe by modern scholars. Instead of being concerned with "overcoming" nihilism, we might come to appreciate its recurrent experience as something that contributes to our ongoing spiritual education.

Let us now look at the evidence for ourselves.

Part One

SCRUTINIZING NIHILISM

Chapter One

GERMAN AND RUSSIAN NIHILISM

The urge for destruction is also a creative urge!
—Mikhail Bakunin, "Reaction in Germany"

The term *nihilism* has undergone an evolution throughout the history of its usage, and it is perhaps partly because of this growth and change that the word is, as Nietzsche writes, "ambiguous."[1] Michael Allen Gillespie points out that "the concept of nihilism has taken on a number of various and often contradictory meanings . . . ,"[2] and because of this, Johan Goudsblom admits that "it is difficult to find one's way in this maze of contradictory interpretations."[3] Given this difficult ambiguity, it is well worth our while to attempt to separate out some of the themes and motifs characterizing things "nihilistic" before grappling with the substance of this abstruse subject. In the process of briefly examining the applications of the term in various contexts and times, we will find that its meanings do tend to converge and gesture toward a number of associated issues that, when considered together, comprise a familiar pattern.

GERMAN NIHILISM

One of the first things that should be noticed about the word *nihilism* is that it is often used to do more than simply describe states of affairs. It is also frequently used to pass judgment on those conditions. "Nihilism," then, is not simply a descriptive term. It often also has an evaluative dimension.

There seems to be some dispute and disagreement in the literature as to when this term first came into use. Stephen Wagner Cho traces its first serious philosophical application to attacks on German idealism by such writers as Obereit, Jenisch, and Jacobi in the eighteenth century.[4] In this context, the term takes on a largely abusive or derogatory meaning, being intended primarily as a label of condemnation directed toward the consequences of Kant's distinction between the noumenal and the phenomenal worlds. Kant, recall, claimed that what humans can "know" is only the phenomena that arise out of interaction between the noumenal self and the noumenal world. All human knowledge is, thus, perspectival rather than a direct intuiting of "things in themselves." Though there is a "Ding an Sich," we can't know its essence. We are forever trapped in our human perspective, processing sensations through a series of categories that yield only subjective (rather than objective) certitude. Kant grants us certainty and knowledge, but only about the world of phenomena. We cannot possibly know anything about the world beyond phenomena.[5]

"The thrust of Obereit's primary critique of Kantian idealism . . . is directed towards the latter's relegation of human knowledge to the realm of phenomenal appearances . . . , which thereby leads to the eternal banishment of humanity from reality itself."[6] Obereit's reaction to Kant is to accuse him of nihilism, or of cutting humanity off from the ultimate, objective reality of the Ding an Sich. If Kant is correct, then humans must despair of anything but a subjective kind of knowledge. But this subjective knowledge, Obereit claims, is really empty and worthless, since it is isolated from the absolute reality of the extra-human world. His condemnation of Kant as a nihilist, in this early appearance of the expression, is motivated by what he sees as Kant's rejection of the possibility of true, nonsubjective, certain knowledge of ultimate reality. This epistemological alienation was felt as a moment for despair not only by Obereit but by many others as well,[7] and in the later critiques of German idealism by Jenisch and Jacobi, the use of the term *nihilism* is "almost invariably taken up as an incisive attack, as a derogatory term of censure and abuse, as an invective or polemical epithet to condemn and disparage."[8] This derisive use of the term reached an influential peak in Jacobi's *Letter to Fichte* in 1799. Following Obereit and Jenisch, Jacobi attacked the subjectivist position of the Kantians in general and the extreme brand of Fichte's absolute subjectivism in particular. According to Jacobi, idealism, by doing away with everything beyond human consciousness, transforms reality into nothing, and so he repudiates it as "nihilism."[9]

The negative or "polemical" employment of the term *nihilism* thus seems to be among its earliest usages. The charge that Kant and his followers (especially Fichte) are advocating a system of thought that leads to a kind of alienation from ultimate reality is seen by these critics as a self-evidently bad thing. Kantian philosophy is "nihilistic," they claim, because its conclusions leave us disconnected from the "ultimate," and this is a distasteful state of affairs.

RUSSIAN NIHILISM

Most commentators seem to agree that the development of the concept of nihilism in German philosophical circles in the eighteenth century was quite separate from its development in Russian circles during the nineteenth century.[10] This would help to explain the dissimilar natures of German and Russian nihilism, as well as giving us an insight into some of the ambiguities associated with the word. Many authors attribute coinage of the term *nihilism* to the Russian writer Ivan Turgenev, [11] who uses it in his novel *Fathers and Sons,* first published in 1862, though as we have already seen the term, in fact, appears much earlier in Germany. Whereas German nihilism tends toward the theoretical and philosophical, the Russian form of nihilism is more closely associated with radical, revolutionary political movements, and, at least for Turgenev, is not necessarily a term of derision. In Turgenev's depiction of nihilism, we find it transformed into a clear-eyed, unromantic, and action-oriented form of protest against the old and decaying forms of Russian political and social convention. Though often Turgenev's nihilists exhibit the callousness and one-sided dogmatism of fanatics, they are, in general, treated with a kind of fondness by the author. This is especially clear with the main character Bazarov, whose energy, intelligence, and dedication to the cause of social justice mark him as a rare and noble figure.

The novel *Fathers and Sons* is, in essence, a story about the gap between older and younger generations. It focuses on the characters of Arcady and Bazarov, two college students who, upon returning home from school, come into conflict with the traditional folkways of their families, communities, and cultures. Arcady has met the nihilist Bazarov at college, and has fallen under his spell. Bazarov is in training to become a doctor, but he is a most unusual type of medical student. He is a nihilist who claims that he believes in nothing. The kind of nihilism that Bazarov advocates, however, seems to be based upon principles of materialism, hedonism, and utility, sounding very much like a more modern variant of ancient Greek cynicism. Bazarov flouts all convention, is engrossed in the dissection of animals for the sake of curiosity, womanizes and drinks hard. He is against all forms of liberalism and romanticism, instead seeing himself as a tool for the preparation of a new stage in the development of history:

> "In these days, negation is the most useful thing of all—and so we deny."
> "Everything?"
> "Everything."
> "What? Not only art, poetry . . . but also . . . I am afraid to say it . . ."
> "Everything," Bazarov repeated with inexpressible calm.[12]

Bazarov's nihilism, though it is met with horror and fear by the older generation, is met with excitement and exhilaration by his peers. Both young men and women find his powerful arrogance attractive. They admire his self-confident calmness and easy dismissal of authority. Although Bazarov claims to hold no stock in logic or reason, he seems very much the model of a down to earth logician, unaffected by emotion or whimsy (at least until he crosses the path of Mme. Odintsov). These characteristics are the very ones that lead to our own ambivalent feelings about Bazarov as we read the novel. On the one hand we admire his spirit and irreverence; his rebellious willingness to speak his mind regardless of the consequences. On the other hand, we are annoyed at his disrespect for the feelings of others. He holds all emotions in contempt, and even seems to despise himself when he experiences them. Despite these personal shortcomings, Turgenev portrays the nihilist Bazarov as a character concerned with education, learning, truth, and social justice. His death, as a result of contracting typhus during an autopsy, is a fitting end for a character dedicated to the medical sciences, the progress of knowledge, and the end of unnecessary human suffering.

Alan Hodge writes, "In Turgenev's eyes, Bazarov was the most profoundly sympathetic of his creations. . . ."[13] The Russian usage of the word *nihilism*, then, may not have necessarily had the same reproachful overtones as the German variant. In fact, the Russian socialist Dmitry Pisarev is said to have adopted the label *nihilist* after having been charmed by Bazarov's character, although other radicals, such as Nikolai Chernyshevsky, were offended by the characterization. Chernyshevsky wrote the novel *What Is To Be Done?*[14] in response to Turgenev's book, and it was in his depiction of the "new men" that Russian nihilists found an alternate model for emulation. Chernyshevsky's brand of nihilism advocated a mix of materialism, egoism, socialism, feminism, and an unbounded faith in the powers of science. But the advocacy of these doctrines seems, as Stephen Lovell writes, to have been primarily motivated by the "rejection of existing authority."[15] Russian nihilism, on the whole, was a movement of revolutionary repudiation whose positive doctrines were generally vague and disjointed. Its main thrust was a desire for political action, change, and revolution. Soon it became integrated into the struggles of anarchism, Jacobism, and Bolshevism. It is understandable, then, that Russian nihilism was immensely exciting and popular among young intellectuals, yet feared and despised by the older conservative elements in the country. For instance, Dostoyevsky's novels, especially *Crime and Punishment, The Idiot,* and *The Possessed* reflect a negative evaluation of those who "had been infected by the rationalistic nihilism of the young revolutionary-minded generation."[16] Despite such dissent, the appearance of the term *nihilism* in Russia seems to stem from a source that did not presuppose a negative judgment of the subject matter to which the term was applied. Calling a person a nihilist did not necessarily indicate distaste for that person. It may just as well have indicated respect.

However, Russian nihilism, not having a cohesive program of political action or ideology, was a convenient umbrella under which to shelter a whole collection of radical types, and the label *nihilism* became increasingly associated with terrorism and acts of violence during the latter part of the nineteenth century. A prime example of this trend is to be found in Sergei Nechayev. Nechayev was an associate of the Russian anarchist Mikhail Bakunin with whom he is rumored to have co-authored a notorious pamphlet titled *Catechism of the Revolutionary*.[17] Nechayev was completely committed to the cause of chaos and destruction, seeing himself, like Bazarov in *Fathers and Sons,* as a tool for the revolution. Eventually he was imprisoned for murder in the Peter and Paul Fortress where he died after many years in solitary confinement.[18]

Catechism of the Revolutionary contains the principles and guidelines for would-be nihilist revolutionaries willing to abandon all belief in order to embark on a career of violence and destruction. Such combatants were expected to be dedicated and merciless, having no beliefs of their own, but willing to prepare the way for the revolution:

> (1) The revolutionary is a dedicated man. He has no interests of his own, no affairs, no feelings, no attachments, no belongings, not even a name. Everything in him is absorbed by a single exclusive interest, a single thought, a single passion—the revolution.[19]

The nihilist's commitment to destruction had to be complete, though it was a destruction intended to serve the greater purpose of establishing a better world for the future:

> (3) The revolutionary despises all doctrinairism and has rejected the mundane sciences, leaving them for future generations. He knows of only one science, the science of destruction. . . . His sole and constant object is the immediate destruction of this vile order.[20]

With activists such as Nechayev, the popular understanding of the term *nihilist* gained renewed negative and frightening connotations. Much of the ambiguity that is now present in the word may stem from this historical baggage with a resulting confusion between its descriptive and evaluative content. Today, the term still rings with echoes of terrorism, violence, and negativity thanks largely to its associations with Russian radicalism, and especially with revolutionary anarchism. Nihilist thought, moreover, had tremendous influence on political developments in nineteenth-century Russia, inspiring the formation of organizations such as "Hell" and "The People's Will." Lenin and the Bolshevik movement were also heavily influenced by the nihilism of Turgenev, Chernyshevsky, Nechayev, and Bakunin. The destructive side of Russian nihilism was often mitigated in these movements by a positive social program in service of which negation and rebellion took place, and, indeed, Russian intellectuals such as Berdayev, Herzen, and Stepniak have characterized these nihilists in terms bordering on reverence. We even find Camus claiming, "The entire history of Russian terrorism can be summed up in the struggle of a handful of intellectuals to abolish tyranny. . . . [B]y their sacrifice and even by their most extreme negations they gave substance to a new standard of values, a new virtue, which even today has not ceased to oppose tyranny and to give aid to the cause of true liberation."[21] Russian nihilism, thus, cannot be accurately depicted as a wholly negative and despised phenomenon. By many thinkers, both at that time and at present, it has been viewed as a noble and worthy political movement. Even after becoming associated with terrorism and violence, "nihilism" in Russia, in contrast to the earlier use of the term in Germany, was not necessarily a label of condemnation.[22]

In his entry for the *Routledge Encyclopedia of Philosophy*, Donald Crosby attributes the wide popularization of the term *nihilism*, after around 1870, primarily to the writings of Turgenev, Dostoyevsky, and Friedrich Nietzsche. For Turgenev and Dostoyevsky, nihilism had a predominately political flavor. But for Nietzsche, nihilism was more complex and personal, issuing forth as both a spiritual and cultural problem.[23] Goudsblom claims that "after Nietzsche the concept of nihilism became respectable."[24] Gillespie writes that the concept of nihilism "was given its determinative definition by Nietzsche,"[25] and Karen L. Carr tells us that "Nietzsche, of course, wrote more explicitly about nihilism than any other nineteenth-century figure; his understanding of nihilism has been the decisive influence on twentieth-century usage."[26] With Nietzsche, the German and the Russian strands of nihilism are woven together into a sophisticated whole, yielding an account that, though at times puzzling, is nonetheless profound and perceptive. Coming to grips with Nietzsche's framing of the problem of nihilism is crucial for a full understanding of what nihilism has come to mean for us and our time. As Camus observed, "With him nihilism becomes conscious for the first time."[27]

Chapter Two

Nietzschean Nihilism

A philosopher recuperates differently and with different means: he recuperates, e.g., with nihilism.

—Friedrich Nietzsche

For Nietzsche, the term "nihilism" remains ambiguous. Though he divides the concept into a large number of sub-categories, two divisions are primary:

A. Nihilism as a sign of increased power of the spirit: as active nihilism.

B. Nihilism as decline and recession of the power of the spirit: as passive nihilism.[1]

Active and passive nihilism, according to Nietzsche, form a dyad making it overly simplistic to claim that nihilism as a whole is a purely negative or destructive force. Nihilism is a process that lies at the very core of life, and can be observed in the continual struggle of humans to advance and improve themselves and their culture. Since the struggle for progress is only intelligible against the backdrop of that which is less developed and worthy, spiritual and cultural growth presuppose a hierarchy of higher and lower levels of development. Nihilism is a symptom of the culmination of this growth, as well as of the ensuing decline that must inevitably follow. Nihilism occurs at that point in the history of an individual or a culture when "the highest values devaluate themselves."[2]

Nietzsche saw himself as "the first perfect nihilist of Europe"[3] capable of diagnosing the sickness and decay of humankind. "I describe what is coming, what can no longer come differently: the advent of nihilism. . . . This future speaks even now in a hundred signs, this destiny announces itself everywhere."[4] The culture of Europe, Nietzsche believed, was experiencing a malaise and general decline in vitality, and two of the most evident signs of this decline were the Christian and the anarchist. Nietzsche's examination of these two types makes especially apparent what he thought wrong with humankind, and also illustrates the dynamic operations of nihilism. Since Nietzsche's treatment is fundamental to our contemporary understanding of the problem, it will be useful in what follows to take a look at his approach in some detail, preparing the way for our own handling of the topic.[5]

THE CHRISTIAN, THE ANARCHIST, AND SOCRATES

The Christian, Nietzsche tells us, is objectionable as a symptom of humankind's world-weariness. In rejecting the realm of the here and now in favor of a transcendent, heavenly afterlife, the Christian's weakness is revealed. This weakness was first observed in Judaism whose logic was simply carried out in the development of Christianity. When faced with the question "to be or not to be," Nietzsche tells us that the Jews decided "to be at any price."[6] Their flight from Egypt into the desert, in search of a new homeland, modified their spirit and character, and the price for their survival turned out to be an inversion of natural values and a flight from "Yahweh" into the hands of "God."

Yahweh originally represented the natural state of affairs that prevailed in the world, and the Jews were most noble in their worship of this severe and uncompromising presence. Yahweh was the principle of nature, personified as an arbitrary, all-powerful ruler who creates and destroys on a whim. The exodus from Egypt, however, modified the needs of the Jewish people, and in accordance with this situation Yahweh changed from a natural force that tested the Jewish toughness of spirit into a willful God who erected a moral order with the proclamation of commandments. The priest is the mouthpiece through which this unnatural state of affairs gains a voice, being the one who judges everything stupidly in terms of "obedience or disobedience to God."[7] The priest is a further symptom of decline, inventing sin as the condition necessary for his own survival, draining the strength of the people, and preparing the way for the nature-inverting onslaught of Christianity.

The Jews at least retained the noble assertion that they were a chosen people. But with Christianity, even this vestige of rank hierarchy was abolished. In this way Christianity revolted against the last thing that was noble in Judaism. Nietzsche interprets Christianity as an attempt to extend, preserve, and multiply the type of human spirit found in Jesus. This project, however, was doomed to failure from the start. Jesus' teaching was about a way to live, not about a way to believe, and the attempt to perpetuate his type through preaching to the masses only led to a perverted and distorted doctrine. The lower humans who followed Jesus reinterpreted his message in their own terms, thereby misconstruing it altogether. The Christian acts in a certain way because it is the law, but Jesus did what he did out of an instinctual physiological sensitivity to suffering, similar to that of Buddha or Epicurus. No one who experiences this sensitivity is able to endure extended contact with the world because they "feel every contact too deeply."[8] The Christian, on the other hand, behaves in accordance with the rules of the church only in order to gain access to heaven and obtain eternal happiness. The difference is an extremely important one. It is the difference between acting in accord with one's nature and rebelling against what one is.

The Christian, Nietzsche claims, is similar to the anarchist. The anarchist also denies the natural rank order of the world in favor of an egalitarian vision of the equality of all souls. This rejection of super- and subordination is a symptom of resentment against reality. It is the dissatisfied cry of the weak who, instead of acting in accord with their own temperaments, revolt against nature and commit a kind of hubris against the world. Nietzsche thought that the socialist doctrines advocated by anarchist and nihilist writers of his time attested to just this sort of weakness of spirit.[9] These advocates of political revolution thought that humans would enjoy expanded freedom and happiness with the abolition of property, leadership, unequal social status, and privilege. But, Nietzsche points out, the complaints and desires of the anarchist are the complaints and desires of those who want revenge on a world that has denied them what they are too weak to seize for themselves. "[T]here is a fine dose of revenge in every complaint."[10] Anarchists try to find someone at fault for their own suffering, and in this fault-finding is exhibited the weakness of one who cannot simply move forward with life. The difference between the Christian and the anarchist is that Christians find fault in themselves while anarchists find fault in others.

A world full of Christians and anarchists is a world in decline. Desiring release from suffering in the here and now, Christians and anarchists imagine the existence of illusory, utopian worlds beyond this one: the Christian heaven and the anarchist collective. In these otherworldly utopias, because everyone is equal, everything is perfect. Since all suffering is the result of the powerful imposing their will upon the weak, in these worlds, all suffering ceases. Pain and want are eliminated, life is happy, fulfilling, and easy. This is a result of the fact that the common structure of these utopias is in perfect synchronization with the capacities of the weak. But, in actual fact, this is a denial of the real structure of the world and a desecration of the earth itself. The desire for utopias is decadent in that they represent a deterioration of the capacity for real world life and living. The Christian and the anarchist are both nihilists in that they reject the only kind of life possible in the here and now, and in this rejection they undercut the possibility of the only type of meaning that ever was or ever will be available to humans.

When the weakest portions of society band together, perverting and distorting the natural order, the situation that obtains is nihilism. Christianity and anarchism are two symptoms of this tendency, but in the example of Socrates we have the quintessential model of the slave revolt against master morality and the most significant antecedent of modern nihilism. The most important thing to know about Socrates, according to Nietzsche, is that he was ugly. This physiological fact accounts for his entire orientation toward life in the Greek polis. He sought to take revenge upon the beautiful culture of the Greeks, and in a "masterful" departure from nature, he developed the art of dialectic. It was in the practice of logic and argumentation that Socrates saw his opportunity to overpower the authority of those around him and thus to secure a position of moral superiority to them. Anyone can learn logic, and since logic is directly opposed to appeals to authority, Socrates and his followers were advocates of a kind of anarchism that invited the lowest common denominator to overthrow and subvert the commands of those in power. It was the perfect weapon for the weak who had no other means of enforcing their own preferences.[11]

As this logical tendency spread throughout the Greek world, Socrates got his revenge. The Greek instincts began to change and the aristocratic bearing of the culture was destroyed, becoming democratic in its political and aesthetic tastes. Tragedy deteriorated and humans became "absurdly rational."[12] Socrates was both a symptom of an emerging Greek nihilism and an instigator of modern nihilism, according to Nietzsche. He stepped onto the scene at a time when Western culture was facing the question that the Jewish people had faced upon their exodus from Egypt: "To be or not to be?" Socrates offered an answer that the world came to accept and embrace, namely that "with the clue of logic, thinking can reach to the nethermost depths of being, and that thinking cannot only perceive being but even modify it."[13] This Socratic imperative reaches all the way into the present, and with it Socrates wreaks his revenge.

APOLLO AND DIONYSUS

Nietzsche offers more than a symptomatology of the modern malaise. In addition to pointing out the various sores and ailments of Western culture, he identifies the common cause of these symptoms. In the spirit of revenge lies the urge to distort the natural order of the world, and this disposition is caused by a lack of Dionysian vitality.

For Nietzsche, the natural world is a chaotic flux of unorganized energy that has no purpose or meaning except the expression of the power that makes up its being. "The total character of the world . . . is in all eternity chaos. . . ."[14] Though this chaotic flux is a never-ending process, some of its fluctuations are distinctive. Humankind is one such distinctive fluctuation. The human world is a symptom of the natural impulse toward the expression of power, and humans cannot avoid the struggle and battle that is at the root of their very being. With Heraclitus, Nietzsche sees the world of change and passing away as the only real world there is. To deny this is to deny the nature of the universe.

Though humans are a part of nature, they are also unique. They are like a wave on the surface of the ocean. A wave comes into being and disappears, but for those moments when it is in existence, it has a unique identity. Likewise, humankind erupts out of chaos and briefly moves across the surface of Being, exhibiting a certain form and direction. In this way it is part of the nature and makeup of the universe. However, humans also possess the peculiar feature that they must have meaning in life. Just as a wave must have a shore to break on, so must humans have a purpose for which to live. This need for purpose and meaning is simply a consequence of humankind's nature as a power-expressing species. The manner in which humans express this "will to power" is through the interpretation of the world.

In accordance with Kant's "Copernican Revolution," Nietzsche conceives of our phenomenal world as arising out of the relationship between our minds and the "Ding an Sich," which for Nietzsche is "chaos." By imposing order on chaos, humans "falsify" the "objective" world, producing an unfaithful representation of the reality that surrounds them. This representation, in its static and comprehensible appearance, does not really correspond to the chaos that underlies it, but nevertheless what we call "knowledge" is just the outcome of this imposition of structure on the world's disorder. Thinking and contemplation is, thus, more akin to a process of interpretation than it is to the simple apprehension of objective reality. Knowing, thinking, and cogitating are all acts of creation. They necessarily involve activity and effort pursued from a particular perspective in order to bring a subjective reality into existence. "We cannot look around our own corner: it is hopeless curiosity that wants to know what other kinds of intellects and perspectives there might be."[15] As we navigate through the world, we are tied to the prejudices, structures, and endowments of our own perspectives. The human mind, in organizing and sifting through the data of experience, is at all times involved in a creative act of the interpretation of reality.

Nietzsche introduces two concepts in order to attempt an analysis of the structure of human interpretation. The Apollonian and the Dionysian are two opposite psychological tendencies that pull humans back and forth in a struggle between the need for order and contemplative representation and the desire for uninhibited frenzy and expression of energetic impulses. The predominance of the Apollonian impulse is exhibited in the painter, sculptor, and epic poet. It is characterized by a certain restraint in representation that allows us to look at and linger on the product of interpretation. It forms and shapes life in the same manner that our minds give shape and form in dreams to the impulses from our unconscious. The Apollonian is the *principium individuationis,* organizing reality and making it representable. The Dionysian, on the other hand, is the failure and destruction of the *principium individuationis.* It resists the imposition of form and structure, delighting instead in the uninhibited expression of frenzied activity. Dance, drunkenness, and music exhibit a predominance of the Dionysian impulse.[16]

Both the Apollonian and the Dionysian impulses are necessary in any act of human interpretation. The Apollonian contributes structure and form while the Dionysian contributes energy and intensity to interpretive undertakings. Like Aristotle's form/matter duality, the two are conceptually distinct, but in fact normally appear in some admixture of one with the other. The product of such a nexus may end up being a well-balanced compromise between the two, as in the highest forms of Attic tragedy, or it may end up being an unbalanced mixture that leans too far toward one extreme or the other. If it leans too far toward the Dionysian, the product will be a confusing frenzy of undisciplined activity. If it leans too far toward the Apollonian, it will be an overly static and lifeless representation.

The human world is full of interpretations that lean one way or the other, but it also possesses a few examples of interpretations that are well balanced. The tendency of Western civilization since Socrates, however, has been to neglect the Dionysian in favor of the Apollonian. Nietzsche's dissatisfaction with this development is more than simply a distaste for the products of these interpretations. It is more importantly an observation about the types of humans that predominate in the world. As one is more insistently called toward the Apollonian, one is called away from the Dionysian, and it is Dionysus rather than Apollo who provides the content and vitality of life. Whereas Apollo offers structure, "by the mystical triumphant cry of Dionysus the spell of individuation is broken, and the way lies open to the Mothers of Being, to the innermost heart of things."[17] The Dionysian is the vital energy and activity lying at the heart of reality. It is the unstructured and overpowering chaos that perpetually threatens structure and order. The Freudian notion of the Id comes close to depicting the Dionysian. It is the power and energy that drives our mental machinery, being held in check and channeled for useful purposes by the Ego, which is itself a notion paralleling the Apollonian. Whereas the Ego should serve the Id, directing and shaping its urges in a manner consonant with reality, an Ego that exists at the expense of the Id is like the Apollonian holding dominance over the Dionysian. It signals the sickness, neurosis, and decline of the organism. For Nietzsche, the proliferation of Apollonian interpretations of the world, then, reveals an underlying general disorder in humankind. It suggests that those who exist in the world have exhausted their spiritual energy and vitality. It signals a lack of spiritual depth.

Nietzsche's diagnosis for modern human beings is that they suffer from a lack of the Dionysian. This is apparent in those interpretive products that attempt to erect illusory representations of utopian worlds that cannot be made to exist in the here and now. These purely formal speculations ignore the single most important evidence against them; namely, that humans are part of nature and must struggle and express their power as long as they remain living. Without struggle and contest, humans degenerate and become sick. Those who become sick instinctively retreat from struggle and contest, and in commiseration with them, the rest of humankind becomes infected. In obtaining the pity of the strong, the weak gain a type of control over the world and invert the natural order of things. With this inversion, the weak seek to bring an end to the cycle of struggle. By banding together they become collectively strong, and as Nietzsche observes, "What is strong wins: that is the universal law. If only it were not so often precisely what is stupid and evil!"[18]

HEALTHY CULTURE AND THE WELL-ORDERED SOCIETY

Nietzsche is as explicit as he can be about what is wrong with the culture that he observes around him. "What is bad? But I have already said this: all that is born of weakness, envy, of revenge. The anarchist and the Christian have the same origin."[19] Of course these are only two among "a hundred signs," but by showing the common origin of the Christian and the anarchist in weakness, Nietzsche offers his diagnosis of modern humankind's disease. It is because of the lack of Dionysian fervor that humankind is sick. Collectively speaking, modern humans are not up to the task of producing "higher humans." Doctrines such as Christianity and anarchism don't even believe in higher humans, and in this weakness is exhibited.

This situation is fatal to higher culture. A higher, healthy culture is one that mirrors nature and its order of rank. Nietzsche seems to follow Plato in the assertion that such a society is naturally divided into three types: the spiritual ones, the guardians, and the mediocre. "A high culture is a pyramid: it can stand only on a broad base; its first presupposition is a strong and soundly consolidated mediocrity."[20] The mediocre ones are the most numerous and least ambitious members of a healthy collectivity. They are, however, indispensable in that they provide society with its basic necessities such as "handicraft, trade, agriculture, science, the greatest part of art, the whole quintessence of professional activity."[21] They are the backbone and the very machines that make collective life possible. It is well in accord with nature that the vast majority of humans are drawn to this sort of social activity by instinct, and there is certainly no need to coerce them into service. The mediocre ones find happiness in this function.

Once the material base of society is secure, there is much that humankind is capable of producing. Just as a strong foundation is necessary in order to support the tallest and most majestic buildings, a strong and healthy mediocrity, free from resentment and instinctually happy with its social role, is necessary in order to support the higher types of humans.

The second in order of natural rank are the "guardians of the law."[22] They are the kings, warriors, and judges who enforce the rule of the most spiritual. As with the mediocre, they are drawn to their position by the instinct that is written in their nature, but unlike the mediocre, they are driven by a sense of duty to the law rather than by a desire for personal happiness. They are not the law's authors, however, and must depend upon the highest humans for direction.

The highest type are the spiritual ones. They are the strongest humans and enjoy the tasks that all others find unbearable, namely the activity of creation and the pursuit of knowledge. Their role is unenviable to the lower humans, and the rewards they receive for their service are of a nature not appreciated by those of a lower rank. These higher humans understand the dignity that comes from the unresentful acceptance of one's role and place in nature's hierarchy and so they in fact feel a duty to the lower humans, treating them with the tenderness and respect that the lower type craves. Yet these highest humans thrive in the outer reaches of human possibility where the conditions are severe and uncertain and so they are often misunderstood by the masses. Despite this fact, they are unable to feel resentment. Their overflowing strength of spirit will not allow them to wish for anything to be different than it is. They love the world and all of the preconditions that have allowed them to exist.

The preceding tripartite division of human types and how they fit into the well ordered society bears an important relation to Zarathustra's discussion of the three metamorphoses of the spirit in the beginning of *Thus Spoke Zarathustra*. It is here that he speaks of the transformation of the spirit from a camel into a lion and finally into a child. What may at first glance appear to be only an admonition toward personal development and growth is actually also a metaphor for the development of the healthy, well-ordered society and a prescription for the treatment of modern European nihilism.

The camel is an animal that feels its own strength by taking on burdens. Like those who make up the base of society's pyramid, the camel has the responsibility to carry someone else's load. This is the nature of a pack animal, and in this is the strength to persevere under the weight of much that is not understood. Because it receives punishment when it refuses to do its job and rewards when it carries through, the camel tends to obey. It follows the direction plotted by the master who gives a destination and purpose to its ordeal.

A good camel accepts its job with the dignity of a beast of burden. It needs its master in order to become what it is and, like the great mass of humans in society, finds happiness here.

The lion is oriented, like the guardians of society, toward the law. However, whereas the guardians are entrusted to uphold and enforce the law, the lion is a mighty "No" sayer, rejecting all values. It is a forceful negator who acts as a ground clearer and, in the manner of Bazarov or Nechayev, generates the opportunity for future freedom and change. Instead of accepting the "Thou salt" of the camel, the lion asserts "I will." Despite what may at first appear to be a departure from the guardian's character, it is this spirit that is actually at its heart. Both the lion and the guardians are ultimately at the service of the most spiritual humans. Neither has the ability to create the values by which they naturally must orient themselves. The lion spirit finds itself in the paradoxical situation that it needs to deny everything, while at the same time needing the existence of something to react against. It relies upon others to create the very values it must deny. In devouring and destroying all the values that it encounters, the lion is still a fearsome upholder of the law. Its energetic pursuit of freedom confirms its place in nature and ends up bringing it to the point where it finds that there is something that it cannot will. It cannot will an affirmation. It cannot create. In the guardians, this spirit manifests itself in the willing enforcement of whatever laws and truths are handed down. A good guardian believes nothing, but wills the world to submit.

The final transformation of the soul takes place in the child. The child has the strength to do what the lion cannot. It can affirm new values. The child engages in an eternal form of play and experimentation, expressing the "overfullness" of one who is a mirror of nature's endless, Dionysian exuberance. It is at this point that the spirit comes as close as it possibly can to being one with the natural processes of the earth. It ceases to be burdened or to will, and desires nothing else than to be what it already is. For these reasons, Gadamer writes that for Nietzsche it is this transformation of the spirit into the child that is "the true content of his message."[23] The spirit of absolute affirmation and creation, this child's spirit, is that possessed by the highest humans in any culture. These higher humans are made possible by the development of the lower tiers of society, but likewise the lower tiers of society need these "Übermenschen" as the progenitors and source of all value in the world.

In this way we can see that there is an interdependence between each of the stages in the development of the spirit, and that there is a corresponding interdependence between the various castes in the well-ordered, healthy society. The development of the spirit that Zarathustra and Nietzsche speak about, however, is not simply a transformation and metamorphosis, but an ascension from a lower, more common form of existence, to a higher, more exceptional form of existence. This ascension of the spirit is both a collective and an individual pursuit.

ASCENT, DECLINE, AND THE ETERNAL RETURN OF THE SAME

The stages of decline that Nietzsche has identified in the history of humankind not only exhibit similar symptoms, they reveal a recurrent process in the workings of life. Just as a culture that is in ascent must traverse the stages from camel to lion to child, so must a culture in decline travel through these same stages, except in a different order. The poles of ascent and decline are relative to one another, so to detect an ascent in culture is to detect movement away from a lower toward a higher form of existence and thus is cause for hope and optimism. On the other hand, to detect a decline is to sense a movement from a higher to a lower position, and so is a cause for concern and pessimism. The latter scenario, the thought that all that lies ahead is decline and decay, is the most abysmal thought imaginable for Nietzsche. However in thinking it, one is led to work out the logic of the eternal return and to transform the dark, brooding anticipation of all that is objectionable into an enthusiasm for what has already been produced and must be produced again.

"Human society is a trial: thus I teach it—a long trial; and what it tries to find is the commander."[24] This "trial" of society in its search for a "commander" is the struggle of the group toward higher transformations of the spirit. The conditions of life are such that transformations cannot help but occur; the only question is whether they lead to ascension or decline. Now, the judgment on whether a society is in ascension or decline must take place from the point of view of one who is embedded in a perspective. No one can step outside of one's own perspective, and this perspective is made possible by the sum total of the history of the culture. Depending upon the stage of ascent or descent, what the culture seeks and moves toward will be different. A low culture has nowhere to go but up, and when it looks for higher types, it doesn't have to look very far off. An advanced culture, on the other hand, has produced so many higher humans during its ascent that it becomes increasingly difficult for it to overcome and surpass these types. Thus, the rapidity at which a culture in its higher stages ascends is less than that at which a culture at its lower stages does so. A low culture can look forward to much, while a high culture may either revel in what it has already produced or look forward with pessimism toward its own decline. This is a depressing thought for those who, from an elevated perspective, have the vision to see all that a culture has produced and what it is now capable or incapable of producing.

But the choices between affirming the moment or despairing of the future are not the only options for higher humans. There is a third possibility that emerges when the psychological experiment of "thinking the most abysmal thought" is carried through to its completion. This third option consists of recognizing the overall struggle of Dionysian vitality that underlies everything. When this realization occurs, it no longer makes sense to despair of the future. On the contrary, with this insight one can only affirm all that ever was or that will be. To take delight in one single instant of human history is to desire everything that made that instant possible to recur again and again. The web of occurrences connecting everything that happens is so tightly spun that a tug in one location forces a reaction in another location. When we judge that a culture is in decay, the logic of ascent and decline tells us that our perspective must be situated at some degree of elevation since it allows us to make lofty determinations. Furthermore, since we recognize the strength of our perspective only through the exercise of its powers of valuation, we naturally wish to affirm its worth. Affirming the worth of our perspective necessitates affirming all that made our perspective possible, and what has done so is all that has ever occurred. For this reason, at the end of the third book of *Thus Spoke Zarathustra*, Zarathustra exclaims over and over again "For I love you, O eternity!"[25] upon accepting the doctrine of eternal recurrence. That everything eternally recurs is "the most abysmal thought" only from the perspective of weakness. From the perspective of exalted strength and wisdom, the eternal return of everything is the ultimate affirmation of the spirit, humankind, the earth, and the universe.

Though it contains hints of both, the doctrine of the eternal return is more like a psychological imperative than a cosmological description. It teaches us, in a manner similar to the Golden Rule or Kant's Categorical Imperative, to take our feelings and actions seriously, and to consider them not as isolated and disjointed moments outside of the cycles of life, but as integral parts of the universe. "Can you live in such a manner that you could will your life to repeat infinitely into the future?" This is the challenge offered by Nietzsche's doctrine of eternal recurrence. It asks us if we are up to the task of finding value even in the most painful and unpleasant moments of our lives. To affirm life, even in its most monstrous manifestations, is a goal that few can approach, and which none can actualize at every moment. However, in the aspiration toward this ideal, Nietzsche tells us that we go a long way toward a spiritual cleansing that makes us more noble and capable of living in harmony with nature.

With the proclamation of the eternal return, Zarathustra and Nietzsche have become who they were always meant to be. "[B]ehold, you are the teacher of the eternal recurrence—that is your destiny!"[26] With the acceptance of the underlying truth of this doctrine, both Nietzsche and Zarathustra take a step toward the overcoming of resentment and weakness, allowing their spirits to take on the child-like characteristics of the highest development of the soul. But there is an irony in accepting the eternal recurrence. When one reaches this highest point of development, decline is imminent. Life will not allow a soul to remain statically elevated. There is no eternal world of enlightened bliss. The elevated one must always fall again, and it is that frenzied, Dionysian scramble back up to the pinnacle that defines spiritual height. Height, individually or collectively, is measured in distance, and so Apollo plays a role in spiritual need no less than does Dionysus. It is the tension between distance and activity that allows progress toward goals and the recurrent struggle for superiority demands decline as a part of ascent.

What Nietzsche calls "nihilism" is tightly bound together with the battles fought in the name of the eternal return. As one who felt himself in a position to make judgments about the ailments of culture, Nietzsche must have struggled with ambivalence toward a world that was capable of producing him and his philosophy as well as the philosophies of Christianity, anarchism, and Socrates. Yet, the logic of the eternal return provides the solution to this seeming inconsistency. Through it the Dionysian impulse is represented as a process aimed at no final purpose. It finds satisfaction only in the repetition and perpetuation of activity. The decline of culture and spirit is thus a natural part of the life of a culture or spirit, and nihilism is part of the very nature of the world itself. "Let us think this thought in its most terrible form: existence as it is, without meaning or aim, yet recurring inevitably without any finale of nothingness: 'the eternal recurrence.' This is the most extreme form of nihilism: the nothing (the 'meaningless') eternally!"[27]

The sickness of modern humans is a symptom of nihilism, but nihilism is also the ultimate cure. The inversion of the natural order, and thus the submission of Dionysus to Apollo, is the root cause of humankind's spiritual and social ills, but it is also a symptom of the natural process that makes up Being. Slave revolts must happen from time to time in order to produce strong masters, and the strongest of masters are those who recognize in these revolts the necessary conditions of the ongoing struggle for earthly power. The human who can unresentfully claim "What does not destroy me, makes me stronger"[28] understands the import of the doctrine of the eternal return. Such an individual confronts nihilism in one's self and in one's culture by thinking through the logic of decline and ascent, mirroring nature and standing as an example to all the world of what humankind is capable. To will everything again, even one's own destruction, is the surest symptom of a human being who has lived life well.

Nietzsche's prescription for the sickness of humans is to think the most abysmal thought of the eternal return through to its logical conclusion in order to realize that the eternal struggle of nature's forces is the only purpose, goal, and meaning that humankind can ever truly discover. Any philosophy or doctrine that tries to deny this reality is nihilistic in that it denies the necessary conditions of all life. Christianity, anarchism, and the philosophy of Socrates are all examples of philosophies that attempt to deny life by asserting the ultimate end of struggle through flight into a utopia. They are expressions of resentment against reality, though they are also expressions of life; albeit life on the decline.

To realize that all life is a struggle between the forces of frenzy and representation is to affirm the basic logic of ascent and decline. Humans must interpret the world out of which they have sprung, for this is how they express their power, but these various interpretations are in battle with one another for dominance. The development of the human spirit from its most passive, camel-like state to its most active, child-like state is made possible by this entire history of interpretation. Spiritual ascent is a quality measured by distance from all things lower and earthly, not by reference to a God or some otherworldly ideal. The Übermensch is a product of the entire history of humankind, capable of thinking the eternal return, and in so doing pushing the frontier of human possibility farther than it has ever been pushed before. But in accomplishing the superlative human feat, this individual is doomed to an ensuing decline.

Nietzsche's inquiry treats nihilism less like a philosophy or intellectual movement and more like a force at work in human history. Struggle and contest are at the root of life, and all development and progress in human history is necessarily accompanied by eventual decline and decay. Active nihilism, or the increase of the power of the spirit, only makes sense in relation to passive nihilism, or the decrease of the power of spirit. The two forces complement one another, and together they constitute the engine that drives history. In this picture, we see a synthesis of the strains of nihilism briefly discussed in the first chapter. Nietzsche's account paints a picture of the world owing much to the Kantian philosophy to which Obereit, Jenisch, and Jacobi originally applied the term *nihilism*. For Nietzsche, humankind is, as for Kant, cut off from the ultimate. Humans are finite creatures whose only hope for knowledge comes from the perspectival interpretation of the world. This situation, however, does not imply that all interpretations of the world are equally legitimate or correct. On the contrary, some interpretations are "nihilistic" insofar as they reject, or represent an inability to cope with, this necessary human circumstance. Nietzsche in this sense, on the one hand, uses the term *nihilism* to characterize a kind of metaphysical condition that he believes describes the human situation, while on the other hand he uses the term as a criticism of those interpretations that turn their backs on this condition. Nihilism is a force of decline that is double edged in its consequences. From the perspective of the eternally recurring cycle of history, nihilism is a component of the life drama necessary in order to propel progress, growth, and development. However, from the perspective of the individuals who are immersed in the ongoing struggles of history, nihilism appears as "the most abysmal thought," or a depressing reminder that nothing is permanent and that all is eventually destined to decay and dissolution. Active nihilism recognizes this fact, while passive nihilism ignores it.

These theoretical elements that Nietzsche culled from early German discussions of nihilism are combined by him with the political nihilism of the Russians in order to draw out their cultural and social implications. Just as an individual may experience nihilism, so may a culture or society. In the individual,

Nietzsche found symptoms of nihilism in the Christian, the anarchist, and Socrates. However, individuals are to a large extent shaped by their cultures, and so the existence of these individuals is a further symptom of the forces of nihilism at work in society as a whole. Russian nihilism sought the destruction of the current political structures in order to usher in a new age of total freedom in accordance with human nature, and Nietzsche borrowed from this movement the potentially frightening insight that the enhancement of the human social and cultural situation may require revolutionary political action and the absolute negation and eradication of past institutions and systems of governance. This too is nihilism, but as for Bazarov and Nechayev, it is a nihilism that serves the future. As Keith Ansell-Pearson writes, "What Nietzsche seeks to do as a thinker, I believe, is to prepare us for change. He shows that humanity has a history, that it has been (de-)formed in a particular way, and that the end of the Christian-moral interpretation of the world offers the possibility of another beginning."[29] Nietzsche, like Aristotle, accepts the fact that humans are social animals, and consequently he must recognize that the development of a culture and its individual members are tied to one another. Spiritual change and transformation is both an individual and a collective pursuit, therefore it has not only psychological but political implications.

Nietzschean nihilism is a complex affair. It involves the intermingling of a variety of related topics and concerns spanning the gaps between epistemology, sociology, politics, ethics, theology, and cosmology. It is, at different times, both descriptive and evaluative. Given that Nietzsche's discussions of the topic have ranged over such a wide intellectual terrain, it is no wonder that there exists so much confusion and disagreement over what he meant when using the term *nihilism*. Regardless of these confusions and disagreements, the influence of Nietzschean nihilism has reached into the present, informing and inspiring the thoughts and actions, for better or for worse, of not only Europeans, but (for better or for worse) of intellectuals everywhere in the world.

HEIDEGGER AND NIETZSCHE

One of the most influential and notorious of these figures is the German philosopher Martin Heidegger. Heidegger established himself as a pivotal figure in contemporary philosophy with the publication of *Being and Time (Sein und Zeit)*, a work that turns away from the traditional epistemological questions of Western philosophy and instead focuses on a fundamental, ontological investigation into the world of human existence. David Farrell Krell has claimed that "Nietzsche lies concealed on every printed page of *Sein und Zeit*."[30] Whether or not this is true, Heidegger was obviously quite inspired by, and preoccupied with, Nietzsche. He was particularly concerned with developing and extending Nietzsche's discussion of the role of nihilism in Western history.

In a sense, the Heideggerian perspective on nihilism is a rediscovery of the simple and straightforward complaints first put forward by Obereit, Jenisch, and Jacobi against Kant. Heidegger understands nihilism to be, primarily, an ontological issue. It is the situation that prevails when humans become "forgetful" of Being by focusing their attention on beings instead of remaining mindful of Being as such. This forgetfulness has the consequence that Being becomes "covered over" and obscured, thus leading humans into an inauthentic and deluded mode of existence. Because humans fail to think about and to understand what truly "is," they lose a sense of their ontological grounding and become existentially separated and alienated from the world.

The entire history of Western metaphysics since Plato, Heidegger complains, is the gradual unfolding of nihilism, and it was not until Nietzsche that this fact became unmistakably obvious. "[T]he metaphysics of Plato is not less nihilistic than that of Nietzsche. In the former, the essence of nihilism is merely concealed; in the latter, it comes completely to appearance."[31] All metaphysics, in fact, is nihilism according to Heidegger. This is because the metaphysician is concerned with representing Being as the totality of beings, and not with "thinking" Being itself. The whole point of metaphysics is to represent that which "is" as a thing-in-itself existing independently and transcendently. However, Being is not a being. It is not a thing. According to Heidegger, we are guilty of nihilistic thinking any time that we fail to recognize the fact that language, and the rational and logical tools it utilizes, necessarily chops up what "is" into fragments, and so falsifies and "covers over" Being itself. In the struggle to articulate and clarify the essence of what "is," we entangle ourselves in language and so necessarily conceal the very thing that we hope to reveal. Yet, this concealment is not total. Since Being touches everything that "is," even in concealment there remains the possibility of a fleeting and transitory glimpse of Being, distorted though it may be by the limitations of the human perspective.

Heidegger uses the term *Da-sein* in order to refer to the uniquely human manner of "being-in-the-world." Da-sein is not simply objectively present in the world as an extended thing. Its possibilities are what uniquely define it as "who" it is. Da-sein is singular among all other beings in that, first of all, it is able to raise the question of Being, and secondly, in that it can choose to relate itself authentically or inauthentically toward Being. This latter characteristic is why Heidegger claims that "the being which this being is concerned about in its being is always my own."[32] Rocks, watermelons, and even dogs are incapable of this kind of existence since their essence lies not in their possibilities but in their actuality. They have definite natures that can be summed up categorically. This is why Heidegger calls the characteristics of beings unlike Da-sein "categories."[33] Da-sein, however, is purely potential, and its characteristics are distinguished from those of objectively present things by the term "existentials."[34] It distinguishes itself in the course of existing by constantly running ahead of any categorical summing up of its characteristics. While things that are objectively present are referred to as "whats," Da-sein is referred to as a "who." It is, in sum, what we think of when we think of "human-being." It is the site that makes the appearance of Being possible.

Human-being, or Da-sein, is the "clearing" that makes room for the appearance of Being itself. Being erupts and manifests itself through the conduit that is Da-sein, and insofar as humans allow this to occur, they experience direct and intuitive commerce with Being. However, the other side of this coin is that Da-sein crowds out Being, and so distorts and falsifies that which "is." In this way, Da-sein both allows Being to make its appearance and corrupts that appearance. Think of the way that a rock, when dropped into a placid pool of water, creates eddies in that water. The entrance of the rock into the pool makes something of the water's nature visible to the eye, yet it does so only by disturbing the unbroken uniformity of the pool's surface. Da-sein is like the rock and Being is like the pool of water.

However, Da-sein is also a part of Being itself, and so our analogy might be a bit misleading. Perhaps a better image would represent Da-sein as a piece of ice that has been frozen out of the waters of the very pool that it is dropped into. Being permeates all that "is," and Da-sein is no less a part of Being than anything else. Da-sein may even melt back into Being under the right circumstances, completely obliterating the distinctions that allow it to stand out as a being among other beings in the first place. This would be the death of Da-sein, and in fact it is the inevitability of death, and our anxiety about it, that makes humans aware of the fact that our existence is not a thing but an event.

The most authentic form of existence for Da-sein is achieved in being-toward-death. With the awareness that our lives are finite and end in nothingness, Da-sein experiences anxiety. Life comes and goes, and Da-sein's uniqueness among all other beings consists in an awareness of this fact. "Anxiety reveals the nothing. We 'hover' in anxiety."[35] It is with the feeling of anxiety that we "dis-cover" the "nothing" at the ground of our very being. "Nothing" is the negation of all individuated beings. It is a part of Being itself. In fact, "nothing" and "Being" are one and the same. In both, the differentiation between beings is forgotten and the common ground, the unbroken and undifferentiated sameness of all that "is" comes to the fore. "Da-sein means: being held out into the nothing."[36] It is the "nothing" that creates space, an opening, for the occurrence of beings, and it is the prereflective awareness of this fact, according to Heidegger, that constitutes the most authentic understanding of Being itself.

Though some commentators, such as Rosen, have pointed to this emphasis on "the nothing" in Heidegger's philosophy as a nihilistic element, Heidegger himself does not consider it as such. Rather, for Heidegger nihilism is the "covering over" of the Being of the "nothing" by way of concentrating on beings. Heidegger equates philosophy with metaphysics, and he considers both to be nihilistic endeavors insofar as they attempt to think "beings as a whole."[37] Especially in the Western tradition, this has translated into a lack of care for the underlying matrix that unifies everything that exists. Philosophers are more concerned with making distinctions than they are with understanding unities. The final consequence of this sort of preoccupation, Heidegger believes, is a fragmented and technical way of looking at the world emphasizing subjectivity and the manipulation of individual beings.

Nietzsche's philosophy represents the ultimate culmination of this sort of thinking, according to Heidegger, and so he considers Nietzsche's "system" to be both the fulfillment and the end of Western metaphysics. In Nietzsche, the question of Being is transformed into the question of becoming. Being becomes nothing more than becoming through an inversion of Platonism and the interpretation of the world in terms of four interrelated concepts: The Will to Power, The Eternal Reccurence of the Same, The Revaluation of Values, and Nihilism. Each of these concepts shares an intimate relationship with the others, according to Heidegger, and the manner in which they are interconnected demonstrates Nietzsche's own concern with the "question of Being," while also revealing his hopeless entanglement in nihilism.

According to Heidegger, will to power is what Nietzsche takes to be the most basic essence of all beings. "Will to power . . . involves the Being and essence of beings; it is this itself."[38] This essence expresses itself as a force of overcoming and energy. It strives for enhancement, heightening, and gain. All beings, then, are involved at the very core of their Being with activity and the struggle toward progress and advancement. At each moment, every thing wants to be more than it actually is. The Being of beings is just the constant and unending pushing forward of force. In fact, according to Heidegger, the term *power* is simply a clarification of the essence of the term *will*, so that the phrase *will to power* is really somewhat redundant. Will is power, and power is will.

Will to power is both creative and destructive at the same time. As it strives forward, it cannot avoid trampling over and dismantling both its own past instantiations and anything that tries to halt its dynamism. In the struggle for activity and overcoming, the will to power perpetually overtakes itself, quite in the manner of Heidegger's own description of Da-sein. It opens possibilities by never resting satisfied with stasis or intermission. Its very essence is, in fact, directly opposed to these states. Will to power *must* transform itself at each instant into what it "feels" is better, stronger, and more advanced. Heidegger claims that for this reason it is a kind of "passion" that not only is engaged in activity, but is engaged in activity that is oriented in a particular direction and for a particular end. Will to power, in its very essence, is a kind of valuation insofar as it "chooses" to move in one particular direction rather than another. But since it is unquenchable in its force, it is also always involved in a revaluation. Will to power never stops its energetic push toward the next step up the ladder of success. In this way, the doctrine of the reevaluation of all values fits together neatly with the doctrine of will to power.

The nature of beings is a never-ending flow of force from one state to the next. All Being is just a flux of becoming. Yet, Heidegger observes, this manner of thinking about the world is disquieting to one caught in the Western tradition that begins with Plato. According to that tradition, "truth" means that which is stable and unchanging. If the nature of Being is a constant becoming, then there is no truth to Being. "Being" is illusion and falsehood. How is one to endure this thought? Heidegger tells us that for Nietzsche the answer lies in the doctrine of the eternal return. By stamping "Becoming with the character of Being"[39] Nietzsche offers a means of thinking about Being in a fashion that, while not quite authentic, at least approaches authenticity. Nietzsche's thought of the eternal return is still a kind of metaphysics, since it conceives of Being as a being, but it is the culmination and last gasp of metaphysics. Because of this, Heidegger tells us, "it performs the grandest and most profound gathering—that is accomplishment—of all the essential fundamental positions in Western philosophy since Plato and in the light of Platonism."[40] Nietzsche's philosophy reconciles Being with becoming, but at the price that it introduces nihilism as an unavoidable component of human existence.

"Nietzsche's metaphysics is not an overcoming of nihilism. It is the ultimate entanglement in nihilism."[41] Nietzsche certainly attempts to "think the question of Being" according to Heidegger, but he also offers an answer to that question that makes it impossible to ever truly encounter Being on its own terms. Being must always remain "covered over" so long as we think of it in terms of the eternal return. The eternal return is a mere being that attempts to encompass Being as the totality of beings. It is a kind of closed circle that cuts off possibilities with the claim that everything that will be has already been. Nietzsche avoids thinking about "the nothing" by means of the eternal return, and so is doomed to an inauthentic relationship to Being itself. Being is nothing. But nothing has Being. The anxious recognition of this allows what "is" to manifest itself freely through us, according to Heidegger. Without the "nothing," no room is made within Being for Da-sein to gather together its world and to continue the inquiry into Being itself.

The four-volume *Nietzsche* is the single longest work ever written by Heidegger and must be approached with caution. Often enough it has been observed that there is more Heidegger in *Nietzsche* than there is Nietzsche, and much of what Heidegger has to say here about Nietzsche's "system" is almost incomprehensible without a previous familiarity with *Being and Time*. Furthermore, Heidegger's interpretation is based predominantly on Nietzsche's unpublished notes and on the aphorisms that make up *The Will To Power*. He claims that these late writings contain the mature thought of Nietzsche and that "Nietzsche's philosophy proper, the fundamental position on the basis of which he speaks in these and in all writings he himself published, did not assume a final form and was not published by him in any book. . . . What Nietzsche himself published during his creative life was always foreground."[42] As a result of this approach, the bulk of what Heidegger accomplishes in these four volumes is largely a creative reading and attempted systemization of some of Nietzsche's most fragmentary writings.

However, the sometimes enlightening and very often inscrutable musings that Heidegger has given us do play a key role in this present stage of our investigation. Heidegger's interpretation and elaboration of Nietzsche's doctrines became, and remain, quite influential, not because they offer an entirely accurate picture of Nietzsche's philosophy, but because they give us an insight into a certain manner of thinking that has come to be called "Heideggerian." Heideggerian thinking attempts to orient itself toward Being while disregarding the incidental details of particular beings. It tries to uncover the Ding an Sich as it permeates the very structure of our existence, thereby allowing us to transcend Western metaphysics, philosophy, and nihilism. The most unique and constructive insight of this form of thinking as it relates to our current inquiry is that nihilism itself may offer us an insight into Being itself. As a being among beings, nihilism participates in Being. Insofar as nihilism "is," it tells us something about reality. For this reason, Heidegger thinks that it is misguided to attempt to "overcome" nihilism. "The will to overcome nihilism mistakes itself because it bars itself from the revelation of the essence of nihilism as the history of the default of Being, bars itself without being able to recognize its own deed."[43]

All of Western thought, according to Heidegger, is nihilism. It is a legacy that has encouraged distance, subjectivity, and the aggressive interrogation of nature with the result that Westerners have come to accept a strange, narrow, and distorted picture of themselves and of the world. Western philosophy and science have mistaken the accidental qualities of our world for the world itself, and in focusing on these qualities have perpetuated an inauthentic mode of existence. The "covering over" of Being is the history of our collective Da-sein. Yet, to reject this history is again to "cover over" part of our Being and so to restrict and distort our existence in an inauthentic manner even further. Heideggerian thought implores us to accept everything that "is," and simply to allow Being to speak to us through its beings. Instead of actively rejecting and overturning the way that things are, it asks us to open ourselves to the possibilities of what might be. It requests that we listen to Being and come to understand its full potential.

There is an element of optimistic passivity involved in Heideggerian thought that seems almost diametrically opposed to the thought of Nietzsche. For Nietzsche, an ongoing and active battle against the chaos and absurdity of the universe offers the only meaningful option against nihilism. However, because we are finite and exhaustible creatures, nihilism will always reassert itself. We are always bound to fail in our struggle for perfection, and to fall short of our highest aspirations for power. The sheer activity of the will is the only thing that can bring meaning and purpose to life, yet this struggle is ultimately fated to decay, dissolution and ruin. Whereas Nietzsche claims that he is "warlike by nature,"[44] Heidegger seems more serene and acquiescent in his thinking. Note that Heidegger abandons the term *philosophy* and adopts the more ambiguous term *thinking* as a name for his existential endeavor. Instead of a "love of wisdom" he pursues a "love of Being." In this endeavor, there is no failure or struggle, but simply a "letting be" of that "which is." True thinking is not so much an activity as it is an event that happens:

> But thinking is an adventure not only as a search and an inquiry into the unthought. Thinking, in its essence as thinking of Being, is claimed by Being. Thinking is related to Being as what arrives. Thinking as such is bound to the advent of Being, to Being as advent. Being has already been dispatched to thinking. Being is the destiny of thinking. But destiny is itself historical. Its history has already come to language in the saying of thinkers.[45]

Nature, the world, and Being are not forces to be fought against. Rather, they are standards by which our thinking should be guided. Nihilism, itself an expression of Being, is thus for Heidegger more of a curiosity than a threat, and so it is a thing that warrants investigation and close inspection. We should allow ourselves to be drawn toward it and to be "claimed" by it as we are "claimed" by Being as a whole. This passive orientation toward the phenomena of thought and existence at times approaches an almost mystical and quasi-religious mode of expression. Karl Löwith, a student of Heidegger's, has written that the "fascination with Heidegger's thinking is based primarily on this religious undertone. . . ."[46] Being comes to sound more and more like God, and Heidegger's writing, especially in his later years, becomes increasingly uncanny. One starts to get the impression that Heidegger is on his way toward some sort of beatific vision, and that the tools of language are unable to adequately express the glory and the power of what is making its appearance through him. In Nietzschean terms, the Apollonian seems to recede and the Dionysian rushes in to take its place.

There are provocative parallels to be drawn between Heidegger's and Nietzsche's late life and writings. As is well known, Nietzsche collapsed into insanity in 1889, and his writings leading up to this collapse became more and more eccentric and polemical. His last five books—*The Case of Wagner, Twilight of the Idols, The Antichrist,* and *Ecce Homo*—were finished in 1888, and are among the strangest he ever wrote. For instance the chapters of *Ecce Homo,* [47] Nietzsche's intellectual autobiography, bear the following titles: "Why I Am So Wise," "Why I Am So Clever," "Why I Write Such Good Books," "Why I Am a Destiny." Walter Kaufman counts these late works of Nietzsche's as among his best, calling them "brilliant works of art" that offer a new image for philosophy: "a philosopher who is not an Alexandrian academician, nor an Apollonian sage, but Dionysian."[48] But they also seem to anticipate Nietzsche's approaching break with rationality. After his collapse, when Nietzsche's sister took him under her care, he was enshrined as a mystical prophet, dressed in white robes and worshiped by a circle of followers who took his insanity as a sign of higher genius. The Antichrist became a religious figure himself.

The mystical and religious parallels that may be drawn between Heidegger's and Nietzsche's thought have a major stumbling block, however. Nietzsche's irrationalism was the result of insanity and so his emergence as a quasi-religious figure, and eventually a Nazi icon, was not his own decision. His thought was exploited by others. Heidegger, on the other hand, seemed eager to attain fame and power, and was an exploiter himself. He is infamous for joining the Nazi Party and expelling Jewish scholars from their positions at Freiburg University. His students—including such figures as Hannah Arendt, Karl Löwith, Karl Jaspers, and Jean-Paul Sartre—have struggled to understand these actions, but Heidegger resolutely refused during his lifetime to offer any sort of apology or justification. One suspects that to do so would be inauthentic according to Heidegger. To regret or to attempt to excuse the advent of Being in any of its manifestations is, according to the Heideggerian way of thinking, a kind of "covering over" of Being. Better to let what "is" speak to us itself rather than entangling ourselves in intricate and inauthentic interactions with others. Such entanglement is, of course, nihilism, something that Heidegger believed himself to have transcended, or at least to have been in the process of transcending.

Chapter Three

WORLD-WAR AND POSTWAR NIHILISM

> We are great invalids, overwhelmed by old dreams, forever incapable
> of utopia, technicians of lassitude, gravediggers of the future,
> horrified by the avatars of the Old Adam. The Tree of Life will no
> longer have spring as one of its seasons: so much dry wood; out of
> it will be made coffins for our bones, our dreams, and our griefs.
> —E. M. Cioran, *A Short History of Decay*

World War I was to be only the first of two world wars that would usher in a new "Age of Anxiety"[1] for humankind, and Nietzsche's name is associated with both of these cataclysms. When World War I began in 1914, though Nietzsche had been dead for fourteen years, his *Thus Spoke Zarathustra* became an international sensation. In Germany, it was suggested reading for the soldier in the trenches, while in the rest of the world it was considered the voice of "German ruthlessness and barbarism."[2] During World War II, thanks largely to his sister's and Heidegger's influence, Nietzsche became an idol for the Nazis, and thus again a symbol of violence and evil for the rest of the world.[3] Though debates about the role played by Nietzsche's philosophy in fomenting these wars go back and forth, what is most interesting about this period of history for our own purposes is not so much speculation about the causal mechanisms involved in Germany's aggression, but rather the increasing discourse concerning the issue of nihilism and its full-blown emergence into world history.

William Barrett writes, "August 1914 shattered the foundations of [the] human world. It revealed that the apparent stability, security, and material

43

progress of society had rested, like everything human, upon the void. European man came face to face with himself as a stranger."[4] Barrett is not alone in this reading of history. The world war and post–world war years are conventionally thought of as a time when the West's optimism and faith in development, progress and rationality came into question. With World War I, and especially after the horrors of World War II, the assumption that humankind was on an unblocked path of perpetual and unfrustrated advancement became untenable, and the problem of nihilism became more of an urgent concern. Nietzsche's formulation of the problem as a complicated spiritual and cultural phenomenon, despite his bad popular reputation, gained increasing recognition for its subtle insights and influenced the writing of some of the most important voices and movements of the twentieth century. As Keiji Nishitani writes, "The First World War exposed the profound crisis of Europe, and at the same time Nietzsche's nihilism came to attract more attention than the ideas of any other thinker."[5]

THE NATIONAL SOCIALISTS

Shortly before the outbreak of World War II, Hermann Rauschning, a former National Socialist writing in Paris, published a book condemning the Nazi party titled *The Revolution of Nihilism: Warning to the West*. In this work he offers an analysis of the Nazi movement as a movement not of nationalist spirit, but of nihilism in the Russian sense. According to Rauschning, Hitler and his elites were quite unconcerned with the development of a positive program of economic and political renewal. Behind their rhetoric, he claims, was hidden the most extreme form of nihilism that sought not the reconstruction of Germany but the total destruction of all order and established institutions. "The first thing to realize is that the purpose of National Socialism is actually the deliberate and systematic destruction of the social classes that have made history, together with the last vestiges of their established order."[6] Rauschning's work not only offers an insider's view of the Nazi party, but also characterizes the nihilism of this movement, in a somewhat Nietzschean manner, as a spiritual and moral problem. Any explanation of this moment in history, he claims, must include an account of the decline and distortion of the German spirit and its lost ability to create positive and lasting social goals. The war years, in other words, represent a historical symptom of the nihilistic forces at work in German culture.

Rauschning tells us that Nazi propaganda was largely a smokescreen for a movement that sought not the establishment of a well-ordered state, but the institution of a "permanent revolution."[7] According to this analysis, Nazism held much in common with Russian nihilism and its emphasis on the total destruction of the present order. The Nazis, like the Russian nihilists, sought a "tabula rasa," but unlike the radicals of Russia, these nihilists, according to Rauschning, had no inclinations for the future reestablishment of peace and order. The Nazi revolution was a revolution that advocated constant action, movement, and war.[8] Through violence, it sought to unleash the primal "dynamism" of the German people, and thereby to conquer and destroy everything in the world. In doing so, this movement pursued the exhaustion of the human spirit. All of the racial, political, and social doctrines that the Nazis claimed to advocate were simply the lies of an elite hurtling headlong into the abyss of nothingness. Like the broken treaties and promises made with other nations, Nazi doctrine was a means to an end, intended to motivate the Germans toward action and destruction, while gratifying the will toward oblivion of its leaders. The enthusiasm with which the masses followed Hitler demonstrates, above and beyond all else, that the collective spirit of the German people desired to be used up, depleted, and emptied out. The problem of Nazi nihilism involves both leaders and followers, and is rooted in their ultimate weariness of this world. It was a movement that, in a last frenzied and furious purgation of energy, sought the quietude and silence of nothingness. "The nihilist revolution evades every spiritual impulse, and sees in reason and the things of the spirit its mortal enemies. . . . The purpose . . . is . . . the total destruction of the last and most deep-rooted support of the forces of conservation."[9]

Rauschning's employment of the word *nihilism* is intended as a label of abhorrence. In National Socialism he sees a force of destruction aimed at no positive, ultimate goals. Destruction for a purpose might be understandable, just as disregard for the truth might be justifiable for the sake of conserving a comfortable, safe way of life. However, Nazism wants neither of these. It, instead, wants the dissolution of spirit, the extinction of life, and the oblivion of the void. But in its raging dash toward dissipation it must summon up and use all of its existing force of spirit. Before it can be done with life, it must use up life. Though Rauschning doesn't use the Nietzschean terminology, he does seem to be thinking along the lines of what in the previous chapter I called the logic of ascent and decline. In order to become passive nihilists, the Nazis had first to become active nihilists. Their energetic quest for destruction was a necessary condition for final dissolution and rest. Spiritual weakness spawned a kind of short-term strength, in the form of violence, that was like the final sprint of a lemming toward the edge of a cliff. In the long run, however, lemmings have not become extinct, and neither have human beings. If there is any truth in Rauschning's analysis of Hitler and the Nazis, then their brand of nihilism had necessarily to fail according to Nietzschean standards. To seek deliverance from the eternal struggle of life's forces is impossible, and so the Nazi desire for total oblivion is no less a pipe dream and sign of decadence than are the utopias of the Christian heaven or the anarchist collective.

CAMUS AND THE EXISTENTIALISTS

Though the Nazis have been so labeled, "One does not need to be guilty of atrocities to be called a nihilist,"[10] and so figures of much higher moral standing than Hitler have been placed in this category. Following World War II, philosophers in the movement that became known as existentialism concerned themselves with coming to grips with their postwar understanding of the problem of nihilism. Far from advocating the total destruction and dissolution of the human race, these postwar existentialists sought to confront a situation that seemed to them to be the unavoidable human condition. Following Nietzsche, this intellectual movement saw in humans the type of creatures that struggle endlessly for meaning, purpose, and achievement in the face of a cold, objectively valueless world. The problem for them, and the problem of nihilism as they came to understand it, was how to live in such a world.

To attempt to address existentialism with any sort of comprehensiveness would not only lead us on a long detour in our investigation into the topic of nihilism, it would also inevitably fail. The thinkers involved in this movement disagreed among themselves as to what existentialism is, and still others tried to distance themselves from the label altogether. There have been theistic and atheistic existentialists, those who have advocated passivity and those who have advocated activity. Perhaps Walter Kaufman is correct in his assertion that existentialism is "not a philosophy but a label for several widely different revolts against traditional philosophy."[11] Keeping this in mind, there is, however, one thinker traditionally classified as an existentialist who sums up some of the important themes wrestled with in this movement as well as acting as a passionate spokesperson for the postwar generation.

Albert Camus has offered us one of the most vivid images of postwar nihilism in his reflective depiction of the Myth of Sisyphus. Sisyphus is a Homeric hero whose crimes included stealing the secrets of the gods, kidnapping and chaining Death, and refusing to return to the underworld when so commanded. As punishment, he is condemned to push a rock up a mountain, only to have it roll back down when the top is reached. He must endlessly repeat this task for all eternity as punishment for his hubris. This image of endless, meaningless, and absurd toil is intended by Camus to characterize the human condition. Following Nietzsche, and as the atrocities of two world wars had confirmed, Camus finds that "God is dead," and in the absence of an overarching and unifying principle of the universe, humankind is left to pursue its activities in a meaningless and uncaring environment. Like Sisyphus, humans exert themselves in the pursuit of projects that, in the grand scheme of things, mean nothing, accomplish nothing, and help no one. This is Camus's version of the eternal return: a vain struggle of ceaseless travail whose only escape is death.

Drawing upon the insights of thinkers ranging from Nietzsche, Heidegger, and Sartre to Jaspers and Husserl, Camus finds the world to be a place where "contradiction, antinomy, anguish, or impotence reigns."[12] The world is irrational, but humans demand order and sense, and so the encounter of humans with the world produces an absurd situation. Humans have a need for meaning, but the world will not offer them what they need ready-made. The world, in fact, stands in opposition to this need, disappointing and frustrating human desire at every turn. As a result, the encounter with reality produces "a total absence of hope . . . a continual rejection . . . and a conscious dissatisfaction."[13] Humans stand in opposition to a cold, valueless world that makes no logical sense, but which offers the material with which they must struggle if they are to continue living. Thus, "the absurd," which Camus takes to be his primary datum, is comprised of three components: (1) the world, (2) human beings, and (3) the struggle of human beings with the world. If any one of these elements is eliminated, the absurd situation is dissolved, and the uniquely human condition evaporates.

Camus tells us that "one does not discover the absurd without being tempted to write a manual of happiness."[14] Others have sought this happiness with the dissolution of the absurd in one way or another, but such attempts are ultimately unsatisfactory since they are an escape from that situation that spurs humans on to activity and creative struggle. The Nazis tried to escape the absurd by seeking the world's destruction. The suicide seeks personal death as an avenue of escape and many religious thinkers and philosophers, Camus thought, looked for escape through philosophical understanding, which amounts to a religious flight from intellectual struggle. Camus rejects all of these "solutions," recommending, rather, that happiness be sought within the absurd and in the ceaseless confrontation between humans and the world. Sisyphus, we are assured, experiences a kind of joy in his situation, and so, potentially, do all humans who engage in a struggle with the world. In acting, humans create their own fate, write their own stories, and derive their own conclusions. At those moments when Sisyphus pauses to begin yet another cycle in his endless task, he may feel sorrow, but he may also feel a happiness derived from contemplating his own unique endeavor in all of its details. The rock is his own. "The rock is his thing."[15] Though he has not chosen his situation, he has chosen to continue in that situation, absurd as it may be, deriving a kind of joy from his personal decision.

Camus's own assessment of the "human condition" led him to advocate a stance of "rebellion" over that of "revolution." The revolutionary, in contrast to the rebel, is one who seeks to silence the voices and strivings of others in order to establish a particular interpretation of the world as final and solely legitimate. In so doing, the revolutionary sets the stage for murder. Since the revolutionary interpretation of reality ultimately rests upon nothing other than an individual confrontation with the world, it is, in effect, suspended over a void. There is no final, unchanging, and universally convincing justification for the revolutionary interpretation, and this being the case, its enforcement and defense ultimately have nothing to rely upon other than violence. In the end, there are no objective reasons to be discovered that justify one system of beliefs over another, and so the final court of appeal for anyone who wishes to convince others of the necessity of a certain set of doctrines is the stick. The arguments of all revolutionaries reduce, in the final evaluation, to *argumenta ad baculum*.[16] Furthermore, when the force of violence is appealed to against others, it legitimates violence against oneself. Insofar as the sacrifice of life is seen as necessary for the service of a cause, legalized murder leads to mass suicide. Camus finds the "most striking demonstration of this" revolutionary logic in "the Hitlerian apocalypse of 1945."[17] So, along with Rauschning, Camus sees National Socialism, on account of its revolutionary stance, as a nihilistic movement propelled toward the extinction of all life.

Rebellion, on the other hand, involves a recognition of the ongoing nature of interpretation and struggle in the human condition, and though it strives toward truth and certainty, it never achieves its final goal. Like Sisyphus, the rebel never ceases to strain against the weight of life's burdens. Unlike the revolutionary, the rebel is never content with a final resting point. The rebel reminds one of Nietzsche's camel; a creature that takes on many burdens without fully understanding them. But one is also reminded of Nietzsche's lion, since the rebel is also a "No" sayer. "What is a rebel? A man who says no, but whose refusal does not imply a renunciation. . . . [T]he rebel slave says yes and no simultaneously."[18] Like a good Nietzschean, Camus sees the human attempt to interpret and make sense of the world as a never-ending battle between Apollo and Dionysus. Frenzy and representation perpetually reinforce one another, and the rebel, though immersed in action and the striving that characterizes movement toward a final goal, nevertheless is never satisfied with the end product of these exertions. Such an individual yearns for that which is worthy of effort and is driven to continue searching for value, yet is doomed to fail in capturing anything but the type of meaning and value that emerges in the moment of engagement with the world. This moment of struggle and trial is, according to Camus, what comprises human nature. Here he departs from an existentialist such as Sartre who completely rejects the notion of pre-given human essence, yet in spirit the two are not so alien to one another. For though Sartre claims that "it is impossible to find in each and every man a universal essence that can be called human nature," he nevertheless allows that there is "a human universality of condition."[19] This condition is just what Camus calls human nature. For this reason, when a human affirms this condition, solidarity is also affirmed between that human and the rest of the species. In rebellion, which is just the recognition of, and the willing participation in, humankind's shared struggle within the absurd condition, humans find solidarity, shared dignity, and community. In a twist on the Cartesian cogito, Camus sums up his own absolutely certain discovery: "I rebel—therefore we exist."[20]

The difference between the revolutionary and the rebel is, for Camus, the difference between nihilism and absurdism. Nihilism consists in that path leading humankind toward extinction, while absurdism is that path that leads toward continued, lively exertion. Camus groups all of history's revolutionaries, from de Sade to Nietzsche, from Marx to Sartre, from the anarchists to the fascists, as nihilists of one stripe or another. All wittingly or unwittingly lead the human race on paths resulting in the justification of murder and suicide. Whereas absurdism exhibits a kind of moderation in its acceptance of the contradiction between individual will and the objective constitution of the universe, nihilism does not. Nihilism, in Camus's use of the word, is that situation that results when rebellion becomes revolution, or in other words, when the individual insults human nature by forgetting the shared condition of us all. Any attempt to dissolve the three-part mixture that makes up the absurd is nihilism. Nihilists may have the best of intentions, but, according to Camus, their assertions always eventually lead to degradation, separation, and oblivion.

I have a great deal of fondness for Camus's writing, however I hope later to show that the kind of attitude encompassed in absurdism is not as separate from nihilism as Camus claims. Camus mistakenly treats nihilism as the denial of the world's absurd nature when it is, in fact, the affirmation of something like this claim. Nihilism and absurdism are not so radically distinct, in other words, and so the rebellious attitude recommended by Camus may perhaps function less as a means of overcoming nihilism and more as a cheerful and constructive means of confronting, dealing, and living with the situation that is nihilism. A spirited attitude of good humor, I shall later demonstrate, is the most appropriate response to nihilism, and though Camus comes close to perceiving this, his insistence on characterizing nihilism as a necessarily negative and destructive phenomenon leads him astray.

Despite Camus's insistence that he was an anti-nihilist, and that he was offering a way to "proceed beyond nihilism,"[21] his philosophy and writings are generally held to belong to a tradition that, if not itself wholly nihilist, is at least nihilistic in its flavor. The title of an article appearing in *The Humanist* in the 1950s expresses a common view of the entire postwar existentialist movement: "Existentialism: Irrational, Nihilistic."[22] Existentialism has been characterized as an understandable, if somewhat melodramatic and extreme, response to the great wars of the twentieth century, and so of less philosophical concern than it is of literary and cultural interest. Its exponents, primarily Sartre and Camus, are accused of painting an overly dreary, gloomy, historically and culturally specific picture of humankind. Furthermore, their solutions to the "Condition Moderne" are criticized as encouraging and motivating nihilism rather than curing it. "Like every other response to nothing . . . the existentialist program was doomed to failure. In a senseless world, there are absolutely no guidelines for choice."[23] In this vein, postwar existentialism has itself been regarded as an expression of nihilism insofar as it issues forth from a culture that, having been plunged into the pits of moral decline, is left with nothing but a despairing and desperate exclamation of anguish. The term *nihilism,* thus, in postwar Europe abandons some of its Nietzschean ambiguity, taking on a more clearly negative and derisive flavor that hearkens back to its earliest German usage. After World War II, the positive role of nihilistic decline in the greater processes of life was forgotten by Europeans who had seen and suffered bombings, death camps, and mass exterminations. The strangely optimistic and favorable Russian connotations became submerged as the world feared, rather than looked forward to, what destruction was capable of bringing.

YUKIO MISHIMA AND ASIAN NIHILISM

But nihilism, contrary to the claims of a large number of scholars, has never been a uniquely European phenomenon. In Japan, the experience of wars and their aftermath brought with it conditions that encouraged the emergence of philosophers and authors who also began to wrestle with the problem. Furthermore, the native religious traditions of Asia, especially Hinduism, Shintoism, and Buddhism, have always possessed a sensibility that is somewhat nihilistic, and so the close contact between the cultures of Europe, Russia, and Asia during and after the war years promoted an interest in nihilism combining insights from both East and West. In addition, the influence of Nietzsche's ideas had a great impact on Asian culture, especially in Japan where his complete works were translated into Japanese between 1916 and 1929. It is, in fact, Yukio Mishima, a self-avowed nihilist and one of Japan's greatest novelists and essayists, who may "be said to have occupied the position of 'moral spokesman' of the new post-war generation, in much the same way as, say, Sartre and Camus did at about the same time in France."[24] Whereas Sartre and Camus sought escape from nihilism, however, Mishima wholeheartedly embraced it, basked in it, and died for it.

Mishima's confrontation with "the void" was characterized by just as much anxiety, emotional tumult, and despair as the French existentialists, yet his brand of nihilism ultimately came to possess an active, political element that he himself associated with the dynamism of Nazi Germany. Publishing his first novel at age sixteen, Mishima early on received an enthusiastic reception from the Japanese nationalist romantics. However, after World War II as Japanese nationalism lost its steam, so did Mishima's writing career. Nevertheless, he soon reemerged as the voice of his generation with a strangely morbid, depressing, and fatalistic work titled *Confessions of a Mask.* Part novel, part autobiography, this book expresses the condition of a young man growing up during World War II. But it is not the war that is the focus of the story. Rather it is the internal life of the narrator who struggles hopelessly against an obsession with "Death and Night and Blood."[25] This obsession, framed in terms of a desperate and irresolvable problematic, provides the substance of the tale, painting a picture of a young man thrown into a world of predetermined necessity that, because beyond his control, fills him with self-loathing.

The narrator of *Confessions of a Mask* begins his story at the very moment of his birth, claiming to remember details that may or may not correspond with reality. Evidence shows that they do not, but even so he cannot help but keep these memories as his own. As he grows, the character begins to experience sexual attraction to members of the same sex, and realizing that this is not considered normal, he hides his desire and develops the ability to construct a "mask" of normalcy. But the mask that he develops confuses him even further, and his identity becomes a fragmented and disconnected disarray of contradictory feelings, desires, roles, and actions. He finds himself in love with a woman to whom he is physically unattracted, while at the same time he finds himself physically attracted to men for whom he has no love. The only unifying aspect of his personality that asserts itself is a vague and disturbing "desire for death." "It was in death that I had discovered my real 'life's aim'."[26] It is unclear just how much of the narrator in this book is Mishima himself, but it does appear that the longing for death was indeed a preoccupation that propelled Mishima not only to create works that would make him a contender for the Nobel Prize, but would also lead him to commit ritual *seppuku* after an unsuccessful attempt to overthrow the Japanese government. For Mishima, the urge for death was an existential reality, experienced at the outset of his life and engaged thereafter as his only focus.

In most of Mishima's later novels there is development on this theme of "Death and Night and Blood," but there is also an obvious attempt to escape from the helpless feeling that initially seems to accompany its intuition. Toward the end of his life, Mishima began to produce a number of philosophical works that are explicit attempts to make rational sense of his desire for death, and it is in these works that he develops his own brand of philosophical nihilism, drawing inspiration from sources as diverse as Nietzsche and Yamamoto Tsunetomo.

In *Sun and Steel* Mishima offers a sober, mature counterbalance to his earlier *Confessions of a Mask;* not that he disavows anything from his youthful novels, but as he writes, "I am twenty no longer . . . I have groped around, therefore, for some other form more suited to such personal utterances and have come up with a kind of hybrid between confession and criticism, a subtly equivocal mode that one might call 'confidential criticism.'"[27] In the course of this critical self-evaluation, Mishima examines his life work, reflecting upon his own intellectual development and clarifying the themes involved in his *Weltanschauung*. For normal humans, Mishima tells us, an awareness of the body precedes an awareness of words. But he finds himself to be far from normal. In his case, it was an awareness of words that preceded an awareness of the body. As a sickly child, he lived with his infirm grandmother and was forbidden to play with other children. Between the times when he was required to attend to his grandmother, he became an observer of the world as it passed by outside of his bedroom window. These circumstances, he believes, first made him feel that he was a powerless voyeur of reality as it was given. However, he discovered a certain means of control in the manipulation of words. By constructing imaginary worlds in novels, stories, and plays, he became a god and creator capable of exercising his power and will.

The problem with words, though, is that they have a "corrosive function."[28] "Words are a medium that reduces reality to abstraction for transmission to our reason, and in their power to corrode reality inevitably lurks the danger that the words themselves will be corroded too."[29] Words, Mishima believes, originally functioned as a means of communication between people, linking humans together in the common experience of reality. Words may have a connection with the world, but they always also distance us from the world of the here-and-now to the extent that they abstract from particular circumstances in order to create readily recognizable generalizations. This is useful and healthy when it fosters connection between individuals and the further uncovering of reality, but too often, as in his own case, the abstraction of words snowballs, and the words themselves become more and more disconnected from their original sources until they possess no discernible connection to reality at all. Writing that begins as parasitic commentary on the work of others encourages the corrosive function of words, spinning off in strange and perverse directions, corroding not only reality but "words themselves" as they move farther and farther away from being representatives of "Truth."[30] Mishima's analysis of the function of language here recalls that given by Nietzsche in *Genealogy of Morals* and especially brings to mind Heidegger's discussion, in *Being and Time* and elsewhere, of our nihilistic "entanglement" in language that acts to "cover over" Being.

This disjunction between words and reality was, according to Mishima, the origination of what was to become the most important question of his life: how to bring together the ideal world of words with the real world of the body and physical existence; how to bring together art and action? Absolutely unmediated, perfect existence is free of words. It is "primordial," to use a Heideggerian term, or "Dionysian," to use a Nietzschean term. But words are capable of acting like a device that reflects reality, though not perfectly, at least closely. The task for Mishima the artist, then, was to use language as a mirror for reality. In an attempt to overcome his abnormal childhood, it became imperative that he develop a physical confidence in his body that would allow him to become directly aware of the world that lay beyond words. He sought a purely physical intuition into the Ding an Sich so as better to approximate it with the tools of the writer's craft. This began his career in bodybuilding.

Because of the distance words create between people and the world, anyone who works solely with words cannot hope to perfectly apprehend truth or reality. The best that a novelist can strive for is to express an original, new, and idiosyncratic interpretation of the world. The bodybuilder, however, seeks to instantiate the universal and classical form of physical beauty that lies hidden in all humans. As an author, Mishima used words in a way that demonstrated his own unique view, his own experience, and his own interpretation of Being. However, as a bodybuilder, he used weights in a way that demonstrated to him the form that lies latent in everyone. His individual will could have no say in the emergence of the various muscles that must make themselves known when exercised. In the "language of the body," "The limiting factors, ultimately, are the harmony and balance on which the body insists. . . . They also, it seems, fulfill the function of taking revenge on, and correcting, any excessively eccentric idea."[31] As opposed to the "depth" of the artist, the bodybuilder concentrates on surfaces, remaining "shallow" yet scrupulously faithful to reality. It is just this shallowness, furthermore, that allows a bridge to be built between one individual and others. Whereas the artist accentuates the individual and eccentric, the bodybuilder accentuates the common and the shared shapes that all humans recognize and appreciate. Mishima's participation in group exercises at the gym, at his military unit, and in carrying a shrine in the Summer Festival all attuned him to the direct, shared, physical connection of one human with another, bringing him into contact with "a joy akin to terror."[32] But what was this terror?

The sun of the outdoors and the steel of the bodybuilder's weights taught Mishima to see that he was like other humans in at least some respects. Despite many detractors and enemies,[33] his writing likewise touched some common chord in the reading public and in certain critical circles. But although his writing may have been successful in communicating a variety of feelings and emotions, Mishima tells us that it was absolutely incapable of communicating the single most basic, common, and universal feeling that bonds all humans together in community. That feeling is physical pain. Physical suffering, pain, and discomfort must be experienced by the body, and when they are experienced they open up an awareness of mortality, dissolution, and death. Mishima's life-long literary preoccupation with "Death and Night and Blood" was, thus, a murky, profound, yet detached and unreal encounter with the brute fact of physical distress as a signal of impending death. "However much the closeted philosopher mulls over the idea of death, so long as he remains divorced from the physical courage that is a prerequisite for an awareness of it, he will remain unable even to grasp it."[34] The perfectly formed muscles of the weightlifter are perfectly formed for a purpose. They have evolved for action, for countering opposition, for the expression of the "will to power." The better toned and honed they are, the better able they are of sensing and responding to finer and more specific stimuli. They also become more attuned to their own condition as they fluctuate between development and deterioration. When death is approaching, the well-trained body senses it first. Like the war factories that the young Mishima worked in during World War II, and like the Kamikaze pilots who gave their lives for the emperor, the human body is dedicated to one final end—death. All of the efforts of this life terminate in the void of nothingness that waits at the end of life. Strong, noble humans are aware of this, and they become more clearly aware of what this means in all of its details the stronger that their bodies become. For this reason, "the cult of the hero and a mighty nihilism are always related to a mighty body and well-tempered muscles."[35]

Mishima found in the seventeenth-century Japanese code of Samurai ethics *Hagakure* confirmation for his association of a "mighty nihilism" with the physical prowess of a noble warrior. "The Way of the Samurai is found in death,"[36] wrote Yamamoto Tsunetomo, author of *Hagakure,* and with Mishima this notion gained a modern convert. The Samurai believes in nothing, but dedicates his life to the service of his lord, or *daiymo.* This may seem a kind of inconsistency, for how can an individual who believes in nothing serve anyone? But there is, in fact, no real inconsistency in this situation since "Human beings in this life are like marionettes."[37] They are driven by forces that they don't truly understand, but this does not absolve them of the responsibility to fulfill their duties, and the Samurai's duty is toward service and action. Again, here we are reminded of Nietzsche's discussion of the guardians in the well-ordered society and the camel who takes on many responsibilities that are not understood. The nobility of such creatures is derived from the sheer dissipation of energy in their struggle and engagement in tasks.

The European "death of God" was paralleled in Japan after World War II when the Japanese emperor renounced his divine status. Mishima expressed his despair over this situation in a verse quoted by Marguerite Yourcenar:

> Brave soldiers died because a god has commanded them to go to war; and not six months after so fierce a battle had stopped instantly because a god declared the fighting at an end, His Majesty announced, "Verily, we are a mortal man." Scarcely a year after we fired ourselves like bullets at an enemy ship for our Emperor who was a god! . . . Why did the Emperor become a man?[38]

Toward the end of his life, it was the reinstatement of the emperor as divine ruler of Japan that Mishima chose as his goal. In ways it seems like a very strange cause to take up, but in light of Mishima's particular brand of Samurai nihilism, there is sense to be made of this decision. As in Yamamoto Tsunetomo's time, Mishima thought that the culture of Japan was in the midst of decline and decay. Money makers, celebrities, and politicians all were symptoms of this decline that was caused by a general trend toward "Westernization." Whereas the war had allowed for the liberation of the drive toward death, in the postwar world, mass consumption and the desire for a long life overthrew this constant awareness of mortality. Japan had become "femi-nized,"[39] decadent, and weak. The Samurai, by contrast, possessed a "deep, penetrating and yet manly 'nihilism.'"[40] The remedy for Japan's sickness, then, was to reinvigorate the latent Samurai spirit lying asleep in the heart of Japan-ese culture. As with Nazi nihilism, Mishima equated the Samurai spirit with pure action and the dissipation of human energy. But reactivating this spirit on a mass scale required the manipulation of culturally available, relevant, and emotionally evocative symbols. The emperor was such a symbol.

On November 25, 1970, Mishima entered the Self-Defense Headquar-ters of the Japanese government with four of the one hundred members of his private army, "The Shield Society." After barricading the doors and tying up General Mashita, Mishima demanded to address the troops, hoping to moti-vate them to revolution. When this failed, he committed ritual *seppuku,* in the manner of the Samurai. The ritual did not, apparently, proceed as smoothly as planned. While Mishima drew his sword across his belly (starting from the left and moving to the right, five inches across and two inches deep according to the autopsy reports), his second, Morita, was supposed to decapitate him. But Morita either slipped in Mishima's blood or was simply too shaky and nervous to take accurate aim. He ended up inflicting two superficial wounds to his Sensei's back and neck. Furu-Koga, another of the lieutenants, then stepped in, successfully finishing the job. Morita had also planned to commit *seppuku.* However, he was unable to plunge his sword deep enough, and instead only scratched the surface skin on his stomach. Furo-Koga decapitated him as well.

Yukio Mishima died at age forty-five. The world had changed so much in so short a time that very few people could understand his actions. The press was dumbfounded, and the prime minister, Eisaku Sato, is quoted as saying, "He must have been *kichigai,* out of his mind." Mishima's friend Yasunari Kawabata remarked, "What a waste!"[41] Only his mother seemed to understand when she said, "Don't grieve for him. For the first time in his life, he did what he wanted to do."[42]

NIHILISM IN AMERICA

In the figures we have examined so far, it has become apparent that nihilism is not a phenomenon tied uniquely to Western Europeans. Russians and Asians have also struggled with nihilism, and America today has itself emerged into an age of preoccupation with the topic. In the writings of Charles Taylor, Cornel West, Alan Bloom, and Michael Novak there is an explicit intellectual engagement with a particular form of cultural nihilism that they find to be pervasive in various sectors of American society. This sug-gests that the issues lying at the core of the problem are more universal and

common, and less tied to a specific tradition or history, than has conventionally been thought. In the space remaining here, it will be useful briefly to
review some of the relevant works by Bloom, Taylor, and Novak in order to
illustrate more generally the emerging face of American nihilism.

Calling the phenomenon "Nihilism, American Style,"[43] Alan Bloom's
best-selling book, *The Closing of the American Mind*, bemoans the relativism
that he has found to be rampant among American college students.[44] This relativism, Bloom tells us, manifests itself in an essentially ethical character, taking the form of "a moral postulate, [and being seen as] the condition of a free
society."[45] An attitude of cultural relativism, modern college students seem to
believe, is necessary in order to promote the attitudes of openness and toleration that are required for a free, democratic society to prosper. Because they
believe that the values people adhere to are relative to their own particular circumstances and preferences, Bloom finds that American students commonly
claim that it is not only useless, but wrong to try and argue about such issues.
Everybody should be left alone to believe what it is that they want to believe,
and any attempt to influence others in this regard is understood as an
infringement upon personal autonomy. Bloom sees this attitude as the domi-
nant imperative among young people in America, and he is quite critical of its
potential for encouraging fragmentation and a disregard for truth, nature, and
reverence for the Good.

Bloom argues that American culture, and the university system in particular, has experienced a "Nietzscheanization," moving away from a traditional
emphasis on the "Great Books" and toward a kind of intellectual anarchy that
treats all ideas as historically conditioned, produced, and equally legitimate.
The belief that the human mind is able to touch and comprehend permanent,
ahistorical truths has been eroded and undermined by the influences of historicism and pragmatism. Tradition, and our common confidence that there
exist things that are truly good and evil, has been lost. "The longing for the
beyond has been attenuated. The very models of admiration and contempt
have vanished."[46] All of this has made us "narrower and flatter." Americans are
becoming self-centered relativists, unconcerned with finding permanent
truths, but overly concerned with finding a "lifestyle" that suits them and constructing a "self" with which they can be comfortable. "It is nihilism with a
happy ending."[47]

What Bloom sees as an emerging form of nihilism in America really
amounts to a kind of soft relativism. Everybody, this way of thinking claims,
should be left to value and believe in whatever it is that they want to believe
in without interference. As Charles Taylor suggests in his book, *The Ethics of
Authenticity*, this American form of soft relativism has at its basis a quite laud-
able, moral ideal that he calls "authenticity." The ideal of "authenticity" holds
that self-fulfillment is a good and worthy goal for individuals to pursue. However otherwise misguided, soft-relativism is premised on this noble belief. The

retrieval of a genuine understanding of this underlying moral imperative is our best hope for a rescue from the kind of "inarticulacy" and fragmentation that has characterized the American decline into nihilism.

Unlike Bloom, Taylor is not so quick to join together with those he calls the "knockers" of the modern culture of authenticity. The upholders of this ideal, after all, support the politics of liberalism and tolerance. However, there is a dark flip side to this coin that Taylor calls "the three malaises about modernity": "'the loss of meaning' . . . 'the eclipse of ends' . . . a loss of freedom."[48] These malaises are the nihilistic outcome of a slide away from a genuine understanding of the moral ideal of authenticity. As this ideal has become degraded, distorted, and deformed, it has given rise to soft-relativism, which in turn has given rise to a fragmentation of society. This fragmentation threatens in the end to undermine the very conditions that allowed us to come together as members of a liberal and democratic culture in the first place. Taylor's critique of relativism is an appeal to the commonly held, yet commonly forgotten, ideal of authenticity, and his argument is intended to reorient us toward this ideal.

When citizens don't engage in dialogue with one another about issues that are important, they lose their shared "horizons of significance"[49] and so their shared sense of meaning and purpose. But without these things, collective action directed toward important ends becomes impossible and so a major aspect of our cultural freedom is lost. Citizens find themselves unable to get together with one another in order to enact social changes and improvements. Rather than freedom and self-fulfillment, individuals experience feelings of isolation, anomie, and powerlessness. In its degenerate form, then, the ethic of authenticity undermines itself, leading to nihilism. Soft-relativism, though initially followed in order to promote self-fulfillment, ultimately destroys the very conditions that make self-fulfillment possible. Nihilism, or "the negation of all horizons of significance,"[50] is a dangerous yet unanticipated byproduct of adherence to a distorted interpretation of an admirable moral imperative.

Taylor offers some very down-to-earth and practical solutions for fighting the drift toward nihilism that are also advocated by Cornel West. The decentralization of highly bureaucratic states is one important measure. Putting the power of government and organization back into the hands of those most directly affected by official decision making will help to alleviate the sense of powerlessness that only aggravates withdrawal from public discourse and involvement on the part of citizens. By getting people more intimately involved with collective decisions, they will develop more of a stake in the political community, and thus come to feel less disconnected from the concerns of their fellow citizens. With this renewed feeling of political potency, citizens will be more confident about participating in debates that touch on a variety of important issues involving public policy, as well as the direction of institutional and technological development.

These more theoretical exchanges of necessity involve philosophical reflection concerning basic values, and so will involve citizens in a much-needed return to the public debate concerning ethics and morality. Shallow relativism and its destructive progeny, nihilism, will thus be defeated.

Taylor calls for a "complex, many-leveled . . . intellectual, spiritual, and political"[51] struggle in the battle against nihilism. In agreement with Bloom, he recognizes that nihilism is more than simply an intellectual or political problem. It involves a question of the spirit. However, whereas Bloom offers the model of Plato's *Republic* as a cure for this malaise, Taylor suggests a recovery of the true spirit of authenticity and an open, popular dialogue concerning its nature. In opposition to Bloom's pessimism about America, Taylor optimistically claims that our social institutions continue to rest upon an undeniably meritorious principle. Though we may have strayed from the best path, we are not completely lost yet.

In 1994, Michael Novak was awarded the Templeton Foundation Prize for Progress in Religion.[52] His formal address, *Awakening from Nihilism: In Preparation for the 21st Century—Four Lessons from the 20th,* echoes some of the sentiments we have already heard articulated by Bloom and Taylor. Novak claims that the wars and struggles of the twentieth century have taught us a number of lessons about the importance of truth, capitalism, and democracy. Yet there is still a lesson that has not been learned. This unlearned lesson concerns the dangers of vulgar relativism, or "nihilism with a happy face." "Vulgar relativism is an invisible gas, odorless, deadly, that is now polluting every free society on earth."[53] According to Novak, this cultural threat promises to undermine Western democracies unless we are able to find our way back to the wisdom and virtues found in the works of Ancient Greece and in the Bible.

Novak's conservatism appears similar in character to that of Bloom's. However, at least one of his earlier writings, *The Experience of Nothingness,* is much more sympathetic to the condition of those who struggle with the problem of nihilism than we might expect. In this work, originally published in 1970, we find Novak actually advocating the "experience of nothingness" as a means of clearing away the illusions and myths of modern society. This experience consists of the realization that there "is no 'real' world out there, given intact, full of significance. . . . Structure is put into experience by culture and self, and may also be pulled out again."[54] In this, he recalls the Russian nihilists, and their advocacy of destruction as a means for opening the way to a better future. However, unlike Bakunin or Nechayev, Novak is a firm believer both in God and the democratic state. The experience of nothingness that he advocates seems to consist in a kind of Socratic skepticism about the world of shallow convention. It manifests itself as "[t]he choice to remain faithful to the drive to question,"[55] and through the exercise of this activity, Novak feels confident that one will ultimately come to discover that which is unquestionable: Truth, God, and Goodness. Through this experience, then, all that is doubtful will fall away, leaving only that which remains firmly rooted in the real.

It is the honesty encountered in the experience of nothingness that Novak has respect for. He encourages this form of honest self-reflection, and sees it as an important part of a meaningful and full spiritual life. However, he also finds it repugnant when this experience becomes codified into a system of belief. Thus, he sneeringly refers to European authors (among them, presumably, those we have already discussed) who promote "nihilism" as a world view. "European thinkers, of course, immediately turned the experience of nothingness, which began to 'infect' Europeans with increasing frequency in the nineteenth century, into an 'ism'; they spoke of it ideologically, as nihilism."[56] This, according to Novak, is unacceptable. The unquestioned embracing of nihilism can lead nowhere. As he was later to proclaim at the Templeton Address, "Nihilism builds no cities."[57]

Despite his enthusiasm for the constructive and positive powers of capitalism and democracy, Novak is first and foremost a Christian religious thinker, and as such predicts a final reckoning in which all that we mere humans have built will disintegrate into nothing. Both his Templeton Address and *The Experience of Nothingness* end on apocalyptic notes: "Free societies like our own, which have arisen rather late in the long evolution of the human race, may pass across the darkness of Time like splendid little comets, burn into ashes, disappear."[58] And again, "Who ever promised us that the world would not end?"[59] Perhaps Novak fails to consider that such comments themselves, when regarded from the standpoint of the atheist, resound with nihilistic overtones.

The modern American discussion about nihilism seems invariably to consider it as a threat and a menace to the stability and functionality of our democratic institutions. There is an air of foreboding and a prophesy of danger associated with this literature that proclaims that American culture is in trouble. Americans have a general lack of confidence in the rightness and goodness of their traditional ideals, and this, so the critics claim, opens the way for the possible subversion of our present freedoms and way of life. The contemporary American critics of nihilism place a heavy emphasis on the potential harmful impact of cultural relativism, and in fact seem to think of nihilism as little more than its most extreme and destructive form. Among mainstream American academics, Novak is perhaps one of the few who comes close to recognizing the potential that the experience of nothingness, if not its close relative nihilism, has for being a useful, transformative, and spiritually uplifting experience.

The preceding chapters, while not pretending to be a comprehensive survey of all of the figures relevant to the topic, have presented a handful of individuals, movements, and philosophies that illustrate the major themes involved in the problem of nihilism. Granted, there are many who have been passed over in the treatment so far, but up to this point I have been trying to restrict my attention to those writers who have explicitly dealt with the topic of nihilism, lived through its experience, and who help to illustrate the themes and issues that recur in this literature. As we proceed in our investigation there will be ample opportunity to examine the works of others who may help to finish off the rough edges of the pattern that is beginning to emerge.

In the chapter that follows, I shall summarize the ground that we have covered so far, and separate some of the various themes that traverse and connect the thinking of nihilists and their movements from the pre- to the postwar periods. Once this is accomplished we will be in a position to understand better what nihilism is and to offer a definition that cuts to the essence of the problem.

Chapter Four

Nihilistic Incongruity

A nihilist has to live in the world as is, gazing the impossible
summit to rubble.
                    —Robert Lowell, *The Nihilist as Hero*

Nihilism is like a quilt that, having been assembled over many years by many
different people and movements, is a patchwork of scraps and hand-me-
downs. Though the origins of these patched-together legacies may have been
long forgotten by their heirs apparent, an investigation into ancestry reveals a
recurrent pattern of related issues and concerns. As with any exploration into
family history, ugly facts that we would rather forget may be unearthed. The
integrity of this quilt, however, depends upon leaving its main threads intact,
even if what results is not harmonious or pleasant to look at. This having been
said, let's take a look at what we have so far unraveled.

Nihilism, as we encounter the idea today, is an ambiguous concept that
has its roots in at least two separate places. First, the earliest German use of
the term *(nihilismus)* was directed toward Kant and his followers, and was
intended to describe that situation in which individual, human knowledge and
experience is alienated from participation in the Ding an Sich, or absolute
reality, as a consequence of the bifurcation of the world into phenomenal and
noumenal realms. Beyond being a simply descriptive label, the early German
use of the term also placed a negative evaluation on this state of affairs. The
earliest use of the term *nihilism,* then, involves two conceptually distinct components, one descriptive and the other evaluative.

Second, the Russian use of the term, which may or may not have developed independently of the earlier German variant, places emphasis on destructive political action pursued without a positive goal in mind. The Russian nihilists, though, possessed a strange kind of optimism in the future, seeing themselves as ground clearers for a better tomorrow. "The urge to destroy is also a creative urge," claimed Bakunin, and as the destructive tools necessary for dissolving the rot and decay that stood in the way of progress, these revolutionaries were looked upon in a not unfavorable light by many in Russia. They exerted a powerful influence on political developments in that country continuing on to the present day. The Russian use of the term, then, does not necessarily carry the negative valuation intended in the German use of the term.

The themes in German and Russian nihilism were brought together by Nietzsche, who reinterpreted the concept, and in it found the symptom of something profound and monumental at the heart of human culture. In it, Nietzsche saw one half of the logical process involved in the eternally recurring ascent and decline of civilizations. With Nietzsche, thus, nihilism became an individual intellectual and spiritual concern as well as a social and political concern, with the two being inextricably linked to one another. The collective striving of a people for progress and excellence tends to produce not only greater and greater group accomplishments, but also greater and greater individual accomplishments within those groups. But these accomplishments only make sense against the backdrop of all that is less meritorious. Cultural and spiritual ascent presupposes the struggle against decline as part of the engine that drives history, and oftentimes it is only a descent into the void that motivates humans to engage in the active battle of creation and achievement. Nietzschean nihilism is either passive or active; it is active when it creates and strives, and it is passive when it submits and gives up. With Nietzsche, nihilism becomes a force of history, instantiated in the endeavors of human beings and played out against the backdrop of the abyss, or the void of nothingness. Nature is the chaos with which human beings must struggle, but there is no final "truth" to be discovered "out there." There is only the recurrent ascent and decline of spirit and its resulting interpretations.

Nietzsche can be regarded as prescient, for the great wars of the twentieth century were both a symptom and a further cause of nihilism in the world, representing a dramatic crisis in the spirit of the human race. The seemingly senseless and ceaseless destruction of human life involved in trench warfare, death camps, and mass bombings opened the eyes of a whole new generation to the importance of confronting the breakdown of their highest values, and to wrestle with the problem of how to live in a world in which hope, along with God, had died. In the world-war and postwar years, the various aspects of Nietzsche's nihilistic world view found their way into the philosophies of thinkers the world over.

Perhaps the most devastating and shocking manifestation of the nihilistic impulse was to be found in Nazism. Many thinkers are united in their assessment of Hitler's political movement as the single most destructive force of nihilism in recent history. Its cost is measured not only in human lives, but in the legacy of fear, suffering, and moral uncertainty that even today remains with us. Nazi nihilism exhibited many of the characteristics of Russian nihilism, especially in its drive for destruction and the unleashing of the pure energy and dynamism of a people, but unlike Russian nihilism, Nazism has been represented, at least by Rauschning, as a pessimistic, rather than an optimistic, movement. Whereas even the most destructive of the Russian nihilists saw themselves as tools for the eventual rejuvenation of society, the Nazis were committed to a "permanent revolution" that would end only with the extinction of humankind. This difference between Nazi and Russian nihilism might be suppressed if Nazi propaganda is taken at face value, and its heralding of the new age of a thousand-year "Reich" is taken seriously. In that case, Nazism might be thought of as fitting the mold of Russian nihilism quite neatly. In fact, the intensity of the political, social, and moral repercussions in Russia and Europe as a result of both of these "nihilisms" is comparable, though in Russia this involved an integration of the program of the nihilists, while in Europe it involved a rejection of that program.

Nietzsche's name is unjustly, yet inextricably, tied to Nazi Germany. In its details his philosophy contradicts most of the dogmas of the National Socialists, but what was attractive and influential to the Nazis was not so much his "system" as a whole, but that strain of Russian nihilism that he inherited, elaborated upon, and to which he gave a distinctively German voice. Crane Brinton, writing during the war in 1941, sees the use Nietzsche was put to by the Nazis as an attempt to develop some sort of philosophical can(n)on in support of Hitler's central text, *Mein Kampf*. The fit was far from perfect, and was accomplished mainly by way of emphasizing Nietzsche's radicalism and exploiting his ambiguous language. "Whatever their ultimate destiny, the Nazis are revolutionists, and they are revolting against a society Nietzsche had earlier revolted against. . . . Nietzsche's contempt for the nineteenth century and all its works, his attacks on Christianity, on humanitarian movements, on parliamentary government, that 'destructive' part of his writings which in verve and clarity is the best of his work—all this is just what the convinced Nazi wants to hear."[1] The interpretive work undertaken by individuals such as Elisabeth Nietzsche and Martin Heidegger at the Nietzsche Archives was instrumental in promoting this inaccurate and irresponsible picture.

Whereas the nihilism of the Nazis is associated with their political drive for action, war, and destruction, the nihilism of existentialism is associated with its position that the world "in itself" is meaningless, worthless, and without value. Humans are "thrown" into this world and must make their way in it. Humans, however, demand that things make sense and have meaning, and so, as Camus claims, the human situation is one that is "absurd." Humans must continually struggle against an inflexible and valueless world, endlessly squaring off and doing battle with a universe that has no objective purpose. It is this picture of alienation that gives the nihilism associated with existentialism the flavor of early German, rather than Russian, nihilism. The position of Kantian philosophy, which separates the finite individual from participation in the objective, ultimate truths of reality, is taken for granted by the existentialists, and their struggle against the negative consequences of this situation is a major preoccupation. This is very pronounced in Camus, but it is a theme that runs throughout all of the existentialists. Even for Heidegger, who believes that the conceptual split between Da-sein and the world is a mistake, humans are still mere "windows" to Being, through which ultimate "truths" are concealed at the same time that they are revealed. Humans are finite. Being is not. The two cannot be reconciled.

At one level, the existentialists give expression to, and embrace, a theme that Obereit, Jenisch, and Jacobi called nihilism, but at another level they seem to reject this label. With its view of a world resisting our comprehension and which is, by its very nature, unfathomable to our understanding, the existentialists proclaim the reality of our ontological alienation. They hold the view (and this is also, it seems to me, true of the theistic existentialists) that there is a vast abyss, a nothing, that separates "human being" from "absolute Being." Humans are forever alienated from their world. They are "strangers" to it and to one another. Here, as a consequence of their ontological premises, we furthermore detect a kind of skeptical, epistemological attitude emerging; the view that knowledge of the world is impossible. Nietzsche held to such a doctrine, claiming that the best we can have are "interpretations" of reality consisting of a mixture of the Dionysian and the Apollonian. Knowledge, in the sense of the true correspondence of a mind to an independently existing reality, is impossible since humans are radically cut off from that reality. We see the world through our own particular lenses, and so our lives are necessarily perspectival.

The emphasis in existentialism upon certain moods, emotions, and feelings that might be characterized as negative is connected with this ontological and epistemological situation. Anxiety is a feeling that, in its vague and undirected manner, alerts us to something that is out of alignment in our very nature. Despair emerges when we find that all our hopes and desires for comfort and "being at home" in the world are doomed. There is no final enlightenment or perfect correspondence of mind with universe. The human condition demands struggle and endless striving as part of its constitution, and here we find a hint of one of the themes that also characterizes the Russian strain of nihilism. Just as Bazarov, Bakunin, and Nechayev emphasized the need for action, so too do the existentialists see struggle within the world as an essential component of what it is to be alive and human. In atheistic existentialism there is a pessimism about the ultimate worth of this struggle, while in theistic existentialism there is an optimism. Thus, the ontological themes of existentialism converge with epistemological and then political, or action-oriented themes that may be either optimistic or pessimistic in mood.

However, existentialists invariably claim that the thrust of their project is to overcome and to leave nihilism behind. They can't, of course, mean that they wish to change or deny the ontological structure of reality. That is, according to them, simply given. To "leave it behind" would entail falling into "inauthenticity" or "bad-faith." Instead, the nihilism that existentialism seeks to overcome is that nihilism associated with a negative evaluation of the human situation in the world. Camus, for instance, wants to affirm the struggle of human will against the objective world and not fall into despair and depression. He wants to engage in the activity of life in the manner of a joyful Sisyphus. This is, he claims, "absurd" without being nihilistic. Yet we might also say that it is ontologically nihilistic without being existentially nihilistic. The lived, existential experience of the absurd need not necessarily be one of despair and depression. At this level, existentialism rejects the traditional label of nihilism as found in the early German usage of the term. In this manner, the existentialists seem to be advocating what Nietzsche called "active nihilism" over "passive nihilism," and in active nihilism there is a convergence of the ontological, existential, and action-oriented themes of nihilism inherited from both the Germans and the Russians.

The Western Europeans and Russians are not the only ones to become engrossed in the problem of nihilism. Nietzsche himself claimed that Buddhism was the Asian equivalent to European nihilism, and so it should be no surprise to find in India, China, and especially Japan a tremendous interest in the topic. For instance, Buddhism rests upon "Four Noble Truths," the first of which is *dukkha,* or the assertion that life is "suffering." "Life . . . is dislocated. Something has gone wrong. It is out of joint."[2] The Second Noble Truth asserts that this suffering is the result of *tanha,* or "desire." The Third Noble Truth finds the solution to life's suffering in the extinction of desire, and the Fourth Noble Truth offers "The Eightfold Path" toward the elimination of desire. In *nirvana,* or "extinction," the Buddhist practitioner experiences the bliss of dissolution, as the personal ego is lost in that absolute nothingness that is at the ground of all Being. In this tradition (which some people hesitate to call genuinely "religious") we find characteristics of a "nihilism of emptiness"[3] that brings together some of the ontological, political, and existential themes we have discussed. In terms of Camus's philosophy, Buddhism (at least the Theraveda variety) might be grouped together with those types of nihilism that seek to escape the struggle of life, and to so elude the uniquely human condition.

Traditional Buddhist writings don't use the term *nihilism,* but as we have seen, certain Asian writers influenced by Buddhism have used the term, and there has been a great deal of energy focused toward looking at the problem of nihilism from an Eastern perspective, as well as looking at Buddhism as nihilistic. In Yukio Mishima we discovered a Japanese author who explicitly dealt with the issue of nihilism, struggling with it existentially, the ultimate result being that he was able to transform himself from a passive into an active nihilist over the course of his lifetime. His suicide might be seen as an attempt to avoid the inevitable decline into decay that necessarily lay ahead for him personally, or as an attempt to bring back the collective sense of meaning and purpose that was lost for Japan when the emperor renounced his divinity. In either case, Mishima's actions put him in the same camp as those Buddhists who search for an end to the cycle of ascent and decline in nirvana; a final place to rest with the dissolution of struggle.

Mishima's nihilism exhibits certain characteristics with which we have already become familiar. As is associated with the early German usage of the term, we see that one of Mishima's central preoccupations centers around a disjunction between the objective nature of reality and the capabilities of human reason to comprehend that reality. Language abstracts, but existence is concrete. This predicament places humans in a position where they must despair of ever creating an accurate representation of the world in terms of art, literature, or for that matter, science. We can never truly understand the world in all of its details and intricacies, and all of our attempts to do so necessarily fall short of the goal. Worse than this, such attempts do damage. So long as they remain ungrounded, words corrode and distort reality, moving our understanding farther and farther away from the world of concrete existence. As we attempt to construct more and more abstract systems out of our language, we produce fantasy worlds that become more and more disconnected from the "truth."

Culturally, furthermore, Mishima's Japan exhibited many of the "nihilistic" symptoms that Nietzsche had discovered in prewar Europe. A kind of crisis of legitimate authority pervaded the country as the emperor renounced his divinity, and the cause for which so many people had died lost all meaning. A cultural and spiritual void was opened up, and until Mishima learned "the language of the body" he felt this lack as a sense of self-loathing and disgust that is expressed through his early novels. Only later is he able to convert this feeling of "passive nihilism" into an "active" or "manly" nihilism. Roy Starrs, in fact, interprets the entire body of Mishima's work in terms of this "deadly dialectic."[4]

In his active confrontation with the void, Mishima expresses yet another characteristic of nihilism that we have seen before. The movement toward militarism, action, and destruction that characterized Russian and Nazi nihilism is found in Mishima's political phase. As a ground-clearing device, political nihilism seeks to eliminate existing institutions, sometimes as in the Russian case, with an optimism for a better future, and sometimes, as in the

Nazi case, with an unrestrained urge for total extinction. Mishima's political nihilism falls somewhere in between these two cases. His desire for the rejuvenation of the Japanese spirit seems to suggest an optimism for the future. However, there is also evidence that his final political persona was nothing more than one more mask meant to cover his own insatiable desire for death and oblivion, in the same manner that Rauschning has argued was the case for Hitler and his officers.[5]

The contemporary American use of the term *nihilism,* as found in the writings of Bloom, Taylor, and Novak (as well as West), emphasizes forms of cultural, epistemological, and moral relativism that are considered destructive and dangerous to the stability and health of our modern democratic institutions. As with the early German use, this current employment of the term is intended to disparage and condemn its targets. Bloom, Taylor, and Novak seem to think that Americans have unwittingly stumbled into nihilism, rather than actively choosing it. In our enthusiasm for equality, individual freedom, and self-fulfillment, we have fallen prey to a form of soft-relativism that has finally manifested itself as a lack of confidence in any sort of assertion about the rightness or wrongness of values. As cultural fragmentation has progressed, these writers feel, the ability of Americans to come together in order to exercise their collective, political will has been eroded. In this way, the epistemological and moral nihilism that individuals have inherited from their culture has contributed to a grander form of political nihilism. American political nihilism, though not calculated as a means of doing away with the present order, is no less destabilizing than Russian nihilism was in the nineteenth century.

It is interesting to note that the contemporary charge of "nihilism" as leveled by Bloom, Taylor, and Novak stresses the destructive passivity of modern American relativism rather than the active dynamism and force of energy associated with the fully conscious single-mindedness of Russian and Nazi nihilisms. Americans are depicted by these authors as a people perhaps well intentioned, yet spiritually misguided. Like young Mishima, they are in need of a cause or a purpose around which to rally. Without such a cause, so the criticism goes, they will fragment into a multitude of subcultures and subgroups having no common bond, but each interested in promoting only their own special interests. American nihilism is thus depicted as an unintended consequence of relativism, rather than as a calculated program of revolutionary zeal.

Whereas the nihilism of the existentialists is associated with negative emotions such as despair and sadness, critics sometimes characterize American nihilism as "happy," presumably in order to illustrate its shallowness and unreflective nature. These happy Americans, however, would most probably reject the charge of nihilism, just as Kantians would dispute the charges of Obereit, Jenisch, and Jacobi. "American nihilism" is considered such only from the disdainful perspective of the cultural critic, and those most prone to making such criticisms seem to be conservative commentators who bemoan the decline of traditional values and morality. The current, American use of the term is, thus, associated with a kind of anxiety about change, and specifically with the sort of change that signals a new lack of confidence or seriousness concerning tradition, authority, and Truth. Nietzsche's proclamation, "God is dead," has finally reached the ears of the masses on this continent.

A general theme that runs through this "quilt of nihilism" we are inspecting expresses itself in a sentiment that might be called "immoralism." Certain ontological, epistemological, existential, and political pains are bearable if a person has faith that there is a larger meaning to the universe. Where the Greeks and medievals thought that they detected some sort of divine order and harmony, the nihilist individuals and movements we have examined so far often speak as if the universe has no ultimate meaning, or that if there is some ultimate purpose to the universe, it will forever elude us. The proclamation "God is Dead" is, in this context, more than simply a theological assertion. It is an observation that traditional standards of authority, structure, and order are no longer available. In its most extreme expression, this situation may lead to the call for destruction and chaos; the Russian response. However, less extreme responses have also been evident in Nietzsche's demand for the "revaluation of all values," in Camus's advocacy of heroic absurdity, in Mishima's disciplined pursuit of "sun and steel," and in the American call for recovery of a common, shared foundation for values. In each case, however, there is the recognition that, as Dostoyevsky wrote in *The Brothers Karamazov*, "[i]f God does not exist, everything is permitted." Ethical nihilism, or the view that all ethical judgments have lost, or never had, legitimacy, thus may be the final outgrowth of other forms of nihilism. If ontologically separated from ultimate reality, humans are incapable of participating in "The Good." The epistemological skepticism following from this separation calls into question the ability of humans even to know what truly ethical behavior is. We live in a darkness, according to the nihilist, that isolates us from any sort of certainty concerning the "truth," "goodness," "reality," "order," or "justice" of the universe. The existential experience of this uncertainty may manifest itself as despair and longing, or conversely, as joy and a sense of freedom. There may also be a middle ground that contents itself with this uncertainty. Again, pessimism, optimism, and indifference all seem possible affective responses to the nihilist's world view, and ethical nihilism does not necessarily translate into a call to sadism and debauchery, though neither does it offer any justification against such excesses.

THE DESCRIPTIVE, NORMATIVE,
AND FATALISTIC PREMISES OF NIHILISM

As this summation demonstrates, there are a variety of recurrent themes that run through and permeate the thought of nihilists. Their literature again and again concerns itself with a very particular description of the world and the place of human beings in that reality. Since the first disparaging usage of the term against Kant, *nihilism* has come to be associated with circumstances in which there is some sort of disjunction between the way things are and the way that humans wish things to be. A contrast is highlighted between what is believed to be the actual state of affairs in the world and what is believed to be an ideal state of affairs. The actual and the ideal in each instance fail to coincide, leaving us with the impression that humans must suffer a distressing alienation that separates them forever from ontological, epistemological, existential, political, and ethical perfection.

Ontologically, the nihilist claims that humans are disconnected and alienated from absolute Being by the very constitution of reality. The result of this separation is the inability to participate fully in, and commune with, the absolute. Human beings are cut off and isolated from the true, objective world that lies beyond their own limited and perspectival awareness. There may be a reality lying beyond our subjective experience—a Ding an Sich—but human capacities are too feeble and limited to fully understand this reality, if it even exists. Words falsify it, and indeed the very operations of our thought distort it. The actual state of human being, alienated and separate from the world of objective reality, stands in contrast to an imagined, ideal state of human being in which the ability to have direct commerce with the real, objective world is still a possibility. The very ontological structure of the universe conspires against humans and their desire for pure and unmediated contact with the absolute, according to the nihilist.

We see this pattern repeated in the nihilist's conception of epistemology. Here it is knowledge, rather than objective Being, that stands out of human reach. Epistemologically, the nihilist declares that the actual form of comprehension possessed by humans ranks as incomplete when measured against the ideal standard of full and absolute knowledge. We are never completely certain about anything, so the nihilist claims. Though there may in fact be ultimate reasons and final justifications that tie together the fragmented bits of information and systems of understanding that constitute our learning, humans cannot possess them because of the limits of the intellect. Humankind is incapable of attaining the certainty and complete justification that constitutes the highest and most valuable level of understanding. This ideal, perfect form of knowledge is beyond the actual, frail capabilities of human aptitude. Only a god could really "know" in this very strong sense of the term, and so our highest epistemic desires are perpetually frustrated.

Existentially, this pattern of contrast and incongruity is continued. In this case, the disjunction that is highlighted concerns the opposition between the quality of the actual, lived lives of human beings and an ideal conception of the "good life." Ideally, life should be fulfilling and satisfying. It should have purpose and meaning that shapes and directs the activities involved in day to day living. Existentially, however, the nihilist proclaims that in actual fact, there is no meaning or point to life. In the end, after a lifetime of striving and activity, we are all destined to die, and at death consciousness is extinguished. There is no afterlife from which we may appreciate our completed lives and be rewarded for doing good or punished for doing bad. The world is ultimately at odds with our desire for meaning, value, and purpose, and though we wish otherwise, our existence is without final significance.

Ethically and politically, the nihilist stresses our separation and alienation from justice and goodness. Ideally, human actions are justified in terms of the "best." However, given the nihilist's world view, no such justification is, in actual fact, available. All human activity must proceed, if it is to be undertaken at all, in the absence of certainty and legitimation. The actual and the ideal diverge in nihilistic conceptions of ethics and politics when the desire for righteousness is undermined by a lack of confidence in one's own actions as measured against the superlative standards of perfect justice or moral correctness. The actions of many of the nihilists we have examined seem to tend toward violence and destruction, and this may be a result of their frustrated desire for justice and goodness. Violence is usually the last avenue that individuals or groups resort to when they are otherwise powerless. Nihilists such as the Russians, the Nazis, and Mishima, in lashing out at the established moral and political orders of their times, may have been engaged in a final, wild, and passionate rebellion against the frustrating constitution of reality. If no actions are ever perfectly good or just, and can never be known to be good or just, then any and all actions, including violence and destruction, might appear equally legitimate ("If God is dead, then anything is permitted"). Camus is one thinker we have looked at who disputed this "logic," claiming that any action leading to murder should be avoided. However, perhaps in this positive admonition against murder, Camus actually departs from a full political and ethical nihilism.

Nihilist literature generally paints a picture of inevitable human alienation. From the finite, human perspective, perfection and final consummation of the natural, human desire for the superlative is simply impossible. Our aptitudes are not up to the achievements that our highest standards of excellence dictate as most worthy of emulation. This contrast is replicated, reinforced, and its consequences amplified, as the various themes of nihilism are brought together. However, there seems to be more to nihilism than a descriptive picture of a universe at odds with human aspiration. Use of the term *nihilism* also seems to suggest a distinctive attitude toward this description of the universe. Charles Kielkopf puts it quite succinctly when he writes that "nihilism is more than a factual claim about how the causal order of the world could go. A statement of nihilism must explicitly state or entail a judgment of values or a normative claim."[6]

In addition to the nihilist's descriptive picture of human alienation from reality, knowledge, the good life, political justice, and ethical goodness, there is a normative judgment passed on this state of affairs. Quite simply put, the nihilist claims that the world as it is in actual fact is other than it ought to be. This sense of dissatisfaction with the nature of reality is evidenced in every one of the nihilists that we have so far examined. Each of them at one point or another expresses a distressed cry of discontent with the world and its constitution. Sometimes this appears as a violent and angry rage against the established order, while at other times it is evidenced as a passive and melancholy attitude of resignation. In either instance, nihilism offers more than a simple, cold, and scientific description of the world. It also intimates that the human relationship to reality is inherently defective.

Victor Frankl has noted, "Nihilism does not contend that there is nothing, but it states that everything is meaningless."[7] This sort of judgment is possible only because the nihilist adheres to a standard of worth against which the things of the world pale by comparison. In light of what we have outlined above as nihilism's descriptive picture of the universe, we might begin to understand this standard of worth in terms of the ontological, epistemological, existential, political, and ethical values that the nihilist adheres to. The specific content of these values may differ, however they all share in common the notion that true worth consists in a complete and perfect fulfillment of their standards. So it is that for the epistemological nihilist, true, real, and valuable knowledge consists in complete certainty. However, nowhere in the world do we find this sort of knowledge, and so all human understanding is, in fact, deficient and worthless. This "all or nothing" understanding of worth seems to be operative in most of the nihilists we have scrutinized.

There is one last, recurrent characteristic that I think can be detected in what we have seen so far in our scrutiny of nihilism. Accompanying the descriptive picture that nihilism paints of human alienation, and the normative claim that the world we live in is worse than it should be, there is also a sentiment of powerlessness expressed in what seems to be the nihilist's belief that humans are ultimately incapable of successfully altering the world and their place in it. Though violent action is sometimes associated with nihilism, what makes such activity nihilistic, it seems, is the belief that ultimately nothing will come of it. When nihilists throw themselves into activity it is with the understanding that its only goal is the expression and dissipation of their life's energy. Any creative product will eventually be consumed by decay. Since there is nothing that humans can do to mend the separation between themselves and reality, they can never actualize their supreme standards of worth and value. This world must remain substandard no matter what we do to try and change the situation.

So it is that nihilists appear to make at least three kinds of claims. (1) They describe a circumstance of human alienation within the world. (2) They make a normative claim that this circumstance is other than it ought to be. (3) They claim that, ultimately, there is nothing we can do to change this circumstance.

Nihilism states that the way the world is, is not the way that it should be, and we humans cannot do anything about this fact. As we have seen in the works so far examined, this is the nihilist predicament. What is to be done when it is recognized that one's highest aspirations are inevitably doomed to frustration and failure? How does one live in a world that will always be less than it should be?

We have come to understand that the real nature of nihilism rests not only in a description of the world, but in a normative and fatalistic orientation toward the situation so described. Despite this, the term has sometimes been used incorrectly by critics to specify what they believe must be the orientation of those who, in fact, accept only the descriptive element of nihilism's view of the world. In other words, it has oftentimes been assumed that the ontological, epistemological, existential, political, and ethical forms of alienation that play a part in nihilism necessarily or naturally imply the normative and fatalistic attitudes that also play a part in the concept. However, this is not the case. One can accept the description of the world that nihilism presents without being led to adopt the other premises of nihilism, as we will see a bit later in this chapter.

We must be careful to remember that the term *nihilism* is sometimes used as a label of derision, while at other times it has been self-consciously adopted as a title of honor. Critics who use the word *nihilism* as an insult are, in effect, saying that if they were in the shoes of those whom they call nihilists, they themselves would be dissatisfied and hopeless about their view of the world. They are, to use a Freudian term, "projecting" their own inferences onto others. This seems to be the case with the critics who accused the Kantians of nihilism. It is not that Obereit, Jenisch, or Jacobi actually believed in Kant's system. Rather, they disbelieved it, and encouraged others to reject it on the basis that if accepted, they would be left with an unfulfillable longing for the ultimate. A satisfied and confident feeling of certainty about the nature of the world would always be missing if Kant's premises were granted, and this, the critics assumed, was a bad thing, since most people were like themselves in considering objective and complete knowledge of reality to be a self-evidently good thing. Because they were upholders of the value of objective epistemological certainty and perfection, they could never be satisfied with the sort of subjectivism that Kant espoused. What Kant had to offer was a pale and worthless stand-in for real Truth, these critics charged. This seems to be the case in the current debate concerning American nihilism as well. It is not that the people making up the American public are self-identified nihilists. Rather, the cultural critics are claiming that they should be, granted their descriptive view of the world.

Insofar as the German idea of "nihilism" has filtered down and been incorporated into later understandings and uses of the word, this sort of inference drawing remains prevalent. Thus, when Nietzsche criticizes the utopian philosophies of anarchists, Christians, and Socrates as "nihilism," he expresses

his own dissatisfaction with their pictures of the world. He finds them in conflict with his own desires and wants concerning life in the here-and-now. If he
were to accept their beliefs, then life in this world would seem meaningless
and worthless. In a like manner, when Nietzsche calls himself a nihilist, he is
intimating that he, at times, also finds this world unbearable as it is. This
sometimes comes through, as it does in Mishima's early works, with a sense of
self-loathing. In proclaiming their nihilism, both Nietzsche and Mishima at
these points express their dissatisfaction and weakness in the face of a cold,
resistant, and objectively valueless world. At these moments, passive nihilism
gives in to the world, recognizing that no amount of human effort will mend
the gap between human being and Being as such. It gives up and so refuses to
act since any action is ultimately doomed to failure and frustration. The world
will never yield to puny, human efforts. We also find Camus using nihilism in
this passive sense as a term of derision, and likewise with contemporary
American cultural critics.

However, we mustn't forget that the Russian nihilists did not intend to
deride or insult themselves by labeling their movement as they did. Instead,
the Russian use of the term is associated with activity and energy; indeed with
an optimism that despite the destruction and violence advocated by their
movement, a new and better future would eventually emerge from the rubble.
The Russian nihilists, however, were willing to sacrifice themselves and their
own personal futures for the sake of a greater opportunity for the rest of their
countrymen. This is most evident in Nechayev and Bakunin's *Catechism of the
Revolutionary,* but we also find hints of this attitude in Chernyshevsky's *What
Is To Be Done?* and in Turgenev's *Fathers and Sons.* In each of these pieces, the
nihilist is depicted as an individual who hates the present order and structure
of the world, and who is willing to move against it, even if this deed amounts
to personal suicide. The Russian nihilists were dissatisfied with the state of
things. The world was not the way that it should be when compared to their
ideal standard of justice. However, instead of passively accepting this state of
affairs, the Russian nihilists acted, and they did so with a violent fury that all
but assured their personal destruction. Despite their hope that the future
would be better for others as a result of their destructive efforts, the Russian
nihilists as a group had no expectation of personal salvation. They had no
hope for their own futures, but this did not prevent them from raging against
the established order.

This active, political form of nihilism has a heroic element to it that many
have found admirable. Those who have adopted the label *nihilism* as a badge
of honor have done so for this very reason. Thus, in contradiction to the negative German use of the term, thinkers such as Nietzsche and Mishima have
at times self-consciously called themselves nihilists in this heroic sense. In
Nietzsche's case, his raging nihilistic activity took place not against a political
order, but against the chaos of the universe. His aristocratic bent led him to

despise Russian radicalism, but in the same spirit of activity he chose to do battle with reality, knowing that with the final dissipation of his "will to power" the world and its Dionysian undercurrent would remain unscathed. This "positive nihilism" counterbalanced his "negative nihilism," and made it possible for him to create his works and vision of the world. As a testament to one's strength of spirit, active nihilism has been understood by some as a title of honor and pride. So it was with Mishima, who in his later life sought a "manly nihilism" in order to do away with his weakness in the face of a world that resisted his desires. If he was not able to change the course of Japanese politics, at least he was able to destroy himself in a final act of heroic protest against a world he hated and despised. Though Camus detests any sort of activity that intentionally or unintentionally leads to murder, he still expresses a sort of admiration for the spirit and dedication mustered by those who, in the face of the void, are able to act and even die for their desires. I don't know if Camus ever read Mishima, but I suspect that he would have the same sort of ambivalent admiration that he expressed toward such figures as the Marquis de Sade, the Russian nihilists, and Nietzsche. Their nihilism, he recognized, was akin to his own absurdism. What separated them was not their bleak view of a world beyond human reach and control. It was rather the nature and content of their ideals. Whereas Nietzsche raged against a world that denied him Truth, and the Russian nihilists raged against a world that denied them Justice, Camus raged against a world filled with suffering and death.

When the term *nihilism* is used as a label of respect, it suggests an approving attitude toward the descriptive, normative, and fatalistic claims outlined above. Those who call themselves "nihilists" do so because they believe there is something valiant and heroic about facing a hostile world with clear-eyed yet dissatisfied fatalism. Those who are unable to understand this attitude tend to use the word as a term of insult or derision, but I think that unless they recognize that authentic nihilism involves more than a descriptive component, they may present a misleading image of those that they so accuse, and in the process intimate more about themselves than they intend.

THE HISTORICAL COMPLICATION

Clarification of the distinctively nihilist philosophy has been complicated by the fact that nihilism is often thought of as part of an ongoing historical process, the stages of which are not neatly distinguishable from one another. We find this in Nietzsche's treatment of the subject where, as a force of decline, nihilism always makes itself known only in relation to a contrasting force of ascent. Though understanding ascent in isolation from decline is impossible, according to Nietzsche nihilism is a conceptually distinct moment in the ongoing and eternal rhythm of history characterized by the progressive decay of confidence in the objective existence of higher values. The individuals who take part in this moment experience these historical changes as a kind of personal conflict and turmoil; an anguish that destroys their confidence in the stability of traditional values while also producing a nostalgia for what seems to have been lost. On this view, authentic, undiluted nihilism stands as the centerpiece of a three-stage process consisting of a past, present, and future, and it may be unclear as to whether or not the stages that precede and follow this most absolute manifestation are properly categorized as nihilism as well.

Alan White has undertaken the task of formulating a typology of these three stages that illustrates the difficulties involved in attempting to distinguish nihilism from other, related philosophical conditions. According to White, the first step on the path of nihilism is what he labels "religious nihilism." The religious nihilist judges that the world of the here and now, the world of becoming, needs a justification if it is to be worthwhile for human beings. Without an ultimate purpose and reason for existing, the world is simply unjustified and so irrational and meaningless. The religious nihilist, thus, posits something like God, Truth, Goodness, Freedom, etc. in order to make life in this world significant. Human activity thereafter becomes important only insofar as it is directed toward one or the other of these ends.

The second stage in the development of nihilism is called by White "radical nihilism," and it is with this kind of nihilism, he correctly points out, that Nietzsche is the most preoccupied. Radical nihilism emerges out of religious nihilism when the sources of the religious nihilist's highest values are exposed as fictitious. God is found not to exist, Truth is not "out there," Good is only the preference of the many, etc. However, the radical nihilist still regards traditional values as worthwhile, and so in contrast the world is transformed into something worthless and without merit. This is the stage of nihilism corresponding to what I suspect is the essential core of the problem. When I refer to "authentic nihilism," it is just this form that I have in mind.

The last stage in this progression is "complete nihilism." Complete nihilism occurs when the radical nihilist stops regarding as worthwhile those traditional values that, in comparison, make the world of the here and now look bad. At this point, the world is reenchanted and becomes valuable in and of itself. The complete nihilist is, in a sense, "beyond nihilism."[8] The longing for something better and more perfect is at an end on this last level. Nihilism has been completed and in this consummation "the complete nihilist, is no longer a nihilist."[9]

It is only the radical nihilist, according to White, who will admit to being a nihilist. The religious and the complete nihilists do not see themselves as such, and they have good reason not to, I think. Among the characteristics that distinguish the radical nihilist from the religious and complete nihilists is an important, psychological fact. The radical nihilist experiences the distress of longing, which is one of the things we have observed again and again in the individuals and movements we have scrutinized. The world just doesn't measure up to the highest criteria that the "radical" nihilist judges as the most excellent measures of worthiness. In the frustration and pain of facing up to the impossibility of actually realizing the superlative standard of worth, the nihilist gains an intuition into the fact that life consists of vain and continuous struggle. Authentic, radical nihilism is bound up with the battle between a desire for the "best" and the belief that the best is never attained. Those values that constitute the traditionally held highest final ends of humankind—Truth, Goodness, Perfection, etc.—are the internalized criteria by which the authentic nihilist can't help but judge the world. Authentic, radical nihilism lies in the incongruity between the way that the world really is and the way that it should be according to the highest human standards.

The "complete nihilist," in contrast, goes "beyond nihilism," dissolving those abstract standards that cause frustration, and in so doing, actually "leaves nihilism behind." This individual confronts some of the same issues as the radical nihilist, but derives completely different conclusions from this encounter. Instead of life appearing as an endless treadmill of vain struggle, the complete nihilist abandons the traditionally accepted highest values and opts instead to accept the world as it is. This individual does not experience a sense of longing for some better world. Rather, the complete nihilist is a pragmatist who is concerned only with the way that things actually are. Anything else is silly dreaming and dramatic romanticism, according to this individual. The only contact that this type has with authentic, radical nihilism stems from a similar descriptive picture of the world in which humans operate. But nihilism in the fullest sense, as we have already found, involves more than just a description of the way the world is. It also involves a desire for the world to be different than it is. As we have already seen, the use of the term *nihilism* is generally associated with some sort of dissatisfaction with the order of the world, and such dissatisfaction presupposes an ideal notion of how things should be. The complete nihilist, in doing away with ideals, is only a nihilist in the sense of "completing," or "being done with," nihilism. While they deal with issues nihilistic, "complete nihilists" are not really nihilists at all. In "leaving nihilism behind," the complete nihilist "is no longer a nihilist."

If the act that marks going "beyond nihilism" is the abandonment of high, unattainable standards of success, then we may have found a clue that will be helpful in leading us to a clearer understanding of what nihilism essentially consists of. In the dissolution of humankind's highest values, the complete nihilist—who might more properly be called a post-nihilist—leaves behind the ideal principles against which the real world looks bad. This situation results not in despondency, frustration, and despair, but rather is a rejection of those feelings. What distinguishes this post-nihilist from authentic nihilists is a refusal to accept this world as being, in fact, worse than it should be. This world, rather, is the standard against which to measure all else, and like a Stoic, the completed nihilist reins in desire in order to fend off possible frustrations and disappointments. The authentic, radical nihilist, by contrast, refuses to accept the world as it is. Frustration, disappointment, and dissatisfaction are part of this individual's experience, and these negative emotions stem, at least in part, from an inability or an unwillingness to do away with very high valuative standards. What marks the radical nihilist as authentically nihilistic is just this incongruity between the real world as it is and the idealized image of a perfect world in which Truth, Goodness, Justice, and Knowledge are fully satisfied. For the authentic nihilist perfection, though desirable and valuable, is forever beyond acquisition.

The religious nihilist is really not a nihilist in this authentic sense either. Such an individual believes that this world is directed toward something better, more perfect and true than that which presently exists, and that this ideal is in the process of being realized. But this is just what the authentic, radical nihilist does not believe. According to the authentic nihilist there is a radical disjunction between the way the world really is and the way the world should be ideally. This disjunction, according to the religious nihilist, however, is just an illusion. There is no necessary split between the ideal and the real. Rather, the real is an aspect of the ideal in the process of achievement. So whereas the complete nihilist dissolves the incongruity between individual desire and the world by getting rid of desire, the religious nihilist never even confronts one of the issues at the core of nihilism as a problem. Believing that our desires are destined to fulfillment, the "religious nihilist" is, if anything, a "pre-nihilist," or one who is possibly on the way to the painful and frustrating discovery that the world resists human ambition. The religious nihilist still has faith (hence the label *religious*) that the world is moving toward a better state of affairs. The genuine experience of nihilism, however, seems to involve denigration of the real world in the face of an ideal, yet absolutely unattainable standard. Even though the authentic, radical stage of nihilism may lie down the road for the "religious nihilist" who loses faith, it does not follow that this stage is itself a form of nihilism. More properly, we might think of it as a stage that might lead up to or precede nihilism.

White's "radical nihilism" is really the only authentic type of nihilism that he discusses, even though he claims "All three positions are 'nihilistic' in important senses."[10] "Complete" and "religious" nihilism may be stages of a historical process through which authentic nihilism emerges and in which it takes part, but this does not mean that the entire process is, as a whole, nihilism. The fact that White's typology places "radical nihilism" at its center, and that it analyzes the other forms only by reference to this central type, suggests that radical nihilism is a core concept telling us something about the essence of nihilism as such. In fact, if we take this as a paradigm, it clears up some confusions surrounding the usage of the term generally. While many philosophies and strains of thought might be considered "nihilistic," what separates pure or authentic nihilism as unique is the unresolved incongruity that exists between the nihilist's desire for perfection and the view that this desire will never be complete no matter what our efforts. The problem of nihilism, in this light, involves the perception of a very high level conceptual incongruity, and philosophies attempting to dissolve this incongruity may be thought of as departing from nihilism. Nihilists, unlike their philosophic cousins, refuse to abandon devotion to the ultimate. The renunciation of desire leads, instead, to more pragmatic theories that, though confronting some of the same issues, are not themselves cases of nihilism.

PYRRHO, STIRNER, RORTY, AND SKEPTICAL PRAGMATISM

Let's look at a class of thinkers who, though they have been labeled nihilists at one time or another, in fact illustrate this key point of divergence between nihilistic and non-nihilistic philosophies. Pyrrho, Max Stirner, and Richard Rorty together represent a trend in skeptical pragmatism that, unlike truly nihilistic thought, offers a solution to, or a way out of, the incongruity lying at the heart of nihilism. A short examination of these figures will be useful in narrowing our discussion and, by way of contrast, helping us to highlight the issues at the core of nihilism itself.

Pyrrhonian skepticism represents one of the earliest, serious confrontations with the issues involved in epistemological nihilism. Pyrrho of Elis proposed a radical form of doubt that began from the observation that every statement could be countered by its own contradictory. This being the case, nothing was certain, including the statement "nothing is certain." Far from surrendering to the pains of ignorant despair, Pyrrho advocated "ataraxia," which is a mental state of peace and restful bliss. The absence of reasonable foundations for any knowledge whatsoever was, contrary to what one might expect, not an occasion for despair at all. Better to recognize and graciously accept the impossibility of justified knowledge than to agonize over the search for a foundation that could never be found.

The skeptic's ataraxia is an attitude of mental quietude intended as a way of facing the lack of foundations in knowledge. The Pyrrhonist gives up the desire for certainty, instead living satisfied and content with convention and the way that things appear to be. This suspension of judgment about ultimate truth or falsehood facilitates navigation through the world by leaving the individual untroubled by the frustration that arises when judging real-world perceptions against the ultimate criterion of absolute certainty. "The Pyrrhonist accepts the conventions of everyday life as a practical criterion without troubling himself over questions about their rational justification."[11] This untroubled attitude promotes serenity and a liberal temperament toward the diverse and competing claims to "truth" of those who argue about such things. The skeptic does not feel threatened or challenged by these claims since they are simply vain attempts to grasp onto what cannot in principle be had. Because the goal of absolute certainty is in principle unattainable one should just stop worrying about it and get on with the rest of life. By becoming free from the desire to judge, the Pyrrhonist becomes free from the disturbances of uncertainty. What begins as a confrontation with epistemological nihilism ends with the surrender of the Pyrrhonist, and it is ataraxia that signals the point of surrender. At that moment, the contrast between the actual and the ideal evaporates and there is a submission to the state of the world as is. Forever after, the hope of transformation, progress, and development is abandoned. In this renunciation we find the skeptical solution to the problem of epistemological nihilism. That solution is to give up the movement and striving toward absolute certainty.[12]

This ancient Greek attitude of renunciation and surrender has been advocated in one way or another by many thinkers who have confronted the themes that we have identified in the basic premises of nihilism. A nineteenth-century variation on this "solution" appears in the egoism of Max Stirner. His only major work, *The Ego and Its Own,* was first published in 1845, and it is here that he proclaims his rejection of all organizing goals and truths as unnecessary constraints upon the unique and personal concerns of individual human beings. Following Feuerbach, Stirner agrees that God does not really exist but is merely an abstraction from the world of material reality. However, against Feuerbach, Stirner goes on to assert that the term *Man* is no less an abstraction than "God." Just as there is no God, there is no Man, but only individual human beings, or "unique ones." The cult of humanity remains the last constraint on individual freedom, and Stirner undertakes as his task the final demolition of this "fixed idea." All higher aspirations, abstractions, and ideals are lies, according to Stirner, and once humans realize this they will become emancipated from the life-denying effects of submission to illusory standards of behavior and achievement. Rather than ataraxia, however, Stirner advocates the unconstrained pursuit of egoistic enjoyment and the exercise of power.

According to Stirner, the history of humankind began with the adoration of "the real." The ancients were like children, thrown into a world that they began to explore and investigate with rabid curiosity. Their investigations, though begun in the naive belief that the truth was to be discovered somewhere "out there," soon led them to the conclusion that the apparent world was really a veil behind which hid an authentic, primordial reality. Through successive and continued waves of abstraction, the search for truth led them to spurn the world of the here and now. Since the unchanging and enduring is more real than the transitory and corruptible, the ancients reached the conclusion that the world of "spirit" was more true than the world of material reality. It was in Pyrrhonian Skepticism, writes Stirner, that the logic of the ancients reaches its culmination:

> There is no longer any truth to be recognized in the world; things contradict themselves; thoughts about things are without distinction (good and bad are the same, so that what one calls good another finds bad); here the recognition of "truth" is at an end, and only the man without the power of recognition, the man who finds in the world nothing to recognize, is left, and this man just leaves the truth-vacant world where it is and takes no account of it.[13]

After this, the door was opened to the otherworldliness of Christianity, which exalts the spiritual and the unseen. As this modern, Christian impulse developed, it became even more abstract, finally culminating in idealism. But idealism then itself embarked upon an ironic development. The idea must find a way to explain the apparent world and to act as its ground, and so it must offer its own account of how it better elucidates all of reality than did ancient materialism. The true essence of the universe, according to idealism, is spirit, and because that spirit finds its expression through human beings, they become the focus of history and the world.

Political liberalism and the desire for absolute freedom represent the further abstract evolution of spirit. But there is an incompatibility between corporeal existence and the call of spiritual perfection that is too large a contradiction to be sustained indefinitely. Humankind is ready, at this point, to emerge into the era of egoism. This development involves the abandonment of abstract categories and collective final ends. Egoism dissolves the "spooks" of idealism, and instead incites each individual human being to pursue those activities that yield personal gratification. Any notion of development, betterment, progress, or improvement is abandoned as false and old-fashioned. They are all abstractions, destructive to the personal awareness of individual uniqueness and power. True fulfillment comes not from following those ideals that by their very definition cannot be made real. It comes, rather, from emptying one's self of abstract content and becoming a "creative nothing."[14] The Stirnerite egoist, like the Pyrrhonian skeptic, abandons those desires aimed at the ideal and in so doing attains a kind of mental satisfaction in accepting the self and the world as is. Life is then just allowed to happen. With this, the inner pain and turmoil involved in trying to strain toward some future greatness may cease. The practical here and now concerns of everyday gratification undermine the inevitable frustration involved in chasing pipe dreams. For these reasons, Stirner tells us, "I have set my affair on nothing."[15]

Stirner's brand of egoism extends the skeptical attack of the Pyrrhonists to all areas of human existence where abstraction dwells. Whereas the ancients tried to "idealize the real" and the moderns tried to "realize the ideal," the egoist simply exists in the world as is, enjoying what is at hand and doing away with the desire for perfection. "'Nothing in the world is perfect.' . . . But we remain in this 'imperfect' world, because even so we can use it for our—self-enjoyment."[16] This is Stirner's version of ataraxia. Self-enjoyment involves the renunciation of those desires directed toward the abstract ends of perfection, excellence, freedom, etc. These things, since they are abstract targets, are never made real, and so are lies. By refusing to orient one's self in relation to these illusory standards, Stirner claims that we can dissolve the dilemma that has always led to human frustration and begin to live life in the manner that it presents itself. Just as the Pyrrhonian skeptic renounces certainty and truth for ataraxia, Stirner renounces all abstract ideals in the name of egoism.[17]

What the skeptic does for knowledge, Stirner does for all other notions of human excellence. This rejection of traditional standards has sometimes been pointed to as a sign that both the Pyrrhonist and the Stirnerite are nihilists.[18] However, I think this rejection also points to a manner in which both of these types diverge from nihilism. Their renunciation of highly valued standards is actually pursued as a solution to what appears time and time again as a central dilemma in nihilist literature, and so, rather than embracing nihilism wholeheartedly, it may be more correct to say that they try to dissolve the problem. Skeptics and egoists confront the problem of nihilism when they give attention to the personal frustration involved in striving toward the unattainable. However, they leave nihilism behind insofar as they offer a way of happily ending, once and for all, the frustration involved in the vain struggle toward perfection. Pyrrhonists and Stirnerite egoists, while accepting the basic descriptive premises involved in nihilism, do not retain the values that are necessary to derive distinctively nihilistic conclusions from those premises. In fact, they explicitly reject those values in arguing against the desirability of stringent, abstract standards and goals for human accomplishment. Pyhrro and Stirner are post-nihilists insofar as they both offer a positive option against the ceaseless toil and struggle of human life.[19] According to them, all is not in vain. We might group them with those religious thinkers and philosophers whom Camus and Nietzsche, conversely, condemned as "nihilists" in another sense; those who seek the dissolution of life's absurd struggles. They claim to have found a final resting place that will relieve the frustrating exertions involved in striving for the ultimate.

Neither Pyhrro nor Stirner discussed the concept of nihilism explicitly, but Richard Rorty, a contemporary exponent of views in some ways similar to those of Pyrrhonists and Stirnerite egoists, has explicitly defined himself in opposition to nihilism. Despite this self-proclamation, others have seen in his views the very essence of nihilism. Rorty prefers to call himself an "ironist."

Rorty's ironism is based in his view of language. All language users, he claims, have become habituated into using certain words in order to construct stories that make sense out of their experiences. These vocabularies vary according to the cultures and subcultures that the individual belongs to, but ultimately they are all rooted in what Rorty calls a "final vocabulary." A final vocabulary is a set of words, different for different groups, that grounds a language. It provides the user with a final line of justification beyond which no speech is possible. "It is 'final' in the sense that if doubt is cast on the worth of these words, their user has no noncircular recourse. Those words are as far as he can go with language. Beyond them is only helpless passivity or a resort to force."[20] Because there is no reasoned justification beyond a final vocabulary, and because different groups work with different final vocabularies, when two language users from different linguistic cultures come into conflict, reason eventually breaks down and argument becomes impotent. The only means of persuasion, short of the force of violence, that is possible in this eventuality is to rehabituate one or the other or both of the individuals into using a different vocabulary.

No vocabulary really picks out the world's true essence, and so there is no criterion for distinguishing between better or worse stories about reality. All stories are, in the grand scheme of things, equally legitimate. However, from inside one language, the descriptions formulated in other languages appear strange. Different ways of speaking inevitably come into contact, however, and over the course of time, linguistic evolution takes place, altering and changing the way that we speak and think about things. Gradual acculturation is what drives the development of language rather than a progressive striving toward Truth. The metaphysicians, in other words, have it wrong if they think that their explanations and descriptions somehow uniquely correspond to the way that things are. There is no final "correct" way of talking about reality, only culturally appropriate or inappropriate ones. The ironist accepts all of this and chooses to rest content in giving up the quest for ultimate Truth in exchange for the gift of endless redescription. Instead of trying to find a "better" way of talking about things, the ironist becomes excited about all of the different ways of speaking. Describing and redescribing experience in different ways is the ironist's preoccupation.

Rorty defines himself as a "liberal ironist" in order to make clear that his final vocabulary contains the presuppositions of liberalism. He advocates the elimination of cruelty as a public good and the freedom for self-development as a private good. As an ironist, he can't offer any argument or justification for why these are goods. He simply accepts them as such and hopes that by his talking in interesting ways about them, others will begin to think of them in this way as well. Of course, there is nothing to preclude the possibility of Rorty himself being won over to another way of speaking, and so he may in the future become socialized into a completely different vocabulary.

Language is a game of power for Rorty. It is the power to describe and thereby to control and manipulate others. "'What is the point of playing the game in question?' . . . It increases our power; it helps us get what we antecedently decided we want."[21] Within a culture, speaking the language of the group allows an individual to navigate and not only survive but prosper socially. For Rorty, then, language is an instrument for self-interested enjoyment, just as it is for Stirner. It is a specific kind of tool whose proper use is the further expansion of one's sphere of influence by facilitating solidarity and cohesion between the individuals comprising a group. In making the interests and values of the collective resonate with those of its individual members, personal prosperity and contentment are, if not assured, at least encouraged.

Like Stirner again, Rorty asks us to renounce many of our traditional conceptions of dearly held values. He is particularly concerned with changing the way that we talk about "Truth" and "Goodness." These words, he wishes to persuade us, have no "natural" justification, but rather are simply formal designations for whatever it is that members of a community decide they value. "[W]e shall call 'true' or 'good' whatever is the outcome of free discussion. . . ."[22] These preferences, which traditionally have been considered the highest of values, are now nothing more than designations for moments of social consensus, according to Rorty, and we should not be terribly troubled by this collapse. What he wants us to be concerned about are those conditions that promote "free discussion," and this for no other reason than he himself values it.

Rorty's position, at first glance, seems very close to an almost complete form of nihilism, combining ontological, epistemological, ethical, and political elements into a rather systematic whole. His world view reminds one, in certain ways, of a liberal counterpart to Mishima's literary/fascistic nihilism,[23] although missing from Rorty is the element of existential anxiety and turmoil that seems such an important part of other nihilist works. "Anxiety or despair over our inability to connect with capital-T Truth is silly, in Rorty's eyes, since there is no such Truth for us to connect with; why berate or bemoan our inability to do something that is impossible because its goal is non-existent?"[24] But it is, I think, just this missing element of anguish that distinguishes Rorty's position as non-nihilistic. Rorty has abandoned respect for "Truth" and "Goodness," and so it is not that troubling for him when he finds them absent from the world. Like Pyrrho and Stirner, he fully renounces the traditional values and background assumptions that, by way of their conflict with his description of reality, would otherwise lead to nihilistic conclusions. He undercuts the problem of nihilism by getting rid of the criteria against which the human situation looks hopeless. The loss of the highest values is not, in this light, viewed as a sign of decline or decay. It is just the way things are.

There is a sense in which Rorty does not even go so far as to confront nihilistic issues at all, but rather evades them altogether. When it comes to questions concerning Truth and Goodness, Rorty tells us that he would like just to change the subject "rather than granting the objector his choice of weapons and terrain by meeting his criticisms head-on."[25] Instead of arguing, he wants simply to speak in a different language, using different words in the hope that others will then acquire the same habit of speaking. The terms that we have found to be associated with the literature of nihilism, we might say, are just not in Rorty's vocabulary. Since Rorty does not use that vocabulary, and since he avoids argumentation and the derivation of conclusions, nihilism is an issue strange and foreign to him. It is just not something that he finds interesting.

My intention in looking at Pyrrho, Stirner, and Rorty has not been to deny that there are nihilistic elements and themes involved in their discussions. Rather, my intention has been to contrast their "solutions" with the more fully nihilistic stances of thinkers such as those examined in the first three chapters of this investigation. There is something non- or even anti-nihilistic in the attempt to overcome and leave nihilism behind, [26] and though these figures may have grappled with some of the issues common to nihilists, it does not therefore follow that they themselves are nihilists.[27] The experience of nihilism takes place from the perspective of individuals who actually possess certain deeply held, traditional values. It is experienced existentially and involves not only beliefs, but feelings and desires. The personal, individual contrast between values and desires on the one hand, and goals and hopes believed impossible, on the other, is nihilistic. At base, thus, nihilism is a personal and subjective battle involving not just the intellect, but the entire impassioned self. The observations of the nihilist are the observations of a living, feeling human who has thus far found the highest goals of humanity beyond reach but who cannot stop wanting those highest of goals to become realized. One cannot give up the desire for the highest, best, and most complete level of attainment and still understand nihilism as a problem. This is, I believe, Keji Nishitani's meaning when he writes, "However appropriate a detached spirit of inquiry may be for other intellectual problems, in the case of existentialism and nihilism it is inappropriate . . . if nihilism is anything, it is first of all a problem of the self."[28] It is a problem, I might add, involving a self that cares about Truth, Goodness, Perfection, and their relationship to the real world.

Much of the ambiguity and vagueness surrounding the issue of nihilism may be the outcome of failing to make some of the distinctions that I have attempted to shape so far in this chapter. While descriptive accounts of human alienation from the world, meaning, and value may constitute part of the picture of nihilism, they do not give the whole story. A full, existential, and psychological confrontation with the problem presupposes that certain background assumptions are also in place. These assumptions involve the belief that humanity's highest values, such as Truth, Goodness, and Perfection, are goals that it is worthwhile to pursue, and that a final achievement of these goals is out of the question. The full impact of the problem of nihilism strikes only when an individual passionately desires ultimate meaning, value, and purpose, but believes those things to be out of reach. Nihilism involves frustration, displeasure, and dissatisfaction, and all efforts to deny the importance of these affective states in this context are attempts to do away with, overcome, or leave behind nihilism as a problem. In order to be a nihilist one must not only have a conception of the world, but also feel a sense of sorrowful dissatisfaction about the way the world is.

A distinctive feature of nihilism is its total rejection of any positive alternative to the continual frustration involved in human struggle toward the ideal. According to the nihilist's philosophy, the world of objective reality is constituted in such a manner that it inevitably must come into conflict with human desire for Goodness, Truth, Perfection, etc. "The philosophical nihilist is convinced that all that happens is meaningless and in vain; and that there ought not to be anything meaningless and in vain."[29] This is a unique kind of incongruity that distinguishes the nihilist from other sorts of skeptics, egoists, and ironists, as well as from cynics, stoics, relativists, pragmatists, and all others who attempt to offer a solution to human dissatisfaction in the renunciation of desire for unattainable superlatives. As so understood, the nihilist is most similar to Camus's sketch of the absurdist; that Sysiphian hero who refuses to renounce the struggle of life's daily undertakings simply because they are "absurd." Nihilistic action is driven by the desire for things to be different than they presently are. At the same time it is accompanied by the conviction that things will never fully be the way that we desire them to be. Struggle is ceaseless, and frustration is inevitable. We constantly fall away from the ultimate in our very battle to achieve it.

As so conceived, the philosophical premises of nihilism can be understood as implying that there exists an unbridgeable incongruity between the highest, most valued human ideals and the real life ability of humans to actualize those ideals. It is a philosophy of struggle and frustration rejecting the view that there is, in fact, a final objective for our earthly exertions, though we wish that there was. The nihilist has both an image of the way that the world is and an image of the way that the world ought to be. These two images are out of sync with one another, and so the real world of the here and now is denigrated in comparison to the ideal, and the ideal is believed to be hopelessly out of reach. Active nihilists gain energy from this situation, always seeing room for improvement and progress in the world of the here and now. Passive nihilists, on the other hand, collapse in despair upon surveying this situation. They see no reason or purpose to struggle if the highest goals are unattainable.

E. M. Cioran, who has been said to embody "the nihilistic-apocalyptic sensibilities of the young generation of Romanian intellectuals,"[30] offers us a vivid and emotional depiction of the personal, painful confrontation with the incongruities involved in nihilism. His writing illustrates the passion of one who recognizes nothing as objectively True or Good, yet who also refuses the renunciation of his desires. In the passage that follows we find an exquisite expression of truly nihilistic ambivalence toward human suffering and frustration. Though he dismisses as factual illusions the "truths" that afford so many people pleasure, joy, and certainty, Cioran also recognizes that to abandon the pursuit of these things simply because they are illusions is a bitter and distasteful decision:

> There is much pride and suffering in every renunciation. . . . The ascetics, who renounced life and fled into the desert, were convinced that they had overcome all human weaknesses. The belief that they had access to a subjective eternity gave them the illusion of total liberation. Nonetheless, their condemnation of pleasure and their contempt for humanity betray their inability to actually free themselves. Were I to withdraw into the most fearsome desert, renounce everything, and live in absolute solitude, still I would never dream of despising men and their pleasure. Since I cannot really enter eternity through renunciation and solitude, since I shall die like the rest, why despise them, why call my way the only true one? All the great prophets lack discretion and human understanding. I witness pain, old age, death, and I know that they cannot be overcome; but why should I spoil another's enjoyment with my knowledge? Suffering and the consciousness of its inescapability lead to renunciation; yet nothing would induce me, not even if I were to become a leper, to condemn another's joy. There is much envy in every act of condemnation.[31]

But, as we have seen, many thinkers have advocated forms of renunciation that, they claim, result in the dissolution of pain and frustration. Human life can be made much more tolerant, comfortable, and pleasant, according to them, by abandoning the desire and struggle for those high ideals and goals that are perpetually out of our reach. This pragmatic orientation toward life promises the dissolution of the problem of nihilism. However, it also comes at a very high price. The desire for perfection is a guard against stagnation, and the struggle toward unattainable, superlative goals is a battle that promotes higher and higher levels of human accomplishment, both on a personal, spiritual level and on a collective, social level. Confronting the painful frustration of failure that necessarily results from the pursuit of perfection allows humans the opportunity for transformation, spiritual growth, and the continued exercise of power. In a world of cold facts and brute forces, the nihilist tells us that it is better to become more, rather than less, passionate about our highest human goals and values, and there may be some truth in this.

In this chapter we have investigated a unique characteristic of nihilism that distinguishes it from other, related philosophical positions. Nihilism involves a picture of the world containing presuppositions of ontological, epistemological, existential, ethical, or political alienation. All humans, the nihilist believes, are in fact separated and cut off from perfect commerce with Being, Truth, Goodness, or Justice. However, not all humans, even if they share this

belief, care that this is so. What distinguishes the nihilist as an authentic pro-
ponent of nihilism is that such an individual possesses a desire for the world
to be different from the way it is believed to actually be, though also convinced
that such a desire is doomed to frustration. The root of authentic nihilism,
thus, lies in an incongruity between the way the world is believed to be in reality and the way that it should be ideally.

Nihilistic incongruity finds expression in the minds and cultures of those
who are unable or unwilling to abandon their highest values even when this
leads to the devaluation of the world around them. Nihilism bewails the distance between humankind and perfection. It longs for Truth and Goodness
and mourns the passing of a time when we could still use these words without irony.[32] Though it is a symptom of shattered confidence and a falling away
from the highest values, nihilism also is a potentially empowering situation
whose very unpleasantness may spur individuals and cultures on to feats of
great courage, accomplishment, and dignity. Distance from the highest values
allows room for movement and may, in fact, act as a motivation toward philosophical reflection, activity, and spiritual depth. In Part Two I shall give closer
attention to the experience that underlies the acceptance of the premises of
nihilism, and in so doing start to uncover the useful potential that lies latent
within the nihilist system of philosophy.

Part Two

DECLINE, ASCENT, AND HUMOR

Chapter Five

DECLINE, DECAY, AND FALLING AWAY

When you have understood the destruction of all that was made,
you will understand that which was not made.

—The Buddha

In the previous chapter we uncovered the basic premises that underlie the philosophy of nihilism, distinguishing it from other, related systems of thought. Authentic nihilists, we found, endorse the following three claims: (1) Humans are alienated from such perfections as absolute Being, Truth, Goodness, Justice, Beauty, etc. (2) This circumstance of alienation is other than it ought to be. (3) There is nothing that humans can do to change this circumstance. Together, these three claims comprise the basic premises that the nihilist takes for granted when reasoning and drawing conclusions about the human condition.

Nihilism has traditionally been considered a philosophy of despair because of the emphasis that it places on the vanity and worthlessness of our earthly struggles.[1] From the perspective of the nihilist, nothing that we do is of real worth because nothing of which we are capable measures up to the superlative standards set by absolute Being, Truth, Goodness, Justice, Beauty, etc. Since the superlative is always beyond reach, all of our accomplishments in this world are, in a sense, substandard. Human life is a constant and hopeless struggle that involves a perpetual falling away from the highest, most worthy ideals. The farther we reach, according to the nihilist, the more painfully we fall away from all that is true, good and perfect. Nihilistic thinking ponders and meditates upon this incongruity between our real-life capacities and the most valued standards of achievement, concluding that nothing we are capable of doing satisfactorily measures up to our highest aspirations.

The trap that past thinkers have commonly fallen into when dealing with the "problem of nihilism" is to conflate all of the negative associations that have become attached to the concept of nihilism with the concept itself. So it is that we find many of the nihilists and commentators on nihilism that I surveyed in both the Introduction and in Part One seeking a means for the "overcoming" of nihilism, and thus, they believe, the overcoming of despair. However, despair is motivated by many factors in human life, and the "overcoming" of nihilism no more implies the end of despair than does the overcoming of poverty. In stipulating the basic premises of nihilism, we have already gone far in clearing away many of the confusing, distracting, and superfluous elements that pull our attention from the core beliefs embodied in the authentically nihilistic philosophy. Our next step is to think through some of the consequences and implications of these premises.

The path that I shall follow in this chapter is an unusual one. Instead of trying to argue for or against the basic assumptions embodied in the nihilist philosophy, I shall instead grant the premises that contribute to this world view and in turn work out some of their consequences. I want to walk along with the nihilist, experiencing the phenomenon from the inside, demonstrating that even from such a perspective, desperation and negativity are not necessary outcomes. I want to show that nihilism may, in fact, be lived with and appreciated. This is an exercise that has rarely been undertaken. As I have already pointed out, it is far more common for critics to attempt to describe a manner in which they believe the philosophy of nihilism might be proven false, "overcome," and left behind. These efforts are ultimately wrongheaded since they convince only those who already dispute the basic premises of nihilism and do nothing to change the minds of nihilists themselves.[2] However, we need not attempt such strong-arm techniques in order to show how nihilistic thinking itself might contribute to an active life approached with an attitude of good humor and a love of wisdom.

The philosophy of nihilism implies a situation that I have called "nihilistic incongruity." Nihilistic incongruity separates nihilists from all that they most highly desire and value, frustrating their every aspiration toward the absolute. We should be careful to note that strictly speaking, "nihilism" and "nihilistic incongruity" are two separate concepts. I shall henceforth use the term *nihilism* to refer to a philosophy that rests upon the three premises reiterated at the beginning of this chapter. On the other hand, I shall use the term *nihilistic incongruity* to refer to that circumstance implied by those premises. If the claims made by nihilism are accepted as true, then we must face the consequence that all that is most highly valued and desired lies out of the bounds of human accomplishment.

What I intend to demonstrate in the remainder of this study is that, contrary to popular philosophical wisdom, the existential consequences of nihilistic incongruity, and of the philosophy of nihilism, are not all terribly negative. By reemphasizing some of the potentially positive philosophical, psychological, cultural, and spiritual ramifications of nihilistic incongruity, we may be able to balance the books, so to speak, and demonstrate that there are, in fact, features of this phenomenon that may act to motivate nihilists to engage in activity, progress, high levels of achievement, and spiritual growth. This being the case, an encounter with the phenomenon of nihilistic incongruity need not be threatening to the meaningful pursuit of life's projects. Encountered as a useful and potentially pleasing sort of incongruity, it may be reacted to with an attitude of good humor rather than with one of despairing anxiety.

In accordance with this general strategy, I shall in this present chapter briefly attempt to explore and understand the inner experience that seems to underlie the nihilist's acceptance of the philosophy of nihilism. I am especially curious to understand why it is that the nihilist remains committed to the second premise of nihilism. We have already come to understand *that* the nihilist cannot abandon loyalty to the absolute. I now would like to know *why*. An understanding of this will give us a point of entry not only into the nihilist's psychology, but into the positively sublime, attractive, and downright amusing consequences that may possibly follow from the contemplation of nihilistic incongruity. Nihilistic incongruity, while promoting distance from all that is most highly valued, nevertheless also has the potential to open up a path of possibility that orients and guides the awareness of the nihilist toward the highest of goals. With this in mind, let us now follow along this path.

According to the first premise of nihilism, humans are alienated from absolute Being, Truth, Goodness, etc. Of course we are not always acutely aware of this, and nihilist authors commonly emphasize the manner in which human beings find themselves distracted from this basic truth about the human condition. One of the primary factors that many of these writers implicate as diverting us from our ontological state of separation from the ultimate is the force of society. Our social duties and projects, though they provide us with various rewards and interesting things to do, also very often encourage us to forget about our own finitude and mortality, thereby "entangling" us in activities that, were we to honestly reflect upon them, would be revealed as absurd. In this regard Nietzsche spoke sneeringly of the human "herd," which acts to disguise individual weaknesses and to shield us from ourselves and our own vain desires. "[D]uring the longest period of the human past nothing was more terrible than to feel that one stood by oneself,"[3] Nietzsche writes. But the comforts offered by the herd against the pains of reality are only shallow distractions that he claims can never fully silence our inner anxieties and our desire for the ultimate. No matter how engrossed we become with our social duties, and no matter how vigorously we attempt to abandon ourselves to the otherworldly promises of a religion, according to Nietzsche we always retain an awareness, muffled and covered over though it may become, of our own finitude and limited amount of inner "will to power." The herd exploits this sort of apprehension, tapping the energy of individuals and utilizing it for its own purposes. In the process, individuals learn to "evaluate as others do, against the inner voice of our taste, which is also a form of conscience."[4] By constraining and directing the energies of its individual members, the herd offers safety, survival, and physical comfort. However, these comforts are offered at the cost of individual freedom, spiritual vitality, and the unsettled, anxious, yet authentic awareness that all life teeters on an abyss of grand nothingness. The culture and conventions of society, along with all of its other wonderful accomplishments and pleasures, are ultimately understood by Nietzsche as attempts by the group to distract its members from the fact that all earthly achievements are doomed to dissolution and decay. As suggested by the second premise of the nihilistic philosophy, despite the pleasurable rewards of fame, fortune, and worldly success, reality ultimately denies us the very things that are truly the most valuable.

Heidegger follows Nietzsche in this regard, indicting "The Crowd" as a potentially corrupting influence upon human existence. According to Heidegger, inauthenticity is the result of our "publicness" which "obscures everything,"[5] pulling us farther and farther away from our own true Being. In overwhelming us with "busyness,"[6] the public world of the crowd forces a wedge between us and an awareness of our highest aspirations toward Being itself. Echoing Nietzsche's cynicism, Heidegger emphasizes the manner in which humans commonly become instruments within a society that pulls them away from themselves. "[B]ecause Da-sein is lost in the 'they, ' it must first find itself,"[7] and it does so, according to Heidegger, by heeding the inner "call of conscience." It is this call that, if heeded, "reveals" to humans that they have been "thrown" into a world in which they are "not-at-home."[8] This realization provokes anxiety and a feeling of "guilt" insofar as it makes us aware that we have allowed ourselves to be pulled away from an authentic relationship to Being itself. The inner "call" of conscience reminds us that we "care" about and desire commerce with absolute Being and yet have allowed ourselves to be distracted from this most important of aspirations.

Though many nihilists devote a large amount of discussion to condemning the corrupting influence of society on the individual, some nevertheless embrace and utilize this same property as a vehicle toward protest, activity, and social change. Mishima, for instance, referred approvingly to the power of "The Group," and its ability to obliterate individuality. In the group, Mishima found "the glorious sense of being the same as others."[9] This sense of belonging provided him with the strength and self-confidence that he needed in order to proceed with his plans for the overthrow of the Japanese government. The more political forms of nihilism, such as Bakunin's and Nechayev's nihilistic anarchism, seek to harness this power of the collective for active, destructive purposes while the more individualistic forms of nihilism, as found in Nietzsche and Heidegger, bewail its constraining and inauthentic nature. Regardless of their different attitudes toward its powers, however, nihilists of all stripes generally emphasize the group as a forceful influence on the individual, which is generally antithetical to uniqueness, individuality, and the pursuit of personal authenticity. Social obligations and duties tend to keep us busy, according to the nihilist, and to distract us from meditating too deeply on our own painful separation from the ultimate.

Mishima writes, "Two different voices constantly call to us. One comes from within, the other from without. The one from without is one's daily duty. If the part of the mind that responded to duty corresponded exactly with the voice from within, then one would indeed be supremely happy."[10] This "inner voice" referred to by Mishima, and recognized by many of the thinkers that we have examined, is experienced by the nihilist as an energetic and unsettled impulse toward the absolute. As they struggle and work toward their worldly objectives, this impulse lies in the background, they claim, providing not only the motivation for striving, but also acting as a standard against which they judge their accomplishments. Its aspirations are very general and very ambitious. It seeks the superlative, the ultimate, and the infinite. It aims toward perfection. It wants to touch Being, Truth, Goodness, and Beauty themselves, and it remains unsatisfied so long as these things are out of reach. It is this aspect of nihilism that has led Gillespie to label it "Promethean."[11] Like Prometheus, the nihilist aspires toward godhood, yet is permanently and pitifully bound to the earth. Camus uses another mythic figure, Sisyphus, to characterize this same situation. According to Camus, it is the innate "appetite for the absolute"[12] that pushes the "absurd man" to engage in the ceaseless, absurd, and rebellious struggle against the world, exhausting life and ultimately "accomplishing nothing."[13] If we are to believe Rauschning's depiction of the Nazis, it was a similar sort of inner "dynamism" of the people that was tapped by Hitler in order to power his "permanent revolution,"[14] and it is quite clear that Bakunin, among the Russian nihilists, held that there is a natural force, or "current of life . . . which manifests itself in all living beings,"[15] and that this force stands behind and motivates the inexorable struggle of humankind toward absolute freedom.

What sometimes appears as a pronounced element of essentialism and vitalism is a recurrent feature of nihilist literature. The most vivid example of this characteristic is, of course, found in Nietzsche's doctrine of the Will to Power, which holds that all of life's phenomena may be analyzed in terms of, and reduced to, the struggle between energetic forces of movement that compete with one another for dominance.[16] Whether or not we ourselves accept this as an accurate description of the nature of humans and the world that we live in, I think we need to be sensitive to the purpose that such proclamations are intended to serve. When authors such as Bakunin, Nietzsche, and Mishima refer to inner drives and forces of life, I believe that they are appealing to these entities not as things that they intend to explain, or as things that they believe permit of objective, empirical verification, but as descriptive metaphors that they find useful for characterizing the feelings involved in their own longing for perfection. Such authors are, in sum, offering reports that describe their unsettled, energetic inner states. To them, it just feels as though some inner force is straining for release and dissipation into infinity. Such authors have hit rock bottom in their search for the reasons that explain why they always want more from the world, and why they must remain unsatisfied with their own finitude. They have reached that point where reflection ceases to yield any further insights, and all that they can do is to report what has been found within. In Heideggarian terms, they have discovered a "primordial" fact about themselves. So it is that Mishima simply considers it "the most natural and decent of all desires, this wish that body and spirit alike should come to resemble the absolute."[17] When asked why it is that they want to experience perfect commerce with the absolute, nihilists can only report that something inside of them naturally drives them toward it. The appeal to inner drives and forces is, I think, an attempt to formulate some sort of characterization of, or explanation for, this primordial fact. According to nihilists, their desire to move closer toward absolute perfection seems as natural a tendency as that of electricity to conduct itself through a wire.

In Kantian terms, the attraction of the nihilist to the ideas of absolute Being, Truth, Goodness, Justice, etc., might be characterized as a kind of "sublime" pleasure. The "sublime" is a feeling of "liking" for that which is "absolutely large."[18] The "absolutely large," according to Kant, is that "beyond which no larger is subjectively possible."[19] Though we can't actually perceive or imagine any particular thing that is absolutely large, we can, through the powers of our reason, conceive of such an idea. Though this superlative exists nowhere in the world of our phenomenal experience, we still have a notion of what the concept means. The experience of the sublime, thus, entails thinking beyond the world of phenomena. It involves an attempted encounter with the supersensible realm of the Ding an Sich. The sublime feeling is the feeling of awe and respect that is experienced when we attempt to touch the absolute reality of the noumenal realm.

Though, as we will see, an encounter with corporeal things is not a necessary component of all sublime feelings, according to Kant the sublime experience often is triggered by encounters with overwhelmingly large physical objects found in nature. By way of illustration, he gives examples of both the "mathematical" and the "dynamical" sublime. The former may occur when our perceptual and imaginative faculties are overwhelmed by the magnitude of certain expansive and vast features of a natural phenomenon. Kant mentions the Milky Way, and the seemingly infinite number of stars and solar systems that it contains, as spurring a sense of the mathematical sublime.[20] When we think of the Milky Way as a whole, we, in a sense, succeed in encompassing the vastness and the infinite number of heavenly bodies that it actually contains into our thought. Even though we can't actually perceive or even imagine each and every one of these bodies all at once, we can think them as "an immense whole,"[21] thereby demonstrating the sublime power of our own minds. The dynamical sublime, on the other hand, is often experienced when we encounter an object, the natural power of which overwhelms us and causes us initially to experience a sense of our own puniness. If we are able to maintain a physically safe distance between ourselves and that object, we may resist its potential for destruction and find within ourselves a sense of "courage" that allows us to feel as though "we could be a match for nature's seeming omnipotence."[22] The sorts of physical objects that Kant mentions as being associated with the dynamically sublime include "bold, overhanging and, as it were, threatening rocks, thunderclouds piling up in the sky and moving about accompanied by lightning and thunderclaps, volcanoes with all their destructive power, hurricanes with all the devastation they leave behind, the boundless ocean heaved up, the high waterfall of a mighty river, and so on."[23] The power and potential for destruction that these things possess is, strictly speaking, unimaginable and beyond our capacity for perception. Yet in our sublime enjoyment of them we experience a feeling of pleasure deriving from an awareness of our own inner strength and its ability to transcend nature's potentially destructive might.

The sublime feeling is rather paradoxical in that while it is a kind of pleasure, it is also associated with a displeasurable sense of being overpowered and with a feeling of discomfort and uneasiness. This feeling is triggered by an unsettling realization that there exists something beyond the apprehension of our perceptual and imaginative powers. These powers must forever remain foiled in any attempt to apprehend the absolutely large. Only by an appeal to the powers of reason can some sort of unifying principle be discovered that is able to comprehend such a supersensible target all at once, and reason provides this in terms of the "infinite." "Infinity" is not a thing in nature, according to Kant, but rather a mental concept that allows us to encapsulate and unify the formlessness of that which would otherwise remain incomprehensible. Though the "absolutely large" resists being encompassed by imagination or perception, with the concept of "infinity," our minds are able to comprehend it, and in a sense to contain and dominate it. A feeling of sublimity is the result of the discovery of this ability in ourselves. It is a kind of respect for our own mental powers and their aspiration toward the Ding an Sich. As we will see, this feeling of respect is one of the keys by which we may unlock the positive value of nihilistic incongruity.

If the sublime experience was triggered only by an encounter with overwhelmingly vast and powerful natural objects, we might rightly be skeptical about the role that this experience plays in nihilism. After all, the nihilist, let us recall, never actually encounters anything worthy of sublime respect in the real world, and it is for this reason that feelings of disappointment, frustration, and despair are often associated with the experience of nihilistic incongruity. However, as Kant is careful to point out, it really is inaccurate to state that the sublime is "in" nature outside of us. Rather, "sublimity can be attributed merely to our way of thinking."[24] What is truly sublime are ideas, not physical objects. The seemingly sublime objects of nature are only triggers that motivate a kind of mental activity allowing us to become aware of the awe-inspiring powers of our own minds to formulate ideas of the "absolutely large." There is, in other words, no necessary connection between the experience of sublimity and a physical encounter with overwhelming objects in nature. What is necessary for the experience of sublime pleasure is an awareness of, and a respect for, our own mental capacity to formulate concepts of the superlative. Nihilists, perhaps to an extent greater than most, are attuned to this very capacity within themselves. Their devout commitment to the ideal realm of absolute concepts is so extreme, in fact, that it often appears as though the actual world is completely incapable of provoking them to feelings of admiration.

Instead of the actual physical objects in nature, it is the experience involved in contemplating the ideas of absolute Being, Truth, and all of the other highest perfections that acts as the trigger for the nihilist's sublime respect. These highest perfections are sorts of "absolutely large" entities that cannot be encountered as anything other than pure concepts. They find no existence in the world of finite reality, but only in the abstract idealizations of the human mind. Because of their supersensibilty, these idealizations possess a power to make the finite individual aware of a quite noble and awe-inspiring capacity; the capacity of the human mind to formulate mental concepts that allow us to hold within our finite selves an idea of the superlative, the infinite, and the absolutely large. This capacity, as Kant writes, "expands the soul,"[25] by releasing the mind from its reliance on the world of finitude.

Kant claims that the sublime experience involves a kind of "moral feeling"[26] that gives us a sort of access to the "Good" itself. In orienting us toward the "absolutely large," the sublime feeling calls our attention to those things beyond which nothing else is conceivable. Our minds, in contemplating this notion, are moved toward the conception of superlatives, and in this a curious and willing desire to progressively encapsulate the various forms of the "absolutely large" under a single, comprehensible idea. In other words, the sublime experience readies our minds to consider the idea of the single, most absolutely large idea imaginable. Just as in thinking of the Milky Way as "an immense whole" we are introduced to our own ability to hold the concept of a vast physical phenomenon in our mind all at once, so in thinking about the totality of our ideas of the "absolutely large" are we able to conceive of the most sublime of all ideas. This idea is "the highest good in the world,"[27] or God, the final cause of all that we experience. Before this most absolutely large of all ideas, Kant thinks that we experience a feeling of fear "without being afraid."[28] The sublime pleasure that comes from contemplating the highest of all supersensible ideals, thus, has the character of an almost mystical wonder related to a sort of religious rapture.

As we have seen in chapter 1, Kant was himself accused of being a nihilist. However, as we see here, this is probably a mistaken accusation. With the sublime feeling, Kant seems to think that the finite human mind discovers a way of thinking that offers it an indirect point of connection to absolute reality. Whether or not this is consistent with the rest of his philosophy is not really relevant to our present discussion. Suffice it to say that Kant, at least in the *Critique of Judgment,* seems to deny the third premise of nihilism.

Furthermore, Kant seems at times to be quite insistent that there is very little danger of anything like nihilistic incongruity developing out of the sublime experience at all. He claims that since the sublime intuition into the ultimate is "inscrutable," it is an essentially "negative exhibition" that we should understand "precludes all positive exhibition whatever."[29] What Kant seems to be getting at here is that because the sublime experience consists not in the imagination or perception of particular things, but in an abstract conception of the absolutely "unbounded" or the "infinite," reasonable people will not be deluded into a desire for the phenomenal experience of any particular "unbounded" or "infinite" thing. He calls such a potential development "fanaticism," claiming that it would involve an irrational "delusion of wanting to SEE something beyond all bounds of sensibility."[30] Kant likens "fanaticism" to a sort of "mania," which is a "disease that deranges"[31] the reason. But in recognizing the possibility of "fanaticism," and its "deep-seated and brooding passion,"[32] Kant also, in fact, inadvertently recognizes the potential for nihilistic incongruity to develop out of the experience of sublimity. Whether we call it "nihilism" or "fanaticism," it still remains that there do in fact seem to be those who have developed an unquenchable and hopeless desire to "see" and experience the perfect realization of unmitigated Being, Truth, Justice, etc.

The nihilist is unable to remain content with a detached and merely aesthetic appreciation of the "infinite." Once the superlative has been formulated as a concept in the nihilist's mind, this individual becomes "fanatically" obsessed with it. The nihilist develops a fanatical and practical interest in pursuing the realization of the ideal, seeking to alter the phenomenal world in accordance with the standards discovered in the absolute. The nihilist becomes devoted to the ideal at the expense of the actual. Despite the warnings of objective reality and the tempting diversions of convention, this individual refuses to rest satisfied with anything less than the ultimate. Nihilism is rebellious in this way, and in the negative affective states often associated with it, we find an ironic illustration of this defiance. If it is believed to be in the nature of things that certain dearly held goals are impossible to realize, why worry at all? Why not just accept the fact that humans are doomed to lives of finitude and imperfection? Why not just be happy with the thought that all of our actions fall short of the highest conceivable ideals? The answer offered by the nihilist is straightforward. To live at peace with the limited and finite constitution of the phenomenal world is to disown a noble and worthy aspiration toward perfection. Even if it is impossible to make the superlative concrete, the nihilist still desires to do so, and no amount of persuasion can convincingly undermine this sublime craving. Negative emotional reactions such as despair announce this condition. They are whimpering objections against the frustrating constitution of the concrete world of experience.[33]

We should note that this sort of rebelliousness in nihilistic thinking in many ways makes it antithetical to aesthetic thinking. We can see this clearly if we follow John Hospers's three-part characterization of the "aesthetic attitude"[34] as being: (1) nonpractical, (2) noncognitive, and (3) nonpersonal. Aesthetic perceptions, he claims, are nonpractical insofar as they involve looking at something "for its own sake and not for the sake of some further end or goal you can achieve by means of it."[35] Nihilistic thinking, however, involves an active desire for the experience of commerce with the object of attention. It is not enough for the nihilist to behold the "absolutely large" ideals of Being, Truth, etc. Instead, this individual possesses a practical interest in the realization of these ideals. So it is that nihilistic thinking is also in contradiction of Hospers's third characteristic of aesthetic thought. The nihilist has an intimate desire to experience the absolute, and thus such an individual's concern is quite personal and interested. According to Hospers, personal and interested concern with an object gets in the way of truly aesthetic appreciation since it pulls us away from the appreciation of the purely perceptual details of the thing itself. This brings us to his second point about the aesthetic attitude. Aesthetic appreciation dwells on perceptual, as opposed to cognitive, experience. Yet nihilistic thinking is almost completely concerned with the contemplation of a nonperceptual incongruity, and thus it is an entirely cognitive undertaking.

Nihilistic thinking is, in some ways, more akin to the religious attitude than it is to the aesthetic attitude. Huston Smith, along these lines, has identified the interested pursuit of "the infinite" as a basic characteristic of those who participate in the vast variety of the world's religions. Hindus, for instance, take it as obvious that what all humans ultimately want is unmitigated Being, knowledge, and joy.[36] Buddhists claim that the innermost desire of human beings is to do away with "the boundaries of the finite self,"[37] while Christians believe that so long as humans remain alienated and estranged from the infinite greatness of the one and only God, they will remain in despair. There does seem to be something very similar in the religious person's admiration for "The Holy" and the nihilist's longing for the absolute. In both cases, there tends to be a denigration of the actual world of earthly existence in favor of an otherworldly realm of perfection. In both cases there is a desire to move closer to perfection, though there is also the conviction that the suffering and torment of *this* world will never end.

However, there is one very important difference between nihilists and those who experience religious longing. Whereas religious adherents believe that their longing for the absolute will ultimately result in successful contact with "The Holy," nihilists believe that the absolute is eternally out of reach. There is, in fact, no God, Brahman, or Nirvana for the nihilist to melt into. There is only a cold, valueless reality that resists desire and promotes frustration and pain. In contrast to the presuppositions of the vast majority of the world's religions, according to the second premise of the nihilist philosophy, reality denies nihilists the very thing that they desire the most: an objectively real "absolute." The ideal aspirations of nihilists are in perpetual conflict with the realities of their actual world, and according to the third premise of nihilism, nothing can be done to transform this imperfect existence into something worthy of admiration. Whereas religions generally claim to offer a path toward the overcoming of pain and suffering in this earthly realm, the nihilist fatalistically accepts that nothing can be done to mend the rift between our finite selves and the absolute.

The nihilist recognizes that the highest conceivable ideals that command our respect and admiration exist nowhere except in our own minds. Whereas Kant takes this as an empowering intuition that attunes us to the power of God within us, nihilists, such as Nietzsche, take this as evidence that "God is dead." Of course this does not mean that God, or any of our highest ideals such as absolute Being, Truth, Goodness, etc., have ceased to be desired and important to us. Rather it means that these ideals have ceased to be considered as objectively present in the world. Just as a child still desires gifts from Santa Claus even after discovering that there is no such person, so too do nihilists still desire an encounter with the absolute even after discovering that the absolute has no objectively real existence. Despair may follow upon this realization. Yet in this experience nihilists may still find a point of departure for philosophical reflection that allows them to reconnect with the sublime and worthy powers of their own highest aspirations.

The Danish philosopher Søren Kierkegaard gives us a model for this sort of reflection. He claimed that all living humans are in despair, and he considered this state to be a "sickness unto death."[38] Because of our necessary, earthly separation from the divine, Kierkegaard held that we are all doomed to live lives that fall short of our highest goals. Yet, a conscious awareness of this fact is worth its drawbacks, he thought, because it establishes an exemplary criterion against which humans may measure themselves and thereby gain the dignity that is appropriate to them as fully developed persons. The individual becomes a "self" only in establishing some standard or ideal against which personal, spiritual development might be gauged. The higher the criterion, the more vigorously and ambitiously does the individual aspire, thought Kierkegaard. Thus, to consciously place one's self before divine perfection and to experience the longing for its fulfillment is to raise the quality and worthiness of one's ambition to the superlative degree. Human beings are "raised up" in their aspiration toward perfection, but at the same time their inadequacies are exposed, and despair is the result.

Despair, according to Kierkegaard, is a state of Being that is inescapable during our earthly existence. It is not something that we can or should avoid, but something that needs to be experienced and lived through to its end in the persistent striving toward godliness. Though despair is a sickness of the spirit, "it is the worst misfortune never to have had that sickness."[39] The experience of despair indicates spiritual ambition and an appetite for improvement. Because it is a symptom of our distance from the highest perfection, it also indicates an awareness of something better than what exists presently. At the same time that it is painful, it is also ennobling in that it orients the soul toward its possibilities. David Michael Levin has used Kierkegaard's very words in describing nihilism as a "sickness unto death,"[40] and though Kierkegaard himself does not utilize the term *nihilism*, his insights have self-evident relevance to our current area of investigation, suggesting a way to conceive of the problem in a manner that empowers rather than destroys, and elevates rather than belittles the individual.[41]

It is neither painful frustration and despair nor earthly suffering and injury that are the worst of human experiences. According to nihilists, no discomfort is more unbearable than the separation and alienation from perfection. They claim, along with Kierkegaard, that the greatest source of human hardship derives from this division, and once we have truly understood and become conscious of this fact, all else seems puny and inconsequential in comparison. While the desire for perfection propels nihilists forward, directing them toward communion with the ultimate, the outside world foils their plans for godhood, impeding their progress and sabotaging their most ambitious aspirations. The world presents obstacles against the free and unfettered pursuit of infinity, and so discontent and despair permeate the human relationship with reality. This nihilists understand to be the normal state of human being.

Feelings of negativity concerning this situation, however, are potential vehicles that might convey the nihilist toward a more positive and enriching state of being. Falling short of superlative standards of achievement forces nihilists to realize just how far they are from perfection. The painful awareness that all that is of the highest value lies out of reach, while potentially debilitating to the human spirit, may also serve to reacquaint it with the very things that are believed to be important, but which have been forgotten or ignored in the course of pursuing life's everyday activities. In the tormenting experience of nihilistic incongruity, awareness is drawn toward the standards against which we feel deficient. This unpleasant feeling of deficiency, like the nausea that accompanies indulgence in unhealthy foods, draws attention to the fact that our lives, like our eating habits, must change. Nihilism is a sign, a symptom, and an indication of our own personal separation from what is most highly valuable to us. However, this separation, and the mournful longing that results, makes us mindful of the very thing that is lacking. Feelings of discontent and despair orient individuals toward their objects of ambition and aspiration. In so doing, these negative feelings may help in the discovery of a focus that acts to organize and direct personal thought and activity. In reflecting upon our deficiencies, we learn to question why we feel ourselves to be deficient, and answers to such questions require that we articulate a standard of value, an ideal state of Being, against which our deficiencies are measured. In the articulation of such an ideal notion of Being, we establish a goal that is considered a worthy and valuable object of pursuit.

In conceiving of such ideal goals as absolute Being, Truth, Justice, etc., the despairing nihilist engages in an awesome task. Just as Kant claimed that an uncomfortable and overwhelming encounter with very large, physical objects might act as a motivation for the individual to realize the sublime powers of the mind, so too might the discomfort of nihilistic incongruity act as a motivation for the despairing nihilist to rediscover the sublime pleasure involved in contemplating ideas of the absolute. Though the nihilist finds no actually existing things that satisfy the desire for perfection, such an experience might be encountered as ennobling and sublime insofar as it attunes the individual to a capacity for thinking beyond the world of our objective, immediate, and finite existence. In formulating notions of the "highest values," the nihilist not only highlights the "fallen" state of our actual existence, but also demonstrates the mighty powers of the human mind to conjure up "absolutely large" ideas that, even as they dwarf our actual accomplishments, may be admired for their capacity to open us up and orient us toward "higher" and "greater" potentialities.

As we discovered in chapter 2, it has been argued by Heidegger that one of the essential characteristics that makes us human is our openness to possibility. This claim has been echoed by thinkers such as Sartre and Camus, and what is meant by it is that the way human being, or Da-sein, exists is different from the way that mere "things" in the world exist. Humans are not simply objectively present in the world as extended things. Rather, "who" they are is defined by their potentialities. "Da-sein is constantly 'more' than it actually is,"[42] writes Heidegger. It involves itself in worldly projects that orient it toward the future and toward the anticipation of things to come. Unlike the unthinking existence of trees or rocks, human beings strive toward the completion of projects, moving forward, and in so doing also always carry with them an awareness of their own finitude and the inevitability of their eventual death. Though this awareness oftentimes gets "covered over" in the course of social living, all of our projects in life are at some level informed by the fact that we are "beings-toward-death." We are aware that we are constantly moving into a future that, even as it makes demands upon us, hurtles us closer to a point of absolute oblivion. Human beings project themselves into tomorrow, making plans and anticipating outcomes. Yet these plans and outcomes, when authentically meditated upon, are recognized as the sorts of things that have no enduring existence of their own. They are part of the subjective world that is created by human beings, and as human beings come to their end, so does the existence of all that seems ultimately important to them.

The nihilist recognizes that the absolutely large ideas of Being, Truth, Goodness, etc., are mind dependent, and despite all of their sublime majesty, nothing can be done to bring them into objective presence. Though, on the one hand, this makes these ideas quite magnificent, on the other, it makes them quite fragile and ghostly. Nihilists, as both Kant and Stirner have quite correctly pointed out, must always fail in their desire to realize the ideal. Yet, from this sort of failure we may be able to retrieve something of value that makes the experience of nihilistic incongruity an occasion not simply for despair and anxiety, but a potential opportunity for the continual opening and interested exploration of human possibility in the sense that Heidegger and the existentialists have claimed is uniquely human. Though the experience of nihilistic incongruity may at times appear to undermine the determination of individuals to continue engaging in activity and the striving toward some better and more full state of being, there is also a sense in which it might cultivate and encourage such a pursuit. This will be the topic of concern in the next chapter.

In this chapter we have explored the nature of nihilistic thinking and have discovered that it involves an admiration for the ideal akin to that experienced in the Kantian Sublime. This insight has allowed us to understand the phenomenon of nihilistic incongruity not as an entirely negative phenomenon, but as one that may potentially make the nihilist aware of a very noble and awe-inspiring power. This is the power to formulate superlatives. While the nihilist's attachment to superlative ideas of perfection often tends to denigrate and belittle the world of actual human accomplishment by emphasizing the failed nature of all earthly pursuits, this attachment also may be used to orient the nihilist toward the highest human potentialities while at the same time keeping open a path in their direction. In the chapter that follows, we will further explore the details of how a nihilistic commitment to the highest ideals might work to open up, rather than to close off, existential possibility.

Chapter Six

AMBITION, ASPIRATION, AND ASCENT

[E]very individual is seized by the striving for perfection, by the
upward striving.

—Alfred Adler, *Superiority and Social Interest*

We have arrived at a point in this investigation where it is now more possible
than ever to understand the real dynamics involved in nihilistic thinking.
Underlying the nihilist's frustration and dissatisfaction with the world of
actual reality is a sort of sublime respect and admiration for some very abstract
ideas. For this reason, it is somewhat inaccurate to claim that the philosophy
of nihilism implies that everything is worthless. Rather, it implies that everything that actually exists possesses a substandard worth when compared to the
ideals of absolute Being, Truth, Goodness, etc. According to nihilistic thinking, since these ideals constitute the objects of the highest value, and since
nothing in our earthly existence can possibly measure up to these standards,
anything that we do in this world is relatively worthless.

We have, thus, succeeded in rescuing a notion of value from the very
depths of nihilistic thinking. Nihilism does not, as Martin E. Marty has
claimed, simply subtract "all elements of affirmation from the universe, leaving a vacuum which it celebrates as a doctrinal absolute."[1] Nihilism is more
complicated than that. It involves an affirmative, yet perhaps unrealistic, commitment to very high standards of ideal worth. By allowing ourselves to think
along with the nihilist, we have come to discover the source of this individual's discontent with the world. However, we have also discovered a point of

leverage by which we may be able to pry nihilism loose from its all too familiar association with unmitigated negativity and despair.

In this chapter I shall explore some of the specific ways in which the
encounter with nihilistic incongruity might actually contribute to the positive
expansion of human possibility. Though it is at times terrible and destructive,
nihilistic incongruity is not necessarily so. When pressed into the service of
life, it may, in fact, function as a motivation for reflection, the clarification of
ideals, and the never-ending pursuit of high levels of human achievement.
Socrates once told a jury of his Athenian peers that an unexamined life is not
worth living. If there is any truth to this statement, then the melancholy and
dejected kind of reflection that is often involved in nihilism, though it may not
be sufficient for a meaningful life, may indeed act as the spur that motivates
the nihilist toward discovering the elements of a life worth living.

We have already discovered that the philosophy of nihilism does not
imply a complete loss of value. What we must now demonstrate is that nihilistic incongruity may itself be considered valuable in light of the nihilist's highest values. What I would like to show is that nihilistic incongruity has the
ironic power, even as it separates the individual from the absolute, to also draw
that individual's awareness back in the same direction. In meditating upon
nihilistic incongruity, the nihilist mentally lingers in the presence of the highest ideals rather than abandoning them altogether. Instead of losing everything, the nihilist retains a relationship with the superlative. Though this relationship, on the one hand, encourages the nihilist to belittle the world of
finitude, it also, on the other hand, acts to bind the nihilist to the ideal; albeit
at a distance. By reemphasizing this positive aspect of nihilistic incongruity we
defuse some of its threatening character and, as we will see in the chapter that
follows, this in turn transforms it into an object not of despair, but an object
of amusement and good humor.

Nihilistic incongruity has the useful potential to attune nihilists to a more
authentic understanding of their own highest aspirations. Such a development
does not promise perfect commerce with the absolute, or perfect understanding of Being itself, but it at least represents a movement in the right direction.
Though the nihilist must always find the world of actual, lived experience to
be lacking in *superlative* worth, this does not mean that it is necessarily lacking in some *degree* of worth. The task that I shall presently undertake will
involve a progressive uncovering of the various levels of positive usefulness
and value that nihilistic incongruity possesses for earthly living. I shall begin
by briefly considering the general role played by frustration and defeat in the
psychological and spiritual development of the individual human being. From
there, I would like to consider some of the potentially negative consequences
that might follow from an overeagerness to flee from the particular sort of
frustration and defeat involved in the experience of nihilism. As we will see,
it is not at all clear that the many "solutions" to nihilism, such as skeptical

pragmatism or postmodernism, offer more "positive" or useful approaches to the problems and challenges that the nihilist encounters in the course of living life. The dissolution of nihilistic incongruity is not, it turns out, an unqualified "good" for nihilists or the communities to which they belong.

Nihilistic incongruity has its roots in the inaccessibility of the ideal. It is a problem that highlights the painful frustration involved at those moments when we come to understand that the highest goals we strive for are out of reach. Falling short of superlative standards of achievement forces us to realize just how far we are from perfection, and this situation signals a point of crisis. Nihilists from Nechayev to Mishima have struggled with a conception of the world that resists their stubborn need for value. A fundamental separation between human being and Being as such assures them that perfect communion with reality is impossible, yet it is this same criterion of perfection against which they must continue to judge their activities in the world. Perfection is never achieved, yet it is still aspired toward as an ideal and as the most valuable state of affairs. The premises of the nihilist philosophy imply that failure and frustration must always remain as signature elements of our lives as human beings. Though we strive and struggle, aspire and aim toward the highest of perfections, in the end, our endeavors will have been in vain.

Sigmund Freud was not the first (nor the last) to claim that it is failure and the frustration of individual desire that constitutes the most basic motivation for psychological, spiritual, and cultural development in human beings. According to Freud, it is because the world offers resistance to the unfettered and undisciplined pursuit of pleasure that human beings develop the ability to "sublimate" their desires, thus becoming psychologically mature and capable of channeling their energies into the long-term projects of civilization. Freud, in truly nihilistic fashion, claims that ultimately humans are *never* capable of attaining "all they desire."[2] This sort of frustration, however, motivates us toward the development of personality, art, culture, and religion.

All human beings have a strong tendency to seek pleasure, claims Freud, yet the external world denies complete satisfaction of this desire. The external world blocks and obstructs the human organism in its unending drive to fulfill the needs of food, comfort, and sex. This sort of frustration, painful though it may be, also has the effect of stimulating the organism to discover strategies and methods for positioning itself within its environment in such a manner that it may make the most of its given circumstances, in the long run reaping the greatest amount of gratification possible. The contrast between an unquenchable drive for pleasure originating from within the organism, and the realities of an external world that grants only limited opportunities for pleasures achieved over a finite period of time, provokes human beings toward activity and, Freud thinks, toward the state of psychological and cultural development that we see in human society today. Humans grow, develop, and evolve in response to the challenges that their environments present. By becoming adept at denying themselves certain short-term pleasures, they become better able to pursue a variety of long-term pleasures that act as replacements for the base and simple bodily enjoyments of childhood. The development of psychological maturity, as well as the pursuit of cultural sophistication, is due largely to this process of repression. All civilized human beings are as a result repressed, neurotic, and sick, according to Freud, yet their neurotic sickness is not of the sort that is unambiguously evil. As we have already heard from Kierkegaard, in fact it may be the "worst misfortune never to have had that sickness."

The most valued ends for human beings, whether they are consciously aware of it or not, according to Freud, are perpetually out of our reach. Deep down in the recesses of our subconscious minds, we are all driven by the contradictory drives of love and death, or Eros and Thanatos, and Freud claims that most of our worldly endeavors and creations are mere stand-ins, or "displacements," that distract us from our unsettled and perpetually dissatisfied inner worlds. All of this should sound very familiar to us by now. The notion that our everyday lives, the lives we lead as public selves, are filled with distractions that take us away from our real inner selves, is a sentiment repeated again and again throughout nihilist literature. The nihilist often seems to convey an attitude of cynical resentment against this situation, emphasizing the inauthenticity that is involved in such a life. Yet with Freud, we are introduced to a more ambiguous, and hopeful, picture of this situation.

Though we cannot ever solve the deeply rooted problems that ultimately trouble us, we can still struggle and strive toward a state of Being in which we understand our plight, in the process becoming psychologically, spiritually, and culturally richer and more textured. "The programme of becoming happy . . . cannot be fulfilled; yet we must not—indeed we cannot—give up our efforts to bring it nearer to fulfillment by some means or another."[3] Nowhere in Freud's writings do we find a more succinct summation of the underlying spirit of psychoanalysis and its nihilistic picture of human existence. There is no end to our failure and suffering in life. However, this need not be understood as a condition that detracts from our own dignity and worth. Rather, it might be understood as the very thing that makes our lives worth living.

Freud emphasized, perhaps more than any other philosopher, the positive role that frustration and dissatisfaction play in human development. Taking a cue from him we might ask the nihilist, what would people who never failed look like? They would probably have no conception of weakness. The world would seem to them like an extension of their will, with no effective distinction being made between wishes and reality. Like newborns, people who never experienced failure would come to feel that the environment naturally conformed to their own desires. Besides the fact that they would have no reason to develop strategies for survival, they would also probably never develop certain characteristics that we normally regard as virtuous, such as the ability to delay or deny themselves gratification or the ability to empathize with the pains and failures of others. The painful lessons of failure are instructive inso-far as they teach us about a world that resists our appetites, thereby pulling us out of ourselves and demonstrating conclusively that the universe is not cen-tered on us. With failure we are taught that sometimes what we want makes no difference, and this is a lesson that serves to imbue us with a modicum of maturity, humility, and modesty.

It is an uncontroversial observation that failure and frustration are unavoidable in life. It does not take a psychologist or a philosopher to under-stand that part of the process of becoming a mature, well-adjusted human being involves developing the ability to face such pains and work through them toward desired goals. Life presents obstacles and hurdles that must be faced and overcome if we are to accomplish anything. None of this is all that controversial or distressing. However, the world view presented by nihilists suggests something a bit more extreme than this. It claims not only that life involves little failures and frustrations, but that life as a whole is one big fail-ure and frustration. The things that we want the most, those things that give life its overall meaning and purpose, are forever out of reach. We may face cer-tain hardships and overcome them during the course of our lives, but ulti-mately we will all die and be forgotten without ever realizing Being, Truth, or Goodness. At the end of our lives, in the final evaluation, everything will have been in vain. The complaint of the nihilist is not that life throws us curveballs once in a while. The complaint of the nihilist is that we are finite creatures, endowed with the ability to conceive of a sublime infinite, and yet this infi-nite must always remain only an ideal; a mere pipe dream. The nihilist's great-est frustration concerns the fact that our lives' undertakings must constantly fall short of this most abstract, and yet magnificent sort of perfection.

Freud disputes that there is any sort of distinct "instinct toward perfec-tion at work in human beings."[4] He does admit, however, that there are those, such as the nihilists we have been studying, who are compulsively attracted to the notion of perfection nonetheless, and that for such individuals, "if it should turn out that life has no [such] purpose, it would lose all value for them."[5] This neurotic attraction to perfection, Freud speculates, may be accounted for in terms of the drive to pursue pleasure, which we have dis-cussed above. The repressed instinct for pleasure "never ceases to strive for complete satisfaction,"[6] and this is experienced by the individual as an unquenchable desire for the absolute. While claiming that the dynamic con-ditions underlying the development of this nihilistic drive for the superlative are present in all human beings, Freud, like Kant before him, seems to suggest that reasonable people normally avoid falling prey to its perils.

Recall that Kant claimed "fanaticism" was the result of a too-enthusiastic desire for the this-worldly realization of "infinity" as first conceived of in the sublime experience. Desperation inevitably lay along this path, thought Kant, since the concept of infinity was an essentially negative idea that did not involve the conception of any particular things. The desire to bring the infinite into concrete existence is doomed to failure, thus, since the phenomenal world of experience consists only of particular things. Freud likewise suggests that the drive for perfection, which is really the drive for infinite pleasure, is doomed to failure since the human organism is finite, and so able to experience only successions of particular pleasures. It is impossible for a finite organism to experience all pleasures at once and forever, and so the desire for perfection is not only irrational, but culminates in despair. In emphasizing the ultimate and necessary frustration that all of our highest desires must meet, the nihilist philosophy has indeed led many an individual down the path of despair. If the worth of a life is gauged only by the standard of perfection, then we are all, and must forever remain, utter failures. This sense of nihilistic hopelessness and despondency is summed up by Cioran when he writes, "The disparity between the world's infinity and man's finitude is a serious cause for despair."[7]

We have, in the previous chapter, shown the nihilist some value in despair nevertheless. As Kierkegaard has demonstrated, despair orients us and makes us painfully aware of the infinite distance between us and our own highest aspirations. In nihilistic despair, people become aware of, and so enter into a relationship with, those things they desire most deeply. Though this relationship is one of distance and longing, it still possesses the power and the potential to draw nihilists toward that which they consider worthy. It gives a focus to the nihilist's struggles in both thought and action. This is all fine and good, but if it is ultimately impossible to consummate the desire for the ultimate, does it, after all, really make any difference? Doesn't the inevitability of nihilistic failure obscure any of the value that we might have discovered in nihilistic incongruity?

The answer is no. Nihilistic failure in fact works to cultivate and sustain the uneasy relationship between nihilists and their most respected objects of value. It binds them fast in an orbit around that which they most passionately desire, keeping the objects of highest aspiration just out of reach, but always in sight. Like a planet that is drawn always inward toward a center of gravity, nihilists never touch the very thing whose invisible tether holds them in place. It is the power of distance that averts planetary disaster, and just as the perpetual movement of our Earth toward the sun creates a system of purposeful activity, so too in nihilistic failure is there the potential to find structure, purpose, and value. Freud has already taught us about the importance of failure and frustration in the maturation and development of human personality and culture. Perhaps if this teaching is applied toward an understanding of nihilistic failure, despairing defeat might be transformed into amused appreciation.

Let us walk through this slowly. The nihilist values nothing more than the superlative ideals of absolute Being, Truth, Goodness, etc. The vain desire that nihilism gives expression to is the longing for the objective and real existence of these absolute perfections. However, as ideals these perfections will forever resist becoming real. Their mode of being is at odds with the mode that the nihilist desires for them. In nihilistic incongruity, thus, we find a situation in which the nihilist must forever fail in the pursuit of that which is most valuable and dearly desired. However, this experience of failure does, nevertheless, have the capacity to reveal something about the objects of highest value, if only in a negative sort of manner. Since nihilistic failure is understood as a falling short of the highest standards of value, in this experience one becomes attuned to those standards of value. If becoming aware of the superlative is worthwhile, then it would appear that nihilistic incongruity itself possesses a degree of value for the nihilist. It makes this individual aware and draws attention to something of great value and importance. Nihilistic incongruity possesses instrumental value insofar as it may act to awaken nihilists to their highest aspirations. Let us call this the "awakening" value of nihilistic incongruity.

Nihilistic incongruity has the capacity to do more than just awaken the nihilist, however. It also grants this individual the gift of perspective and distance. Without nihilistic incongruity, the awakened one would be much like a child who has never been forced to pull away from its mother. As Freud has suggested, such an immature individual would not have the capacity to fully appreciate the consoling and comforting powers of the mother because such an individual would never have been forced to go without these delights. The distance of separation has the capacity to highlight and bring into stark relief those pleasures that might have gone unnoticed were it not for the contrast offered by their absence. So it is for the nihilist that the distance between the real and the ideal worlds allows room for a richer and expanded relationship of proximity to develop. Nihilistic incongruity keeps the nihilist oriented in the right direction while at the same time creating the sort of distance that allows the nihilist to behold and fully appreciate the import of the highest objects of desire. Nihilistic incongruity emphasizes the separateness of the finite individual from the infinite, and in so doing allows the possibility for a mature relationship to be formed between the two. Such a relationship gives the nihilist an opportunity to fully appreciate and admire the sublime power of the superlative in its separateness. Let us call this the "admirational" power of nihilistic incongruity.

Nihilistic failure is part and parcel of nihilistic longing, and without the distance of nihilistic incongruity, there would be neither failure nor longing. Without the revelatory power of distance, the nihilist might never even think about the highest values, and thus, in a sense, be farther away from them than ever before. Heidegger makes this point quite forcefully when he writes about the phenomenon of "dedistancing." His vivid example concerns the spectacles on an individual's face. Though they are:

"sitting on his nose," this useful thing is further away in the surrounding
world than the picture on the wall across the room. This useful thing has so
little nearness that it is often not even to be found initially. Useful things for
seeing, and those for hearing, for example, the telephone receiver, have the
inconspicuousness of what is initially at hand . . .[8]

It is when one loses one's spectacles that they come to mind as important. It
is then that the desire to reacquire them kicks in. Likewise, we might observe
that for the nihilist, it is because the highest perfections are out of reach, or
lost, that they come to mind and are contemplated on account of their distance. In falling away from the ideal, the nihilist becomes aware of just how
valuable it is. Nihilistic incongruity itself has value, then, both in its capacity
to awaken the nihilist to the ideal and to form an admirational relationship
between the nihilist and the ideal.

Furthermore, the frustrating failure involved in the unceasing desire for
the superlative cements the relationship of distant proximity between the
nihilist and those objects of highest value. In refusing to give up the desire for
the absolute, the nihilist is bonded ever tighter to it. Unlike skeptical pragmatists and postmodernists, the nihilist attempts not only to establish, but to
retain a relationship with the ideal, even if this relationship is a frustrating and
painful one. In so doing, the nihilist, in a sense, comes closer to the ideal than
would otherwise be the case. A bond remains in place between the finite individual and the infinite, and this bond of desire connects the nihilist to all that
is most valuable. In light of the highest values, then, nihilistic frustration is
itself of value insofar as it acts unceasingly to draw the nihilist in a valuable
direction. Let us call this the "bonding" value of nihilistic incongruity.

Taken together, the awakening, admirational, and bonding aspects of
nihilistic incongruity may perform a potentially useful and valuable function.
Though they can never mend the disjunction between the finite and the infinite, they can at least act as lines of connection that offer a means of bringing
the accomplishments of this world ever closer to the objects of highest value.
Certainly, all of our earthly accomplishments must ultimately fall short of
superlative perfection. However, that does not preclude the possibility of
endeavoring toward increasing degrees of real-world development and
improvement seen in light of the highest, ultimately unreachable goals. The
"failures" of actual, real-world accomplishment offer a foothold from which
the nihilist may begin to consider what is ultimately of supreme value.[9] From
this foothold, the nihilist may begin the climb toward higher and higher levels of real-world accomplishment that offer better and better approximations
of the absolute. Since the ultimate, final goal that the nihilist aspires toward is
in fact unreachable, a path of unlimited, never-ending, and infinite possibility
may be opened up within this world. The picture that emerges here shares
similarities to that drawn by Plato with his "simile of the line" as discussed in

The Republic, [10] except that in the case of nihilism there is no hope for a final, mystical leap into "The Good" itself. The highest ideals have no objective existence outside of the nihilist's desire for them, and thus the openness of worldly potential *never* closes for the nihilist until death appears on the scene to spirit this individual away forever.

Plato, like most religious thinkers who have come after him, escapes the conclusions implied by the philosophy of nihilism by rejecting its third premise. But we need not reject any of the premises of nihilism in order to uncover the existential value of nihilistic incongruity. If, as Kierkegaard, Heidegger, and the postwar existentialists believe, human beings are defined by their openness to possibility, then in becoming oriented toward future hopes and ideals that are infinitely far away, and in pursuing desires that are perpetually unfulfilled, humans increase their own Being. By multiplying and opening up the possibilities that lie latent within them, humans may constantly and endlessly develop and unfold, emerging into a fuller realization of themselves and their future potentialities. What I am driving at here is that though the nihilist is locked into an eternally frustrating relationship with the absolute, this relationship offers an opportunity to find value in the most profound failures of life insofar as these failures offer a point of contrast that reflects something of the absolute back toward the nihilist. This faint reflection of the superlative keeps the nihilist aware of something greater and more worthy of aspiration that lies just out of reach and in the distance. To always want "more" is to be dissatisfied with the actual and to aspire toward a greater, unrealized potential. If the "essence" of human Being lies in its potentiality, then in nihilistic incongruity we find a means of pursuing the very essence of what it is to be human.

Both Kant and Freud seem to claim that the dynamics involved in nihilistic thinking are irrational, and thus to be avoided. [11] Their arguments reduce to something like this: Since perfection is an unattainable ideal, it is irrational for the nihilist to desire its realization. Furthermore, since it is irrational to desire the realization of perfection, the nihilist should stop desiring such an absurdity. Notice that there are a couple of hidden assumptions involved here. The first is that it is irrational to desire the unattainable. The second is that one should stop desiring that which is irrational. Neither of these assumptions are, of course, self-evidently true. In what follows I would like to present evidence that undermines the first of these assumptions and suggest that the pursuit of unattainable ideals is indeed rational insofar as it may act as a means toward the progressive unfolding of greater and greater human accomplishments. These accomplishments may in turn be found to possess a degree of value for the nihilist insofar as they offer the possibility for a progressively finer attunement to the highest ideals of perfection.

Not everyone accepts the basic presumptions of nihilism as true, and so not everyone consciously wrestles with the painful frustration involved in nihilistic incongruity. For those caught within its grip, however, it seems quite appropriate to ask, "What is to be done?" The nihilist, it seems to me, has at least three options: (1) Abandon ideals altogether, becoming what White calls a "complete nihilist" (or what I term a "post-nihilist"), thus leaving nihilism behind and becoming satisfied with the world as is. (2) Choose new, more moderate and attainable goals, thus avoiding the risk of becoming disillusioned in the future. (3) Remain committed to unattainable ideals, languishing in nihilism and longing for a world that will never be.

Being satisfied with the world of the here-and-now entails the renunciation of longing for a world that could be. "The very word 'longing' tells of a distance between the soul and its end," writes Ralph Harper, [12] and the cessation of longing suggests that a final reconciliation of the individual with reality has been achieved. The state of being satisfied is reached when desire and longing come to an end; when it is felt that there is nothing more to do. On the contrary, the experience of desire gives expression to feelings of imperfection and of shortcoming. When you want something, this is only because you don't already have it. You lack the very thing that you wish was not lacking. [13] Now, deficiency and distance are often characterized as states of Being that are naturally negative, unpleasant, and disagreeable, and so to be avoided at all costs. This is the intuition that drives the post-nihilist to abandon "higher" ends and values. There is always some distance between the individual and the most abstract final goals, as Stirner points out, [14] and so to stop desiring them seems a rational move in the direction of serenity and complacency, as both Kant and Freud claim. Frustration and distress can then be left behind and satisfaction may be achieved. However, this emphasis on the unpleasantness of the negative feelings involved in longing fails to recognize that in longing for a future state of affairs there is not only frustration and distance, but also activity and liveliness.

Future goals and ends act to focus longing in a concrete manner by giving purpose and direction to active desires. Goals establish an objective and a target toward which energies may be concentrated, thereby avoiding the undisciplined and immediate squandering of effort. They give longing a purpose and allow for the engagement in ongoing, lively, and active struggle. In helping to focus attention, goals help us to concentrate upon particular outcomes, encouraging the development of interesting strategies and tactics that give humans something to do during the course of life.

Harry Frankfurt has pointed out not only the usefulness, but the necessity that final ends and goals play in organizing a purposeful life. "We are creatures who cannot avoid being active," [15] he writes, and in our activities we naturally value certain outcomes as superior to others. Since goals help to focus, guide, and direct our activities, they make it more probable that our efforts will get us what we want. But this is only part of the reason why the formulation of final ends is important for human beings. More important is the fact that much of the meaning and fulfillment that we achieve in life comes not from actually accomplishing our goals, but rather from taking part in the struggles toward goals. These struggles are made possible insofar as they are conceptualized in terms of means toward certain ends. Without ends to pursue, there are no means, and without means, there is nothing to do in life.

Frankfurt claims it to be an error of Aristotle's that he failed to recognize the true interdependence of means and ends in terms of their instrumental and terminal values. Instrumental value consists in the usefulness of a thing insofar as it allows for the accomplishment of other goals. Those goals, if they are valued in and of themselves apart from their own usefulness toward other ends, are considered to have terminal value. Means have traditionally been thought of as having only instrumental value and final ends as having only terminal value. This, however, is mistaken according to Frankfurt. Final ends do, in fact, also have instrumental value insofar as they are useful in organizing the activities that fill up the bulk of our lives. We value certain ends partly because of the means by which we pursue those ends. The ends become useful in that they allow us to engage in certain means, which themselves have terminal value. The decision to adopt a final end is at least partly based upon the fact that this adoption will make purposeful activity possible. If this is correct, then final ends are useful and do serve an important function in human life. They serve to organize and direct activity in a focused and resolute manner.

The formulation of goals involves, I think, a couple of different dimensions. First, there must be the conception of a state of affairs different from the actual, present, existent state of affairs. When we set goals, at least part of what we do is to delineate ways in which the future will be different from the present. It is because our goals are things that don't presently exist that we pursue them. Secondly, we pursue these nonexistent states of affairs because we value what they embody and we desire for them to become actualized. A goal, then, is a state of affairs that it is hoped will eventually materialize into actuality through our efforts. However, we must be careful to recognize that while goals are hoped for states of affairs that we strive toward, it is not necessarily the case that they are in fact realizable. Some goals are so grand or unrealistic that they will never be actualized. These kinds of goals or ends might properly be termed "ideals." An ideal is a superlative standard beyond which one cannot go. As we have seen again and again, nihilists desire the consummation of certain ends that are, according their own presuppositions, unattainable. Absolute commerce with Being, Truth, Goodness, Beauty, etc. are the goals longed for by nihilists, yet nihilists simultaneously understand these to be out of the reach of their actual capabilities. We might question, along with post-nihilists, postmodernists, and both Kant and Freud, the usefulness and the rationality of aspiring toward such ideals. Is there any use or value in pursuing goals that are in fact unattainable?

In order to answer this question we need only recall Frankfurt's observation that the most important and useful function of goals is not so much that they allow us to get what we want, but rather that they give us the framework within which we may engage in the activity of purposeful struggle. In aspiring toward the absolute, though nihilists are on the one hand condemned to frustration and disappointment, on the other, they are also assured of a never-ending source of inspiration for further activity. The distance between the actual and the ideal is, for the nihilist, a gap that opens up the possibility for unending struggle and activity. While this activity is purposeful and oriented toward a hoped-for future state of affairs, it is also understood in the grand scheme of things to be in vain. Although the final ends of the nihilist are never reached, they remain useful for the organization of life. The image of Camus's Sisyphus comes to mind once again. It is the rock and the mountain that allow him to do what he does, yet if we think about his situation in terms of goal accomplishment, his task seems meaningless and without purpose. Likewise, the life of nihilists might seem to be in vain so long as we emphasize the unattainable content of their hoped for ideals. If we shift our attention toward the usefulness of perpetuating endless, purposeful activity, then nihilism loses some of its negative, despairing connotations. The life of the active nihilist, if not the passive nihilist, might be preferable to that of the post-nihilist insofar as the active nihilist, ironically, at least has purpose and direction in life. Longing and desire are never extinguished in this individual, and so there remains an inexhaustible reservoir of potential motivation for further activity.

The post-nihilist, in refusing to recognize any standards or criteria above and beyond the state of things in the here-and-now, is in effect not only forsaking ideals, but all types of goals. Things just are the way that they are, according to this individual, including the set of preferences that one possesses or the "final vocabulary" that one has inherited. Consequently, such an individual is destined forever to lack the capacity for growth, development, and improvement. The post-nihilist cannot engage in anything like a career, calling, or life project since any of these things demand a conception of some imagined, future state of affairs that is considered, by some criterion, to be worth pursuing. This individual has abandoned the nihilistic values, and in the absence of some such values, the activities of the post-nihilist must remain undirected, disorganized, and without aim. The post-nihilist, in acquiescence to the world as-is, abandons longing for satisfaction, and in satisfaction there is no desire for betterment.

It might be claimed that even though the formulation of goals and ends is indispensable to a purposeful and active life, the goals that the nihilist aspires toward are simply too high. The criteria for success that this individual establishes are so difficult to achieve that frustration and failure are inevitable. What does this individual expect, after all, other than defeat? Perhaps the setting of less ambitious goals, goals within the reach of real-life capabilities, would be a better alternative to either setting one's sights too high or abandoning abstract goals altogether. Increasingly difficult projects might be undertaken during the course of a lifetime, with one following the other in order of complexity. As the less arduous tasks are completed, the more difficult ones might be undertaken in their turn. This sort of step-wise goal setting might be a more sensible and reasonable alternative to both the nihilist and post-nihilist standpoints. "Set goals, but don't set them too high," might be the advice we could give. This advice, however, fails to recognize some of the aspirations and complexities that are involved in nihilistic thinking.

For the nihilist, the above mentioned advice gets everything backward. It assumes that we can measure the value of our earthly accomplishments from the bottom up. But when the nihilist looks to this world, such an individual finds very little that is worthy of admiration, and even less that may act as a motivation toward future aspiration. For the nihilist, anything in this world that is worthwhile is worthwhile only to the degree that it reflects something of the absolute. It is perfection that the nihilist craves, not a sensible life of moderation. Separation from the ultimate is the greatest pain, and the accomplishments of this world possess value for the nihilist only insofar as they act to transport this individual closer to the absolute. Goals that are set step-wise measure their progress against all that is lower and already done. But this is just progressive mediocrity from the nihilist's point of view. It lacks a grand and ambitious vision of perfection that is truly inspirational.

Nihilists are generally dissatisfied creatures. They yearn for perfection, feeling unfulfilled so long as there remains any room whatsoever for improvement and development. Ideal goals play an indispensable role in this inwardly motivated pursuit of progress. As John Dewey tells us, the ideal is a conception that allows humans to examine the world around them and aggressively alter and change actual circumstances in light of its standards. Ideal goals are "fantasies," certainly, but they are fantasies that offer criteria against which changes may be judged as better or worse. In treating these fantasies as possibilities, humans progress in their achievements, not in the sense of obtaining absolute truths, but in the sense of gaining a more and more sophisticated grasp of their own power to alter and manipulate the world around them. The ideal "is that collection of imagined possibilities that stimulates men to new efforts and realizations."[16] In the struggle to make the ideal real, humans engage in the activities of life.

The pursuit of goals, at least very often, involves some dissatisfaction with the present as well as an ideal notion of what would constitute a better state of affairs worth pursuing. However, we never know until we try whether the goals that we formulate are realizable or not. That takes trial and error, and oftentimes we are in error. Even the lowliest goals are subject to failure due to any number of real-world factors, and failure in life remains a constant danger so long as we pursue any goals whatsoever. Some goals, though, seem more likely to be realized than others. Yet success in the accomplishment of goals is not necessarily the most important or valued reason why we push toward them. Engagement in the activity of pursuit may be an even more important reason to set goals. This being so, it may make sense to set very high, unattainable goals simply to assure ourselves that we will have an ideal toward which constantly to move and to strive. Unattainable goals may provide a non-exhaustible motivation toward action that attainable goals lack.

Beyond this, and related to the nihilist's longing for perfection, is the fact that higher, more difficult goals and standards tend to promote higher levels of excellence and achievement than do lower, less difficult goals and standards. In a review of experimental studies dealing with goal setting and task performance, Locke, Shaw, Saari, and Latham discovered that "99 out of 110 studies found that specific, hard goals produced better performance than medium, easy, do-your-best, or no goals."[17] Their explanation for this finding was rather simple and straightforward: "[H]igher goals produce higher performance than lower goals or no goals because people simply work harder for the former."[18] As a standard of success is set higher and higher, people tend to strive higher and higher, even if they must fall short of superlative accomplishment. Locke and Latham sum up this finding by claiming that there is a "linear relationship between the degree of goal difficultly and performance."[19] These studies verify an intuition already shared by many. Quality of performance is enhanced when higher quality is aimed at.

This appears to follow for a number of reasons. As has already been noted, goals direct attention toward a certain standard. When attention is directed toward a specific standard or goal, it is that end toward which the individual's energies become directed, and this direction of attention is key in the development of specific strategies and methods for working toward the goal or goals desired. The combination of increased attention, persistence, concentrated effort, and detailed planning seem to be associated with elevated levels of performance among those pursuing difficult goals. As difficulty increases, so too does the need for increased effort, and increased effort translates, at least quite often, into increased levels of performance.

Accompanying this increase in performance, however, it has also been found that harder goals lead to an increase in the amount of anxiety and stress experienced by those pursuing those goals. "The harder the goal, the greater the pressure and the greater the chances for failure."[20] This is to be expected, and it is the very problem that has led to the abandonment of high ideals and abstract goals by post-nihilists. The fear of failure, of not living up to the standards that one has come to accept as worthy, is a powerful inducement that may motivate individuals to pursue a number of differing alternatives. But the usefulness of goals is far too great for the nihilist to abandon them altogether. Likewise, the increased quality of human achievement argues against doing away with ideals. Consequently, not only is the post-nihilist solution of abandoning all goals untenable, but so too is the admonition to pursue only lower, more moderate goals.

The frustration that is involved in the experience of nihilistic incongruity, while it may produce a mournful sense of loss, also attunes the nihilist to the very things that this individual considers most worthwhile. Even though the nihilist believes that all of our worldly pursuits are ultimately in vain, the experience of nihilistic incongruity itself might not be in vain. Nihilistic incongruity, in other words, may be useful and serve a purpose insofar as it makes nihilists aware of their own human potential in a world without God. The key to understanding the usefulness of this "most uncanny of guests" rests in viewing nihilistic incongruity as a means rather than as an end in itself, and understanding it as an experience that may enrich the human spirit in its ongoing struggle toward greater things. Nihilistic incongruity might, in this manner, possess some value. It might act as a tool of orientation, a compass whose needle points us in the direction that we want to move.

Those who advocate the rejection of ideals so that the problem of nihilism may be left behind offer a path toward collective satisfaction and contentment, but they also advocate a way of life that is untenable for nihilists. Nihilists long for perfection, and any attempt to placate them with lesser stand-ins is considered insulting. The nihilist regards the skepticism of pragmatists and postmodernists as facile. In it they see the promotion of a bizarre ruse that tries to tempt them with the possibility of a real-world utopia in which perfection plays no part. Pragmatists and postmodernists claim that we can leave the problem of nihilism behind forever by focusing on the here-and-now, thereby dissolving the incongruity between ideals and our real-life capacities. In ceasing to desire those things that we will never possess, they want us to believe that nihilism, and the intimately distressing pain that it provokes, will evaporate forever. No longer will we be tormented by a lack of confidence or a fear of failure. Rather, we will emerge into a new era in which our natures are in perfect consonance with the world around us. Despair will disappear and there will be no such thing as failure. Everything that we do will be a success.

However, this vision is not so attractive as it might at first appear. The frustration, failure, and desperation that is oftentimes emphasized as a negative and unattractive feature of nihilism is only the flip side of a larger process that, as a whole, might recommend the toleration and acceptance of nihilism as a necessary stage in the pursuit of ever higher levels of achievement. Progress does not, and never will, follow an uninterrupted path of upward movement. Rather, it occurs in starts, stops, and periodic retrogression. The eagerness to avoid failures and frustrations can all too easily lead to an enthusiasm to throw the baby out with the bath water, or in this case to do away with decline at the cost of ascent. "There are people who are filled with such horror at the idea of a defeat that they keep themselves from ever doing anything," writes Simone de Beauvoir,[21] but without defeat we don't truly appreciate or understand our triumphs, and for this reason alone perhaps we should learn to cherish the value of nihilistic incongruity. The nihilistic question, "What is to be done?" is more than simply a refrain of despair. It is also an expression of dissatisfaction with the way that the world is. As such, it presupposes an ideal standard against which the world of the here-and-now looks bad. With the feeling of negativity there lies a motivation toward change, and in this a change toward what is considered to be a better state of affairs. Nihilism, or the falling away from the highest values, is a symptom of failure. But it is also a symptom of preceding liveliness and vitality that might be recovered in the future.

Iris Murdoch captures the double-edged character of ideals when she writes:

> It may seem curious to wonder whether the idea of perfection . . . is really an important one, and what sort of role it can play. Well is it important to measure and compare things and know how good they are? . . . A deep understanding of any field of human activity . . . involves an increasing revelation of degrees of excellence and often a revelation of there being in fact little that is very good and nothing that is perfect.[22]

Ideals have the capacity both to illuminate as worthy and to belittle our experiences in the world. But this twin capacity is potentially useful for rational creatures who strive toward some better state of Being. The contrast between the actual and ideal might be thought of as an engine that drives accomplishment, and though the longing and striving involved in the pursuit of ideals may ultimately be doomed to failure, this failure is an unavoidable danger for the nihilist who wishes to remain actively engaged in the struggle for progress and development. A nihilistic battle for improvement involves the formulation of superlative standards as nihilists strive to come as close as possible to that standard, all the while knowing that they must fall short of their final goal. The ideal is like a reward held just out of reach, potentially motivating nihilists to greater and greater heights of accomplishment, while at the same time tormenting them by its inaccessibility.

The argument that I have offered in this chapter concludes with the assertion that ideals, understood as goals that are in principle unreachable, are potentially useful for the organization of life's activities despite the painful frustrations that they may cause. They serve as abstract targets that focus one's efforts, making progress and high levels of achievement more likely, not only by encouraging hard work, but also by promoting dissatisfaction with the current condition of things. It is not at all irrational, as Kant and Freud claim, for the nihilist to strive after the unattainable. This vain quest has the positive power to motivate nihilists toward activity, change, and progressively higher levels of worldly accomplishment. Such a struggle need not culminate in despair but may, in fact, lead toward what to some may seem like an oxymoronic concept: nihilistic progress. In "awakening" nihilists to their highest values, nihilistic incongruity allows them to "admire" these values as forms of unrealized potential. Nihilistic frustration, furthermore, acts to "bind" the nihilist to these values in an enduring and unending relationship of longing. This longing may motivate unending activity that itself appears to possess a relative degree of value in the light of all that is supremely valuable and worthy.

Nihilists, and those who criticize them, have a tendency to emphasize the dark, gloomy, and depressing aspects of nihilism. The very term is, in fact, often used to denote absolute and complete negativity, or situations lacking in any sort of positive or affirming qualities. What I hope to have uncovered in this and the previous chapter is the fact that such uses of the term are erroneous. By descending down into nihilism and trying to understand it from within, we have discovered that the premises and values shared by many nihilistic thinkers lead toward conclusions that might contribute to an enriching and "positive" view of human life. Contrary to the majority of both popular and professional philosophical wisdom, nihilistic incongruity is a phenomenon that may enrich the human soul rather than destroying it. It is a painful yet powerful phenomenon that makes us aware of what we consider to be most valuable. Because the term has been used so carelessly and with so little precision for so long by philosophers, many of these facts have become covered over and ignored.

The preceding excavation, while certainly not the last word on the subject, represents what I think is a quite unique and novel attempt to truly comprehend nihilism, rather than confronting it adversarially and dismissing it glibly. For individual persons, nihilism may offer an opportunity for spiritual enrichment, growth, and development, thus making them better as human beings. Though nihilism stems from an incongruity between our actual capacities and the ideal goals that we orient our desires and energies toward, this incongruity is not, as it turns out, necessarily threatening. In reflecting upon the nature of despair, failure, and personal deficiency, we have found that these qualities may be incorporated into a more general understanding of our experience as creatures who are spiritually full and active. To feel despair over our failures does not preclude a higher order understanding of ourselves that permits a feeling of good humor to prevail overall. Allen Wheelis, a San Francisco psychoanalyst, expresses this sentiment when he remarks, "The laughter I seek is that which looks straight in the eye of despair and laughs."[23] In the following chapter we will join him in this search.

Chapter Seven

HUMOR AND INCONGRUITY

Is there upon earth a more potent means than laughter to resist the mockeries of the world and of fate?

—Bonaventura, *Nachtwachen*

There is nothing in either the philosophy of nihilism, or in nihilistic incongruity itself, that implies the necessity of a despairing stance on the part of the nihilist. Quite the contrary, we have in the course of this investigation come to understand that nihilism is even compatible with notions of value and of progress. Though this may seem strange to the mind that is attuned to the conventional "negative" understanding of nihilism, we have, I hope, been successful in undermining such facile assessments of the phenomenon. The philosophy of nihilism allows for the adoption of any number of differing attitudes toward the phenomenon of nihilistic incongruity. What I would presently like to propose, however, is that there is one attitude, or stance, that represents an especially constructive and philosophically appropriate approach to the situation embodied in nihilistic incongruity. I shall call this approach the "humorous attitude." In order to understand why the humorous attitude is especially well suited to an encounter with nihilistic incongruity, we need to examine the structure of the relationship that exists between humor and incongruity.

In this chapter I shall suggest that the humorous attitude is an active, creative capacity that encourages the interpretation of incongruities in terms of pleasure and enjoyment. Because they embody a sort of disharmony and discord, when incongruities such as nihilistic incongruity come to our awareness, they have the tendency, in varying degrees, to provoke feelings of tension in us. This sort of inner tension has long been regarded by rationalist philosophers ranging from Socrates to Kant as a naturally unpleasant experience, equivalent to anxiety, that human beings reflexively recoil from. However, this is not self-evidently the case. Some incongruities, as pointed out by John Morreall, may produce a pleasurable sort of tension in us that we call "amusement." The humorous attitude, in fact, is that distinctively human capacity that enables us to actively interpret incongruity in terms of amused pleasure rather than painful anxiety. A humorous attitude encourages us to linger in contemplation of various incongruities and to consider them from a variety of differing angles, or perspectives. In the course of this sort of ongoing humorous meditation, we develop the ability to consider incongruities from a wider and wider variety of viewpoints, cultivating an understanding of the incongruous phenomenon within an ever grander, unthreatening context. As we develop the ability to see initially troubling incongruities from a wider variety of viewpoints and perspectives, we exercise our sense of humor. Humor, thus, aids us in facing the world, not by encouraging us to deny or turn away from painful realities, but by encouraging us to work toward the development of an understanding of those pains within a richer context. This is why Morreall likens humor to wisdom. Both allow us to "see things as part of the big picture."[1] The development of this capacity, I shall claim, provides nihilists with a sort of "comic lens" that encourages them to avoid a gloomy overemphasis on life's frustrations and failures. If, as the nihilist claims, nothing that we do is ultimately very important, then it makes little sense to take things too seriously, even our own frustrations and failures. The humorous response to nihilism brings this insight forth and challenges nihilists to take their own world view to heart.

I would like to initiate this chapter's investigation by first probing into the constitution of incongruity. Once having fleshed out some of the details of this notion, its relationship to humorous amusement may then be established. In the course of drawing a distinction between jokes, comedy, and humor, we will come to a clear understanding of the essence of humor as that capacity that allows us to confront an incongruity and interpret it in terms of amusement, thereby transforming the incongruous phenomenon into an object of comedy. I shall then end this chapter with a number of examples that demonstrate how humor functions in this regard.

Incongruity is a phenomenon that is characterized by breaks, interruptions, and discontinuity. As such, it presupposes a separation between two or more things that lack correspondence and fit with one another. Ideas, words, statements, sentences, physical objects, or any other types of entities may be incongruous with one another. When things are incongruous, we can't figure out how they might be connected or brought together. Incongruous things are radically separated and just don't seem to belong with each other. However, though it involves a difference between things, incongruity is also more than this. Whereas things that are simply different might harmonize and complement one another, as do the colors in a rainbow, things that are incongruous conflict and clash with one another, like the colors of a bad wardrobe. As *Webster's Dictionary* points out, the very definition of "incongruous" involves the idea of things that are "incompatible," "not harmonious," "not conforming," "disagreeing," "inconsistent," and "lacking propriety." While simple differences might find harmonious resolution, incongruities resist such resolution. They represent that special kind of difference that emerges between adversarial opposites. Incongruity is, thus, associated with a kind of tension and harshness that arises from the confrontation between incompatibles. It involves an element of discord and friction.

Incongruity may exist in varying degrees. Things are thought to be more or less incongruous depending upon the intensity of the dissonance that occurs upon their juxtaposition. For instance, there is a greater incongruity involved in thinking about a squid riding a bicycle than there is in thinking about a bear riding a bicycle. It is difficult to understand how a squid could possibly mount and pedal such a vehicle. On the other hand, though bears don't usually ride bicycles, they are more physically capable of doing so than squids, and in fact we are aware that there exist circus bears trained to do just that. Squids and bears are not themselves incongruous, but when juxtaposed with bicycle riding, incongruity arises; and this is the case with squids to a greater degree than with bears. The greater the degree of incongruity between things, the greater the degree of dissonance, discord, and incompatibility that exists between them.

Sometimes we speak of an entity as being incongruous not in relation to the things that surround it, but in relation to our own background expectations. A Polish visitor to Canada, for instance, might find the brightly colored and ornate costumes of the Royal Canadian Mounties to be incongruous even though that mode of dress is in perfect harmony with the traditions and culture of the country. In this case, it is the past experience and expectations of the Polish tourist that clash with what is encountered. The disharmony that comes into being has its source in a conflict between the tourist's expectations concerning the normally drab and utilitarian appearance of official police dress uniforms and the Mounties' bright and festive looking attire. Though the Polish tourist might say that the Mounties' uniform is itself "incongruous," we would understand this as an assertion made from the perspective of a particular set of cultural expectations. What in fact constitutes an incongruity in this instance is the discordant confrontation of the tourist's perception of the Mounties' uniform with the tourist's conceptual expectations concerning police uniforms in general.

Incongruities arise when two or more things that cannot be reconciled are brought together in an oppositional encounter with one another. Such irreconcilable differences might exist objectively in the world or they might just be thought to exist by us because of our limited knowledge. Sometimes we believe certain things to be incongruous simply because we have not been patient, astute, or clever enough to understand the harmonies and connections that actually exist between them. Often we find that we are able to resolve certain apparent incongruities by way of study, investigation, or leaps of the imagination. Such successful resolution of incongruity is very often experienced as pleasurable and gratifying because it demonstrates our ability to work through and unravel a previously mysterious aspect of reality. In finding a means of resolution, we eliminate incongruity and replace it with harmonic congruence.

While the resolution of incongruity is commonly recognized as pleasurable, it has often been assumed natural for human beings to avoid and shun incongruity itself. Because an incongruity is discordant, disharmonious, and oppositional, with it we encounter a situation in which our understanding of the connections between things in the world is challenged. Incongruity gets in the way of calculation, manipulation, and prediction, representing a break in a system, or a gap in a pattern. In these general ways, incongruities have often been considered unpleasant disruptions that upset our comprehension and understanding of the world around us. John Morreall cites a tradition beginning at least with Socrates holding that "it is perverse to enjoy the frustration of our reason, which is what enjoying incongruity amounts to."[2] The sort of tension aroused in us by unresolved incongruity, according to this way of thinking, is naturally experienced by us as an unpleasant and anxious sort of discomfort.

The view that incongruity must always be experienced as unpleasant is, I think, implausible and is associated with those philosophers who tend to place an overemphasis on the sort of pleasure we derive during the course of reasoning and problem solving. Incongruity is a type of inconsistency, and it is consistency that has long been regarded by many as one of the supreme criteria of correctness and truth. According to this viewpoint, when we encounter inconsistencies in our thinking, this is a sign that there is something wrong or incoherent about our thinking. The human mind has a natural tendency to strive toward coherence and consistency, this tradition claims, and when the mind fails in this task it experiences dissonance and a sense of anxious discomfort that it recoils from instinctively.

We find an extreme expression of this attitude in Kant's system of philosophy. According to Kant, the faculty of reason is a natural endowment of human beings, and as with all of our other natural endowments it is well suited to its end. Like the organs of the human body, the "organ" of reason performs an important function in the "purpose of life,"[3] and this function is to guide us in thought and action toward living in harmony with the "moral law." The moral law is an end in itself, commanding our respect and admiration regardless of the consequences that we encounter when we live in accordance with its dictates. The moral law is, in fact, something like God itself. It is universally valid, and the closer that we are able to bring our own wills into harmony with this universally valid law, the better we become.

The moral law commands our respect, according to Kant, and part and parcel of such respect is an eagerness to avoid inconsistency and contradiction. In chapter 5 we already encountered Kant's views on the moral law and its relation to the sublime experience. Recall that the experience of the sublime is initiated by an encounter with an idea of the "absolutely large," or of "infinity." As an aesthetic experience, sublimity occurs when we are forced to encounter phenomena that overwhelm the capacities of our imagination and perception. However, this aesthetic experience further opens us up to a moral experience insofar as it allows our minds to harmonize with the moral law itself. The idea of the "absolutely large" is a product of our reason that absorbs, reconciles, and thereby dominates the apparent inconsistencies of the phenomenal world. It allows us to resolve the uncomfortable dissonance that we feel as finite creatures who are unable to perceive or even imagine the infinite vastness of absolute reality. With the exercise of our reason, we become "god-like," but not quite gods, since, unlike God, our thought "always involves limitations."[4]

Though we are never the same as God, according to Kant we should strive in this direction by continually bringing our will into accord with our reason. What this entails is conducting ourselves with reference to our "categorical" duties. I don't want to get into all of the sticky details of Kant's moral philosophy here, but it will serve our purposes to simply point out that for Kant, we human beings are at our best when we act in such a manner that we can will our actions to be universal laws. A universal law admits of no exceptions and is indifferent to consequences. If we could comport ourselves as though we were driven by such a law—by God's law—we would never experience the discomfort that arises from transgressing that law. We would never be troubled by incongruities and inconsistencies between will and reason.

Kant's philosophy, in consonance with the tradition of rationalism that precedes him, overemphasizes consistency, congruity, and and noncontradiction as the highest guidelines for proper thought and action. We all, as rational creatures, have a natural aversion to inconsistency, incongruity, and contradiction, according to this way of thinking. But is this really the case? Can't the frustration of our reason—and I specifically am concerned with that sort of frustration that occurs in the encounter with incongruity—be experienced as pleasurable in and of itself?

By way of answering this question, we should first briefly examine what actually occurs in the encounter with incongruity. Not all incongruities are immediately or necessarily apparent to us, this is true, but when an incongruous phenomenon does come to our attention, the phenomenon has a tendency to stand out more or less sharply, depending upon the degree of incongruity that is manifested, in contrast to all that surrounds it. Incongruity displays itself as a separation in the undifferentiated "flow" of our background experience. It focuses our attention and "breaks" the current of experience, compelling us to engage situations that seem out of the ordinary. Incongruity is marked by conflict, contrast, and differentiation. It is important to reemphasize in this regard that what a person considers incongruous is, however, to a large extent relative to that individual's experience and expectation. Incongruity oftentimes arises out of novel encounters with unfamiliar things, and if we understand that different people have different expectations and familiarities according to their past experiences and understandings, then we can see that differing people may oftentimes find different things incongruous. While there may be truly objective incongruities that exist independently of our experiences of them, there are also a great number of incongruities that are the result of our own unfamiliarity and lack of personal understanding. Many incongruities are emergent phenomena, and they sometimes emerge out of the violation of our taken for granted expectations.

Regardless of the many potential dissimilarities in what people find to be incongruous, creatures with similar sensory mechanisms probably experience the disparate and divergent physical features of their environments in a similar manner. Those of us who have properly functioning eyes are, for example, able to recognize where a sidewalk stops and the roadway starts. We can see the edge of a river, and we recognize the difference that marks the dropoff where a balcony no longer extends. Similar commonalities hold for the other human senses. In order to navigate through our world, an individual needs to recognize physical differences in the environment. In addition, since our environment is not wholly static but goes through changes and alterations over time, a person must be able to recognize and respond to the disruptions that may get in the way of life's patterns. Sometimes sidewalks get blocked or removed, rivers get diverted, and balconies are torn down. Individual survival depends upon these things coming to our attention and upon us altering our behavior in response to such sudden and unanticipated changes in the environment. Our sensory organs and mechanisms, in combination with memory, have evolved in such a manner that they allow us to perceive and recall the details of salient, physical incongruities within our immediate environments.

However, sometimes our attention is called not by the concrete, physical disruptions and disharmonies in the world, but by the incongruity of higher-level concepts that are brought together in novel and unexpected ways. Part and parcel of the development of our rational faculties is the ability to abstract from concrete particulars, and in the development of abstract concepts, a whole new realm of incongruous possibility is created. Experience plays a role in our conceptual expectations no less than it does in our perceptual expectations. The forces of civilization, culture, and environment train and encourage us to think in more or less conventional ways, and as we grow and mature, our conceptual systems evolve and become increasingly complicated. Despite the substantial similarities shared by those raised in similar cultures, conflicts do arise within and between the conceptual systems of individuals. The greater the complication and sophistication in our conceptual universe, the more opportunity there is for incongruity to develop among its components. The juxtaposition of contradictory, contrary, or otherwise logically incompatible ideas is an example of a common kind of conceptual incongruity that, in grabbing our attention, calls for some kind of response. Just as perceptual harmony is often disrupted, so sometimes is conceptual harmony. Thus, incongruity may manifest itself in the conceptual as well as the perceptual realms. In all cases, however, there is a discord and dissonance that manifests itself either between percepts, concepts, or both percepts and concepts.

Suppose, for instance, that I am walking down the sidewalk. As I amble along, cars pass by me on the roadway, just as I expect them to do, and just as I have seen them do every day. Under these circumstances I don't normally take note of the makes, models, or styles of the automobiles as they speed by. I have neither the interest nor the time to notice these particular details since, first of all, I have no reason to do so, and second of all, it would entail remembering far too much information. My memory simply does not have the capacity to store all of the sensory data that is produced in me day after day, and most of that data is superfluous anyway.

But now suppose I witness an accident. The perceptual incongruity between the smooth flow of traffic and the sudden jolting crash is certain to startle me to attention. With my concentration focused on the crash, I now become mindful of the vehicles involved. What is to be done? I can't remain fixed on this anomaly forever. Something must motivate me toward further action, allowing me either to disengage from, or become further involved in, the events unfolding before me. I await some kind of guidance or direction. A feeling like concern, fear, or anger may provide just this sort of guidance. It compels me to do something now that I have noticed an important and potentially threatening feature of the environment.

Traffic accidents occur on a regular basis and so are not completely unexpected in our daily lives. In fact, it is probably a thought in the back of our minds whenever walking down the sidewalk that we may potentially witness an accident. For this reason, while actual crashing cars are startling and incongruous, the higher level concepts of "car" and "crash" are not. We don't find it unusual when the two are associated together since we are quite used to thinking of them in conjunction with one another. But suppose instead of just two cars involved in a fender bender, I observe a collision between two ambulances. This is most unusual, and it raises the incongruity of the situation to a new level. Whereas in the first case the incongruity that drew my attention was the perceptual disharmony of the crash when compared to the previous flow of traffic, or the loud and sudden noise as compared to the previous even hum of passing cars, in this second case there is something extra involved.

The collision of two ambulances is not startling and incongruent for visual or auditory reasons alone. It is also conceptually incongruent, and it is so in at least two ways. First of all, accidents are thought to be accidental. When two very similar things come to be associated with one another under accidental circumstances, we are naturally struck by the coincidence. It may seem, in such a case, that some sort of prearrangement or planning was involved, though we know there wasn't. This circumstance, thus, presents us with an incongruity between the concepts *accident* and *contrivance*. Second, ambulances are normally thought to arrive at accident scenes in order to assist the injured. When ambulances are involved in accidents, and the drivers are themselves in need of help, our understanding of the role and function of paramedics is violated. This discrepancy points to an incongruity between the concepts of "function of an ambulance" and "being in need of help at the scene of a crash."

Suppose that this collision is serious enough to have resulted in life-threatening injuries to the ambulance attendants, but that the patients being carried in the back of the ambulances are not so threatened. The ambulances strike one another in a shower of broken glass, screeching tires, and dented metal. The two pairs of paramedics (two individuals in the front seat of each vehicle) can be seen to slump over simultaneously upon impact like four uniform-clad rag dolls. This initial crash startles me to attention and I react with a feeling of pity and fear for those involved. As I watch, the back doors of both ambulances simultaneously swing open and out stumble the patients who were previously being cared for (one out of each ambulance). They are a bit unsteady, not only because they have been shaken up by the accident, but because they are still hooked up to their IV drips. Despite their unsteadiness, each patient shuffles to the aid of the injured paramedics and starts to perform first aid, all the while being very careful not to rip the needles and tubes out of their own arms. The whole procedure looks very awkward, but soon a number of bystanders intervene and offer their assistance. My own assistance is unneeded at this point, and I would only be a hindrance to the rescue efforts. I must stay at the scene as a witness to the accident, however, and so all I can do is watch, uninvolved in the efforts. What goes through my mind?

Well, on the one hand I can't help but feel concern for the injured. The irony of the situation is that these paramedics, invested with the responsibility of helping the injured, can't carry out their duties but must rely upon those who were previously dependent upon them for help. This is, in a sense, a painfully tragic situation. The noble efforts of these well-meaning people have come to nothing. In the very act of carrying out their responsibilities they have fallen prey to a situation that undermines their continued ability to perform those same duties. Where they once were strong and capable, they are now weak and dependent, and I feel pity and fear as a result of this situation.[5]

On the other hand, since the structure of the predicament is similar to that of a joke, the situation also has the flavor of comedy to it. On their way to helping the sick, an unexpected reversal occurs. It is a ludicrous situation that develops when two ambulances collide, and the absurdity is amplified by the further role reversals. The participants in this farce have become embroiled in a sort of slapstick mockery wherein the normal, "serious" world of professional activity has been turned on its head. I feel a strange sense of amusement at this all too perfect, and seemingly choreographed, violation of my conceptual expectations.[6]

Though this situation is not unambiguously comic or tragic, there are elements involved in it from which we are able to construct comic or tragic interpretations of the situation. The elements that cause our ambivalent disposition toward this situation are the conceptual incongruities involved. We are not only taken aback by the all too perfect manner in which this "accident" has played out, but we feel unsettled by the fact that our expectations about the function of ambulances and paramedics have been subverted. With these incongruous developments we are put into a tricky position. How should we accommodate and deal with this circumstance? The incongruities make it apparent that something is not right, but then we are left to figure out what to do with this information. In assessing the lack of fit between our concepts we are torn between the impulses to laugh and to cry. Dissonance is produced, tension mounts, and this makes us aware that we now have a choice to make. From this choice opens up an entire realm of possibilities more varied than ever imagined by Kant and the rationalists.

It is evident that incongruities generally demand our attention, yet it would be a mistake to treat all incongruities alike. Some incongruities alert us to threatening or dangerous situations while others simply call our attention to novel or unexpected features of our world. For instance, the perceptual incongruity involved in witnessing a car crash calls our attention to a potentially life-threatening situation that demands immediate response in the form of intervention or avoidance. Because of such worldly markers, we are able to navigate through our physical environment, reacting appropriately to occurrences that threaten our survival and prosperity. Many of our responses to these sorts of incongruities have probably become "hard-wired" over the course of our evolutionary development. Certain perceptual incongruities, such as a sudden crashing loud noise, being struck in the face, or a sudden and intense change in light or dark, immediately trigger a startled response without any thought. Our heartbeat quickens, our blood vessels dilate, and we become ready to take action in order to respond to whatever it is that threatens.[7]

However, incongruous "breaks" in our experience are not always as dramatic or as dangerous as these examples might suggest. Our attention is also sometimes drawn to less prominent features of the environment such as gentle variations and gradual changes in sights, sounds, feels, and smells, or to conceptual inconsistencies and disharmonies. While these distinctions may not involve the violence of a sheer startle reaction, they may provide a less intense sort of incongruity that nevertheless calls our attention. Such incongruities might appear puzzling, as is the case for optical illusions and riddles, or downright amusing, as is the case when a friend trips but is unharmed. These sorts of incongruities produce a sort of tension in us, however it is a sort of tension that does not result in an immediate feeling of displeasure. Rather, we respond with puzzlement or amusement and are encouraged to linger with the incongruity in question.

Kant thinks that the pleasant, amused feelings involved in these sorts of situations are related to incongruity, but he claims that they are so related by way of agitation and anxiety. When we laugh at an amusing situation, we do so because "a tense expectation is transformed into nothing."[8] Jokes, for instance, contain conceptual absurdities and incongruities that painfully frustrate our reason, yet the tension and unease that is produced in us as a result finds an outlet through the bodily motions of laughter. It feels good to laugh, claims Kant, because in laughter we experience a sort of catharsis that purges the painful unease of our encounter with incongruity. Note that for Kant, it is never incongruity itself that is pleasurable to encounter. Rather, what is pleasurable is the relief that occurs when we "laugh off" the painful tension that incongruity produces in us.

The biggest problem with Kant's "relief theory" of laughter and humor is that it seems incapable of explaining the sort of pleasurable amusement that we feel when we don't laugh. Laughter does not accompany all, or even most, of our amused feelings. Oftentimes we encounter incongruities that we find amusing without so much as cracking a smile. The pleasure that we experience in these cases is completely separate from any sort of bodily spasms or movements. We just quietly enjoy the feeling that is provoked in us by the incongruity that we are focused upon. Kant surely recognized that this was the case, but he gives scant attention to this simple counterexample. He persists in claiming that the intellectual capacity for "whimsicality," is "closely akin to the gratification derived from laughter,"[9] and leaves it at that. Just how it is that a purely intellectual pleasure is related to the bodily pleasure remains mysterious and unexplained.

Because incongruity oftentimes involves a break in a system and an apparent deviation from the way that we expect things to be, it has a tendency to provoke us toward a tense awareness of a disharmony in the world. However, despite this and contrary to Kant's claim, it appears that not all kinds of incongruities are necessarily encountered as unambiguously unpleasant and threatening. There are some incongruities that possess amusing qualities as well. John Morreall, in fact, has claimed that human beings have at least three separate, natural types of reactions to incongruous situations: negative emotional responses, puzzlement, and humorous amusement. Negative emotions and puzzlement, he claims, are reactions that motivate us toward resolving troubling incongruities, while humorous amusement allows us to linger on those incongruities that are not immediately dangerous or physically threatening to us.

Negative emotional reactions to incongruity impel us toward regaining control over our immediate circumstances. For instance, when we feel fear, our bodies undergo certain physiological changes that motivate us to run away from danger, fight it, defend ourselves, etc. All of these reactions serve to give us some control over what happens and allow us to avoid or minimize injury. Even emotions such as sadness have this practical element to them. In sadness, bodily functions slow down and we withdraw from the situations that caused us pain, allowing us time to recuperate and regain control over our lives. Negative emotions, then, can have a positive, practical function insofar as they motivate us toward regaining control over the world when it has slipped out of our command.

Puzzlement is a reaction to incongruity that shares many similarities with negative emotional responses. When we are puzzled by a situation, we experience a kind of tension and uneasiness. However, unlike negative emotions, when we are puzzled, it is our understanding of the world, and not the world itself, that we want to be different. We have a desire to "assimilate reality" when we encounter puzzling, incongruous situations that don't fit into our understanding of the world. In this drive toward assimilation we strive to increase our control by way of being able to anticipate and predict events. We try to relate the unfamiliar to the already familiar, thereby increasing our understanding, knowledge, and mastery of reality.

Cases of negative emotional reaction and puzzlement, then, share three common qualities: (1) In both there is uneasiness about a situation. (2) In both cases this uneasiness concerns a loss of control. (3) Both reactions motivate action toward changing the situation.

But there is a third reaction to incongruity. This Morreall calls "humorous amusement." Unlike the reactions discussed above, with humorous amusement the tension that results from an encounter with incongruity is not associated either with uneasiness, a sense of lost control, or a desire for active change. Humorous amusement, rather, is more frequently associated with feelings of pleasure and the desire to prolong contact with incongruity. Morreall suggests that an overemphasis on the analysis of joking situations has led some philosophers and psychologists to the conclusion that the resolution of incongruity, as in a punch line, is where humorous amusement lies. He points out that, on the contrary, there are many instances where unresolved incongruity also leads to humorous amusement in certain jokes, cartoons, and real life. Contrary to what is claimed by Kant, the link between humor and incongruity is not formed by way of the relief of a previous pain. But how could there be pleasure in unresolved incongruity?

The answer Morreall gives is that there is survival value in "our drive to seek variety in cognitive input."[10] This kind of variety encourages our curiosity about the world, resulting in an improved ability to adapt and survive. Incongruous situations that do not produce negative emotions or puzzlement are occasions for humorous enjoyment because they are novel yet do not threaten our physical survival or our overall beliefs about the structure of the world. Humorous enjoyment motivates us to linger in our contemplation of certain kinds of novel situations, stimulating our ability to deal with newness and preparing us for encounters with other types of threatening incongruity.

If Morreall is correct, then some incongruities may be experienced as stimulating, invigorating, and just downright entertaining in and of themselves. This conclusion is in clear opposition to the position of rationalists and relief theorists such as Kant, but it is a conclusion shared by another tradition of theorists who adhere to what has come to be known as the "incongruity theory" of laughter and humor. Incongruity theories find the source of humorous laughter in pleasant, incongruous shifts of one sort or another. According to them, we often laugh in sheer amusement at the novel and amusing juxtaposition of sensations, perceptions, or concepts. Incongruity theories turn on the speculation that amusement is the result of some sort of unexpected, yet pleasurable disruption in our patterns of expectation.

One of the more sophisticated, and unusual, theories that illustrates the role of incongruity in laughter and humor comes to us from Henri Bergson. For Bergson, humorous laughter is the result of an incongruity between the natural elasticity and flexibility that we expect from human beings and the inflexibility that we find them manifesting under certain circumstances. For instance, when we see someone trip and fall on the street, such an individual appears comic to us, and thus makes us laugh, because the usual supple and natural movements of the living organism have been interrupted in the manner of a machine that has ceased to function properly. This same effect is at work in any area of human affairs where the human spirit forgets itself and takes on the characteristics of automatism, rigidity, and mechanism. Not only actions and events, but words, thoughts, and character may become comic, and so laughable, when they exhibit the rigid characteristics more appropriate to an unthinking mechanism than to human activity. The mechanical operations of "repetition," "inversion," and "reciprocal interference" are potential symptoms of an underlying clockwork, or automated program, and so when we sense them as being present in human affairs, we think it inappropriate, incongruous, and laughable. Such are the reasons that Bergson defines comedy, and so all that is laughable, as "[s]omething mechanical encrusted on the living."[11]

Bergson goes on to suggest that our laughter serves the purpose of acting as a corrective to inappropriately rigid behavior in our fellow citizens. Since the smooth functioning of a society depends upon the ability of individuals to adapt to and conform with the ever-changing conditions of the collective, it is a matter of the utmost importance that citizens avoid rigidity in action, thought, and character. Since being the object of laughter is a painful and humiliating experience, it serves to dissuade people from falling into a state of easy and unthinking automism.[12] "[I]t is the business of laughter to repress any separatist tendency. Its function is to convert rigidity into plasticity, to readapt the individual to the whole, in short to round off the corners wherever they are met with."[13] Laughter, thus, has within it an element of coercive aggression, according to Bergson. In laughing at others, we belittle them and communicate our disapproval of their behavior.

We are all aware of the fact that humorous amusement may be had at the expense of others, and Bergson's comments on the social function played by laughter fall into line with observations made by such figures as Plato, Aristotle, and Hobbes concerning the fact that, at least quite often, when we laugh, it involves a feeling of superiority on our own part. Aristotle wrote that in comedy we laugh at the imitation of those inferior to us. Comic characters appear "ludicrous" because of "some defect or ugliness which is not painful or destructive."[14] It is because we feel unthreatened by these shortcomings that laughter and amusement, rather than fear or sadness, is the natural response. Those who put an emphasis on the feelings of dominance present in much laughter have been classified separately from those who emphasize the role of incongruity. But such a distinction may bewitch us into overlooking the fact that superiority is itself a kind of incongruity between the superior and the inferior. Even the so-called superiority theories rest upon the recognition that a kind of incongruity is at the root of much laughter and humor. The added element that they bring to the discussion that we should take note of, however, is that in order for an incongruity to be laughable, it seems that it must be somehow unthreatening and beneath us.

Most theories of humor draw, to a greater or lesser extent, on the idea that some sort of unthreatening incongruity is involved in laughter and laughing situations. It is a natural observation to make. Humor, laughter, and associated phenomena such as jokes and comedy do seem, at least a great deal of the time, to involve sudden, unexpected shifts in our patterns of expectation. At the very least, in order for an individual to experience humor, there must be a shift from a non-amused to an amused mental state, and most of the time the phenomena that precipitate this shift are themselves forms of unexpected incongruity. Though surprise may not be a necessary component of all laughter—there are cases of purely physiologically induced laughter resulting from drugs and disease—it is an element indispensable to what we might call "humorous laughter," or that form of laughter that depends upon mental processing in the mind of an individual.

Laughter itself is merely a sound that humans produce under certain conditions, and so it is not as interesting as the processes underlying its production. The philosophy of laughter and humor is not so much concerned with "laughter" as with "laughing about something."[15] Thus far we have run into a tangle of terms that need to be separated out before we will be able to come to a clear understanding of the nature of the distinctively humorous attitude. Toward this goal it will be useful to elaborate upon a helpful distinction drawn by both Immanuel Kant and Sigmund Freud between "jokes," "comedy," and "humor." Focusing on this distinction will allow us to clarify and home in on the nature of the "humorous attitude," see how it is separate from other related phenomena, and finally come to a more detailed understanding of its relationship to incongruity, and specifically to nihilistic incongruity. Let us, then, proceed with an analysis of the difference between jokes, comedy, and humor.

JOKES

Joking situations include those circumstances in which a story or narrative is intentionally constructed in order to evoke amusement. Jokes have been discussed at length by Freud as involving processes similar to those at work in dreams,[16] namely, "condensation accompanied by the formation of a substitute."[17] When following a story or narrative, our minds anticipate an outcome by picking up on the clues embedded in the story by the storyteller. A joke, however, is structured so as to subvert and misdirect our expectations by utilizing various sorts of ambiguity and incongruity. In a joke, there is more than one possible outcome that would sensibly complete the story, and the jokester purposely misdirects the listener toward the wrong conclusion until the very last instant. This deception by the jokester encourages the listener's understanding to form a false expectation that, with the delivery of the punch line, disappears "into nothing." According to Kant, laughter results when the mind, agitated and vacillating back and forth between the punch line and its lost expectation, somehow communicates this movement to the body. For Freud, it results when the "psychic energy" originally marshaled for one purpose is found to be unnecessary, and so is discharged in laughter.

Consider the following joke:

> When the unfaithful artist heard his wife coming up the stairs, he said to his lover, "Quick! Take off your clothes!"[18]

Here the subverted expectation is that an unfaithful man normally tries to escape his wife's suspicion and would certainly avoid being caught in the same room as a nude woman. As the joke begins, we anticipate that the man will try to find some manner of concealing his affair, but our initial expectation of how he will do so disappears "into nothing" when we realize that for a certain kind of artist, being in a room alone with a nude woman is part of the profession and so may be less suspicious than being alone in a room with a fully clothed woman.

Kant emphasizes that in order for a joke to be funny, the expectation of the listener must be transformed into nothing and "not into the positive opposite of an expected object, for that is always something and may frequently grieve us."[19] In other words, the punch line must not simply contradict the expectations of the listener. If the above joke was reformulated as follows:

> When the unfaithful artist heard his wife coming up the stairs he said to his lover, "Kiss me now so that my wife will see!"

the joke would not make us laugh. Simply contradicting the listeners' expectations brings discomfort rather than pleasure. It demonstrates to us that our initial expectations were simply not applicable to this case. In a funny joke, though our expectations may be misdirected, our more general assumptions about the world are validated. The first formulation of the joke is funny because it plays off of our common belief that unfaithful husbands generally try to avoid detection. The second formulation is not funny because it simply contradicts that common assumption. This is a key point that should be kept in mind. Part of the pleasure we find in jokes derives from the mind's ability to integrate unexpected possibilities into the understanding. When we laugh at a joke, we do so because we recognize that an unanticipated outcome sensibly completes the story without contradicting our most general assumptions about what the world is like. We delight in the discovery of new possibilities without being threatened by the dangers of chaos. Our amusement at jokes often seems to rest upon the successful resolution of incongruity, though as we will see this is not always the case with all objects of amusement.

Kant believed jokes to be a subspecies of the beautiful. However, there is a distinction drawn by Freud that may encourage us to alter this classification. Freud distinguishes between "innocent" and "tendentious" jokes. Tendentious jokes are those that give vent to aggressive or sexual drives, and their main purpose is to circumvent psychological blockages standing in the way of the free expression of life and death instincts. Innocent jokes, on the other hand, serve no such purpose.[20] They "begin as play, in order to derive pleasure from the free use of words and thoughts."[21] It is innocent jokes, thus, that do seem to fit neatly into Kant's category of the beautiful. Tendentious jokes, being characterized by the struggle to overcome the repression of hidden drives, seem not so beautiful. This latter form of joke has something of the aggressive in it, giving vent to sublimated urges that are primitive and potentially overwhelming. In the controlled context of joking, however, these sublimated urges are conquered and mastered. Through the ingenuity of the jokester, the power of the Id is harnessed to turn the wheels of laughter.

COMEDY

Whereas jokes are constructed, comedy is found in the world. The most common species of comedy is the "naive." Naiveté is, in a sense, the contrary of joking insofar as no situations involving naiveté involve deception. The naive person has completely innocent intentions, and it would never occur to this individual to disguise them. We laugh at naive people for this very reason. Most of us normally feel compelled to veil our true desires and wants behind a tapestry of social convention, and so our interactions with one another are often mediated by the expectation that we will have to second-guess the true intentions of others. However, when we encounter the naive person, this expectation, to use Kant's terms, "disappears into nothing." Naiveté consists in "the eruption of the sincerity that originally was natural to humanity and which is opposed to the art of dissimulation that has become our second nature."[22]

Kant points out that the spectator, in finding someone naive, reveals the possession of a set of expectations not shared by the object of laughter. In Freud we find some further, very insightful observations concerning this contrast. According to Freud, when a situation is seen as comic, it appears to the spectator that the people involved in the comedy overcome their inhibitions without any effort. This is, of course, because the inhibitions in question are not present in them. At some level the spectator must indeed believe this, otherwise the comedic behavior would instead appear "impudent." But it is this power to judge someone comic rather than impudent that the pleasure of comedy relies upon. "The discovery that one has it in one's power to make someone else comic opens the way to an un-dreamt-of yield of comic pleasure. . . ."[23] To view a situation as comic is, in this sense, not only to discover the ability within one's self to interpret a situation in more than one way, but to opt for the more pleasurable interpretation.

Consider the following scenario:

> A child is in attendance at a party thrown by his parents. All of the guests are marveling at the delicious cake that the hostess has served for dessert. One guest asks for the recipe, and the hostess simply smiles and nods. The child, however, blurts out, "But mommy, you didn't bake that cake yourself! You bought it at the store!"

Our immediate reaction is to see the comedy in this situation. The child appears naively comic because he is inappropriately honest. We laugh because we assume that there is no malicious intent in the comment, only an unreflective adherence to the principle of honesty. We snicker and say, "Oh, he didn't know any better." If, however, an adult had made the same comment, we might not find the situation so comic. Instead we would probably assume that some sort of underlying resentment against the hostess was being expressed. The point remains that regardless of what is in fact motivating certain behaviors, the comic dimension of those behaviors is dependent upon how we as spectators interpret the scenarios. If we think the worst of a person's motivation, we will not find comedy. If, on the other hand, we assume no malicious intent, but attribute only naiveté to the actor, we may discover comic pleasure.

Comedy, as a dramatic art form, rests upon an individual's talent at constructing a drama in which the actions of the protagonists in the drama are portrayed to an audience in a comic manner. Just as in making a joke the humorist must construct a narrative that leads an audience along a path in which their expectations are subverted, so too in a comedy must the comic author construct a plot that is full of amusing reversals and turns of the situation that amuse rather than frighten or confuse the audience. Aristotle articulates this very point in his *Poetics*. The plot of an effective drama, whether it be a comedy or tragedy, must contain interesting twists and turns that lead the audience along a path of discovery.

Comic dramas are written by individuals who intend to give expression to, as Morreall calls it, a "Comic Vision,"[24] and the actions of the characters in such dramas are intended to be viewed within the context of this vision. A comic play is not just a form of artistic expression, then. It is also a means of communication. Like a joke, a comedy presupposes both an author and an audience. The author attempts to present the action of the play in such a manner that the audience may share the author's perspective on these events. What is important for comedy, thus, is not so much subject matter, but *a manner of presentation*. *What* the comic author writes about is not so important as *how* the material is presented. Kaufman claims that "[t]he same material can be made into a tragedy and into a comedy,"[25] and this is the case because the "comic vision," as we have already pointed out in the case of "the naive," rests not upon some objective characteristic of the events that we observe, but on our own ability to adopt a particular sort of comic perspective toward those events.

Aristotle wrote in *Poetics* that the final cause of a drama is found in the feelings that it provokes in the audience. If the audience does not feel the catharsis at the end of a tragedy, then that drama fails to be a good tragedy for that audience. Likewise, if an audience fails to feel amusement during the course of a comedy, then that drama fails to be a good comedy for them. If a comic dramatist is unable to make the audience "see" the events in the manner that is intended, then there is a failure of communication and the drama misses its mark. Sometimes dramas intended as tragedies are instead received as comedies, and vice versa. Many factors can contribute to this sort of failure, and not all of them are in the control of the author. The passage of time can make a drama seem old-fashioned. Changing attitudes and prejudices about particular sorts of people can alter the ability of audiences to sympathize with or be amused by characters in a drama. Recent discoveries about the world might undermine the plausibility of events within the play, etc. All of these factors may contribute to a breakdown in communication between the author and the audience, and the bottom line is that when such communication breaks down, the author's intended vision is not properly conveyed.[26]

Yet it is this vision that lies at the heart of comic drama. The point of a comedy is not, as Aristotle sometimes claimed, to simply "imitate" the actions of ludicrous people. Rather, the point of comedy is for an author to create and manipulate a situation in such a manner that it brings a feeling of amusement to an audience. The particular material through which this is done may differ according to the audience and the author. However, the manner of presentation of that material must allow the audience to experience the situation as amusing. Like the house guests who interpret the verbalizations of an overly honest child as "naive" rather than "rude," the spectators at a comedy must be shown how to view the events in the drama as amusing, rather than painful.

Though the magnitude of a comedy is greater than that of a joke, comedies and jokes share much in common. Both are intended to produce amusement in an audience. Both do so through the use of incongruity and ambiguity. Both rely upon an author that attempts to communicate a particular comic viewpoint. Both may be encountered as either performances or as written texts. There is a major difference between a comedy and a joke, however, that elevates comedy above jokes to a higher art form. A comedy, like all forms of drama, attempts to draw the audience into a new world that has been created by the artist. It not only seeks to amuse spectators, but to bring them into another realm and to show them how to navigate within that realm. A comedy is not just a funny story. It is a demonstration of how the world would appear if we could approach everything with a sense of humor.

Eric Bentley writes, "In comedy, even if one cannot identify one's self with anybody on stage, one has a hero to identify with nonetheless: the author."[27] However, since comedy rests not upon any particular subject matter, but rather upon the manner of presentation of that subject matter, the author that one identifies with need not be the person that wrote down all of the words spoken during the course of a comedy. A joke can be repeated by anyone, and we might still get its point. In order for a comedy to be successful, however, an entire vision must be communicated, and the character of that vision is often affected by the interpretations of such individuals as directors, producers, actors, etc. In Aristophanes' time, by entrusting the production of a comedy to someone else, the writer of a play ensured that his own name would fail to be officially recorded.[28] Even today we recognize that very mediocre material might be produced and performed with comic genius by people possessing the proper talent and vision, and that, conversely, material with much potential can be ruined by a mediocre production and performance. This all reinforces the main point that comedy rests not in a particular subject matter, story line, or set of words, but in the talent or ability to understand any of these things from a humorous perspective. As Morreall writes, "it is precisely in humor that we find the core of comedy."[29]

HUMOR

The attitude that allows humans to make jokes and find things comic is called "humor" or a "whimsical manner." Kant calls the whimsical manner "the talent enabling us to put ourselves at will into a certain disposition, in which everything is judged in a way quite different from the usual one (even vice versa) . . ."[30] Freud likewise writes that with humor, "one spares oneself the affects to which the situation would naturally give rise and overrides with a jest the possibility of such an emotional display."[31] In both cases, humor is characterized as a talent or ability that enables a human being to interpret the world in a manner different from what otherwise might be expected. A person with a humorous manner sees the world differently from those who do not possess such a manner, and is able to find pleasure where others find only pain and displeasure.

A perfect example of the operation of humor involves the story of a condemned man who, upon approaching the gallows, says, "Well, this is a good beginning to the week!"[32] The terrifying situation of facing impending death would normally be thought to be accompanied by feelings of terror and fear. The attitude of this condemned man, however, denies those feelings, or rather rejects them, and instead makes a joke, thereby extracting pleasure from what would otherwise be a painful situation. The humorist is uniquely capable of extracting pleasure from a painful world by interpreting circumstances in a different manner from the way most people would naturally interpret them. In so doing, such an individual may appear comic and bring amusement to himself and others.

Freud thinks of the humorous attitude as a kind of defensive mechanism, and in fact as "the highest of the defensive processes."[33] In displacing the psychic energy naturally summoned for one affect into the service of another, humor allows us to guard against depression and despair in the face of the necessities of nature. Humor empowers us to resist what reality tells us it is hopeless to resist against. This mighty task is not always accompanied by laughter, however. Whereas the measure of the effectiveness of jokes and comedy might be found in the amount of laughter they produce, the pleasure in humor is more subtle and sustained. This is because the possession of a humorous attitude, rather than giving one enjoyment ready-made, instead only allows one to fashion one's own pleasures from the raw material of the world. Because of the extra mental effort and work that is involved in constructing a piece of humor, as compared to simply finding it in a comedy, or hearing it in a joke, the gratification that comes to the humorist is more moderate, less explosive, yet also accompanied by the superior feeling of a job well done. According to Freud, a humorist taps the energy that would naturally be directed toward feeling a certain emotion and instead redirects and uses that energy in order to manufacture an alternative interpretation of the world's phenomena. This, he claims, is why the experiences involved in telling a joke and hearing one are so different. The explosive, surprised laughter of an audience is inaccessible to the joke teller. Instead, the humorist feels a more sustained and superior sense of satisfaction, competency, and command deriving from the clever and creative manipulation of reality's raw materials.

In the humorist, Freud claims that we find an Ego that forsakes the "reality principle" in favor of the "pleasure principle," and in so doing approximates the processes involved in psychopathology. Humor understands reality, but refuses to be constrained by it. Instead, it strives for pleasure, even in the face of overwhelming circumstances. In refusing to suffer in the face of adversity and demanding pleasure from the world, humor rebels against the natural order of things, liberating one from the chains of nature. In these ways, Freud considers humor a form of neurosis. "[T]he denial of the claim of reality and the triumph of the pleasure principle, cause humor to approximate to the regressive or reactionary processes which engage our attention so largely in psychopathology."[34] However, we value the power that humor gives us to reinterpret, and thereby to dominate the world around us. The humorist exerts a supreme interpretational power in refusing to feel the pains of the world as pains, and this is a power to admire and respect.

Freud's discussion and portrayal of humor suggests that humor suppresses, or more accurately, displaces emotions that would otherwise be experienced under certain circumstances. Humor is, in fact, defined by Freud as that pleasure arising from "an economy in expenditure on feeling."[35] Instead of feeling a certain emotion, the psychic energy that would otherwise be "cathected"[36] by that feeling is displaced and utilized to shape a humorous reaction. On this account, humor and emotion are largely incompatible reactions, since in experiencing humor one uses up the energy that would otherwise go into feeling an emotion. Along with Freud, Bergson and Morreall hold too the view that amusement blocks emotion. "[L]aughter has no greater foe than emotion,"[37] Bergson writes, and with this assertion he points to a fairly common, yet mistaken, belief. Emotions seem often to be associated with serious, deep, and earnest feelings. Pity, fear, anger, lust, and sadness are all feelings that seem to presuppose a serious attitude and they tend to evaporate when the amusement of humor encroaches upon their territory. It is impossible to imagine, for example, finding an individual fearsome and comic at the same time.

According to Morreall, it is because emotions and the humorous response have evolved in order to fulfill differing evolutionary needs that they are incompatible. He claims that it is the practical orientation of emotion versus "the non-practical nature of amusement" that "make them not just different kinds of experience, but experiences which suppress one another."[38] Most emotions, Morreall claims, have a very down-to-earth, survival-oriented function to play in the human organism, while humorous amusement, at first glance, seems not to have a comparable, practical function. In fact, amusement appears in some ways to be entirely contrary to survival. In its most extreme form it incapacitates us with laughter and restricts our ability to breathe. Whereas fear motivates us to fight or run away from danger, amusement encourages us to linger on objects and situations, potentially to our physical detriment. Morreall claims that it is because of this contrariety that emotions and amusement suppress one another. We can't be both amused and fearful at the same time, he claims, and it is in this aspect of amusement that he finds its power.

Emotions, in his view, have developed as responses to those kinds of environmental incongruities that we are interested in resolving, while humorous amusement is a reaction that has evolved as a response to unthreatening incongruities that we are unconcerned about resolving. It is our practical concern with a phenomenon that provokes emotional feelings about it, while a nonpractical orientation, as is present in the humorous response, is necessarily devoid of such feelings. Humorous amusement results when there is sufficient emotional distance between ourselves and an incongruity so that the incongruity appears unthreatening. When such phenomena are thought to present no danger to us, we allow ourselves to linger in contemplation of them. Such activity stimulates our minds and our reason, creating pleasure and promoting the ability to deal with other, perhaps more threatening surprises that the world may spring on us in the future. Humor encourages the conceptual association of quite general and sensibly unrelated phenomena, and in this way it reinforces abstract modes of thinking and motivates the development of more and more complicated and sophisticated conceptual systems. Humor, according to Morreall, is, for these reasons, "tied to our race's general survival strategy of being rational animals."[39] It is a higher, uniquely human capacity that, because it involves conceptual abstractness, is more closely associated with the development of rationality than with emotion.

We should note that although Freud and Morreall agree with one another that humor and emotion are simultaneously incompatible, the relationship that they posit as existing between the two types of responses is significantly different. For Freud, humor draws its power from a quantum of energy that would otherwise go to energize an emotional response. The emotional response itself is characterized as being a "natural" response or the "usual" response that we would expect given a particular situation. Humor, however, involves the unexpected reinterpretation of that same situation in terms of the pleasure, rather than the reality, principle. Morreall, on the other hand, suggests that humor and emotion are completely separate reactions that have developed over our evolutionary history as responses to separate classes of incongruities. Humor and emotion, he claims, are necessarily directed toward different kinds of intentional objects, while for Freud they need not be.[40]

The assertion that humor is necessarily opposed to emotion is implausible, and it seems to rest on the mistaken assumption that all emotions are "serious," being irretrievably bound up with a practical orientation toward the world. Morreall, for example, claims that "[e]motions had survival value for animals because they prompted adaptive behavior in situations such as danger and loss."[41] Yet, we humans experience certain emotions that are completely unrelated to the experiences of danger and loss. Emotions such as love, happiness, and joy appear to have the effect not of pushing us away from the world's phenomena, but rather, as Morreall claims is the case with humorous amusement, of motivating us to linger with the objects of our attention. Furthermore, the manner in which we linger on an object in loving, happy, or joyous attention does not necessarily appear to be accompanied by any practical concern with altering or changing the object. Quite the contrary, when I lovingly linger in contemplation of, say, my pet cat, it is with no further concern than to enjoy the presence of that object. I see no necessary incompatibility between feeling both humorously amused and lovingly attracted to my cat, and in fact I have experienced both of these feelings simultaneously.

Most arguments rejecting the idea of humorous amusement as being an emotion point out that humor seems to block out or dissolve certain emotional feelings. However, as Ronald de Sousa observes, just as various emotions are incompatible with amusement, so are certain feelings that are uncontroversially classed as emotions incompatible with each other. Sadness and happiness are virtual opposites, as are love and hatred, yet no one suggests that because of their incompatibility they don't share equal status as emotions. Certain emotions block one another, and so this alone is no argument against classifying amusement as an emotion.

De Sousa calls the view that humor and emotion are incompatible the "Walberg View,"[42] and he believes it to be based upon some questionable assumptions in traditional philosophical psychology. What is presupposed in this view, he claims, is either an Aristotelian/Cartesian or a Platonic topology of the mind. In either case, the mind is thought of as divided into faculties that are incompatible with one another. In the Aristotelian/Cartesian view, the faculties of emotion and intellect are seen as separate parts that make up the mind as a whole. In the Platonic view, the mind is divided, yet dominated by a single faculty. As a consequence of these divisions, emotion and intellect, since they are qualitatively different endowments, come to be thought of as in perpetual conflict, unable to mix or cooperate with one another. They can only push one another around, competing for preeminence.

De Sousa proposes a different picture of the relationship between emotions and humor. Amusement, he claims, is a kind of emotion, and like all emotions it arises during the course of human maturation and development. Beginning in childhood, we are exposed to various "types" of situations and throughout our lives we learn to react to them in ways that are shaped by the influences exerted upon us by our genes, our parents, peers, friends, culture, etc. Emotions come into being as we come to associate different stable complexes of phenomena with the internal feelings they evoke in us. As babies, we learn to anticipate and to associate the reactions of our parents with our own subjective, bodily states. As we mature and are initiated into the folkways of society, we learn how others react to the stories, myths, and tales that are common to the cultural heritage. Our emotional sophistication becomes greater through the ability to talk about and formulate our internal feelings linguistically. In so doing, we become able to make finer and finer distinctions in our interior, emotional lives. Amusement is just one among a whole range of emotions that emerges out of the various "paradigm scenarios" we are exposed to over the course of our lifetime. Though the formal object, or core complex of associations, that humor is focused toward may be different from those of other emotions, it is only for this reason that amusement appears antithetical to other feelings. Like all other emotions, amusement is a feeling rooted in its own paradigm scenario and rationally directed toward a formal object.

The precise manner in which humor and emotion are related to one another is a fascinating question in and of itself, but it is not a question that we need to answer definitively here. What is important for our present investigation is simply to take note of the fact that regardless of whether or not humorous amusement is an emotion, it is a kind of feeling that seems to share an uneasy relationship with those "negative" sentiments that are characterized by displeasure and gloominess. Humorous amusement is opposed to the solemnity and serious-mindedness that are indispensable parts of many other passionate states of mind. Being in "good humor" means not to take things too seriously. It requires the moderation of other intense and forceful feelings through the adoption of an amused interest in the phenomena of life. A humorous attitude shares an affinity with emotion, involving a kind of feeling that colors the way in which we look at the world. But it also seems quite unique in that to look at things humorously necessarily involves finding some sort of pleasure in what is scrutinized. Even if our initial, emotional response does involve some sort of unpleasant feeling, with humor that unpleasant feeling is reevaluated and transformed into material for enjoyment. When we humorously reflect upon experiences that are otherwise painful, we reorient ourselves toward those experiences in such a manner that we gain a feeling of control and mastery over them. In choosing to view unpleasant situations through a humorous lens we demonstrate not only our own interpretational prowess, but also a rebelliousness against pain and negativity. Humor refuses to accept the pains and frustrations of the world as simply painful and frustrating. It demands that they be understood as means toward the end of providing us with merriment.

A fine discussion of the positive, rejuvenating capacity involved in the humorous attitude comes to us from the Russian philosopher and literary theorist Mikhail Bakhtin. In his lengthy discussion of the writings of the sixteenth-century literary figure Rabelais, Bakhtin reconstructs the spirit of humorous laughter that permeated the folk culture of the Middle Ages and the Renaissance and contrasts it to its counterpart in the official, more typically serious, culture of "high ideology and literature."[43] Within the folk culture of Rabelais's time, humor, Bakhtin claims, served a regenerative and affirmative purpose. It was linked to "the change of the seasons, to the phases of the sun and the moon, to the death and renewal of vegetation, and to the succession of agricultural seasons."[44] The laughing humor of the people was especially evident in their interactions during the festivals of carnival. It was during these gatherings that the full and ambivalent character of folk humor became truly evident.

The carnival was an opportunity for the common people to gather together and celebrate their connection with the earth and its powers of creation and destruction. Being tied to the land, they were keenly aware that their livelihoods hung in a continual and uneasy balance between the forces of life and death, famine and feast, growth and decay. During carnival, these forces, and their continuous, ambivalent and unstable relationship to one another, were honored. Normally, it was a feast of one sort or another that served as the pretext for these gatherings: the feasts of Saint Martin, Saint Michael, Saint Lazarus, the "asses feast," the "feasts of fools," etc. In butchering and devouring animals for these feasts, the relationship between life and death was emphasized. The death of the animal made life possible for the people. Their merriment and festive mood rested upon the destruction of life. Consequently, death and destruction could not be viewed in isolation from the wider and more inclusive processes of the world. Death made life possible, and life inevitably led to death. To refuse to affirm the more "negative" elements of the process would imply the desire for the ruination of nature's eternal cycles, which would lead, of course, to the termination of their own livelihoods.

For the people who worked the land, thus, the painful and upsetting realities they faced every day were part and parcel of the overall regulation of life. In the understanding of this fact, the folk learned to knowingly laugh when confronted with degrading and destructive events. Such events were, they knew, always accompanied by a corresponding regeneration and rebirth. The festive laughter of the people thus reflected a wisdom about "the play of time itself, which kills and gives birth at the same time, recasting the old into the new, allowing nothing to perpetuate itself."[45] The carnival was a time when, coming together, the community could rejoice in this wisdom, and they did so, Bakhtin tells us, through displays and antics that the higher, official, intellectual culture of that time (and ours) could not comprehend. Verbal abuses, sexual and scatological references and portrayals, beatings, the indulgence and encouragement of grotesqueries; all of these things were interpreted by the folk as occasions for laughter.

Bakhtin complains that modern theories of laughter and humor misunderstand the phenomenon because they emphasize its negative aspects as seen from the perspective of officialdom. He especially criticizes Bergson's theory of laughter for expounding on "mostly its negative functions,"[46] but this charge is more generally leveled at all those theorists who see in laughter and humor none of its positive, regenerative powers. Official culture is threatened by the ambivalence of folk humor, Bahktin claims, because in folk humor, all that is higher and exalted is understood to be subject to an inevitable decline and decay that brings it down to the level of the lowly and debased. This theme is especially apparent in the travesties and reversals of hierarchical order occurring during carnival in which fools were proclaimed king and clowns were ordained as bishops or the pope. These reversals are part of an overall "topographical logic" in which a shift from top to bottom came to symbolize the relativity of becoming in contradistinction to the illusion of stability and permanence that was entrenched in the official, hierarchical doctrines.

But such debasements, it should be remembered, were not intended simply to belittle and dominate, as the superiority theorists like to claim. Rather, they are intended to regenerate and repair the separation that has developed between life's negative and positive poles. The folk humor of Rabelais is in this way concerned about a rather profound and vexing human problem. How is it that we withstand a world that, being in constant flux and change, offers us no ultimate delivery from suffering? This is a serious question, and it is in fact nihilistic to its core. Bakhtin's comments suggest that the answer to this question may be found in the "universal laughter" of folk humor. The laughter and humor of the people "does not deny seriousness but purifies and completes it,"[47] he writes, and so we see here a depiction of the humorous attitude that does not attempt to cleave it completely from the experience of earnestness and emotional feeling. In its fullest sense, humor complements and rounds off emotion. It interprets emotion by placing it within some grander context, thereby transforming it into an occasion for appreciation and understanding. The feeling of emotion can be overwhelming and it may at times threaten to destroy us unless we are able to gain some sort of distance from it and ourselves. The humorous attitude allows for this sort of distance. While the realities and incongruities of the world may never change, humor allows us the opportunity to shift our way of viewing them, and in so doing to transform all of our experiences, be they good or evil, into constructive opportunities for affirmative enjoyment.

This transformative character of the humorous attitude has been commented upon extensively. Harvey Mindess, for example, emphasizes the fact that the adoption of a humorous attitude "is frequently made as a reaction to painful, distressing problems. . . . [H]umorous creativity affords its creator a means of coping with, and possibly resolving, conflicts and anxieties arising from his personal life circumstances. . . ."[48] Much of the allure of the humorous attitude lies precisely in its power to transform what would from a self-centered perspective seem threatening into an occasion for amusement. There is a psychological conversion that occurs in the mind of a humorist that involves taking up a perspective in which the normally unpleasant phenomena of experience are viewed from a vantage point of semidetached superiority and dominance. From this safe perspective, the dangers of the world appear unthreatening, and so may be humorously appreciated. The sense of mastery and dominance, while not exhausting all there is to humor, does seem to play a role in it, and for this reason Marie Collins Swabey writes that "the perceiver of the comic tends to retain mastery over himself and the situation. . . ."[49] Humor, at least very often, works to transform our painful weaknesses into strengths through an imaginative projection into a psychologically shielded point of view.[50]

The notion that humor and creativity are closely intertwined appears throughout the literature that deals with such topics, and it is generally thought that an important connection between the two capacities has to do with the role that freshness, surprise, and novelty play in both. For instance, Arthur Asa Berger writes, "[W]hatever it is, humor seems to be intimately connected with creativity, whatever that might be."[51] He goes on to suggest that an important part of creativity, and so also of humor, is "boundary breaking."[52] Boundary breaking consists in the ability to "disregard the assumptions we have about things, to break conventions, to look at things from new perspectives."[53] Mindess likewise considers "[f]lexibility, spontaneity, unconventionality"[54] to be indispensable elements in the creation of humor. William F. Fry Jr. and Melanie Allen claim that "there is no problem with humor conforming to the basic definition of creativity," which, following Fabun, they give as "the process by which original (novel) patterns are formed and expressed."[55]

We have already learned from Kant and Freud that viewing things humorously depends upon the creative ability to conceive of them in a manner different than is usual or expected. In those who have highly sophisticated and developed capacities for humor, we can expect to find an equally well-developed competency for adopting unexpected and novel ways of conceiving of the world and its varied occurrences. Though rigidity and narrowness may be the object of our laughter at times (á la Bergson), these qualities will forever be antithetical to the production of humor. The humorous attitude is opposed to all inflexibility. It is instead dependent upon a willingness to step outside of the well-demarcated and explored boundaries of "serious" thought. Humor involves taking delight in viewing things in unexpected, ambiguous, and nonconventional ways, in surprising and astounding us with a new "spin" or "slant" on a subject. In this way, the humorous attitude is involved in a kind of creative thinking.

Not all thinking is creative. Certain types of thought simply involve a noncreative reasoning within a system. By carrying out the preestablished operations that a system sanctions, a person may competently resolve apparent incongruities, solve problems, and come to conclusions that are already latent within that system. For instance, by working with the traditionally accepted premises of Freudian psychoanalysis, a therapist might uncreatively reason that all of a patient's neurotic symptoms are traceable to certain childhood struggles and traumas. In this case, the Freudian model offers a lens through which certain phenomena are made to make sense. The sense that is made results from fitting the patient's symptoms into a ready-made explanatory framework. In some cases such a framework may help to illuminate the phenomena under scrutiny by organizing them according to a set of rules that someone else has created. Symptoms that at first appeared to be mysterious become comprehensible in light of certain theoretical assumptions. But such slavish applications of theory are not truly creative since they work solely within a system of prefabricated method. Creativity, on the other hand, involves something unexpected and novel.

In forming associations between concepts that initially seemed to be disconnected, an individual exercises a kind of creativity. Arthur Koestler calls this ability "bisociation,"[56] and he claims that it is at the basis of all creative thought. For instance, the concepts of psychoanalysis might be used to analyze not just individual psychology, but also cultural and aesthetic issues. So it is that Freud was able to offer a new and creative critique of Michelangelo's *Moses*,[57] and also a creative critique of Christianity in general.[58] In boldly reaching beyond the established boundaries of a discipline or routine ways of thinking, an individual exercises the power of unification by drawing previously separated concepts closer to one another. However, these associations may not always be of the sort that illuminate. At times people draw associations that, far from producing plausible interpretations, instead produce results that mystify or puzzle due to their novelty or absurdity. When results of this type are seen as threatening, others may react negatively with anger, outrage, or puzzlement. The incongruity that is brought into existence by the creative thinker is, in this case, too much to be intellectually tolerated.

However, sometimes the conceptual incongruities that the creative thinker brings into existence are not threatening, but are thought to be amusing, and it is the ability to produce these sorts of juxtapositions where the humorous ability makes its mark. The humorist, in drawing novel and surprising associations, has access to, and thinks in terms of, more than a single, enclosed system of ready-made concepts. In transgressing conceptual boundaries the humorist is able to form playful associations that amuse and

entertain. In switching from one system to another, the humorist has the
capacity to view the points of contact between those systems from differing
perspectives. For those not privy to all of the perspectives that the humorist
draws upon, such insights might appear nonsensical, rude, or just plain false.
However, when the humorist is able to direct an audience's attention skill-
fully, and thus is able to make them see things from the appropriate points
of view, amusement and laughter may result.

The perspectives that the humorist utilizes are not necessarily systems
that possess the formality of mathematics. Probably the most common systems that act as material for the humorist are the complexes of meaning and
symbols utilized by subgroups underneath the larger umbrella of a given culture. Every group develops a way of speaking and thinking that serves to
define it as a "community," and when the specialized meanings and taken-for-
granted understandings of a community are juxtaposed with those of other
communities, hilarity may sometimes ensue. Sometimes, on the other hand,
bad feelings and animosity may also result. The humorous attitude, however,
is the attitude that is able to see such incongruities in the most pleasurable
light. What one person finds humorous, another may find otherwise.

Before moving on to a discussion of the manner in which the humorous
attitude is well suited as a response to the problem of nihilism, I would like
first to illustrate, with the aid of a couple of riddles, how it is that humor relies
upon the availability of alternative viewpoints and perspectives in order to
produce its cheerful effects. The examples that follow demonstrate the point
that humorous amusement requires access to more than a single, rigid way of
looking at things. It requires the flexible ability to move back and forth
between different perspectives whose major point of association is the object
of amusement.

Why was 6 scared of 7? Because 7, 8, 9.

What is it that we find funny in this riddle? We can begin to understand the
details of our amusement, and the humorous disposition that created it, by
first noting the phonic ambiguity involved between the pronunciation of the
symbol *8* and the word *ate*. Within the language of mathematics, 8 (eight) is
a numeral that occurs intermediate between the numerals 7 and 9. But the
pronunciation of the word *eight* is indistinguishable from the pronunciation of
the word *ate*, which seemingly has nothing whatsoever to do with the system
of mathematics. However, the humorist who created this riddle must have
been familiar with both natural language and the mathematical system of
numbers. This familiarity allowed for the association, in terms of sound,
between *8* and *ate*. Such a superficial connection between the two systems of
thought is made more apparent by way of a construction that anthropomor-
phizes the symbols *6* and *7*, leading the audience to entertain the fantasy that

the number 6 could be scared of the number 7. With the initial question as a priming device, the listener's mind is led in the direction of considering 7 as though it was an agent capable of such actions as eating other numbers. Thus, the mind vacillates back and forth between the numerical meaning and the unexpected natural language meaning of the sequence 7, 8, 9.

Note that this connection is accentuated by the writing of the sequence in number symbols. If written instead in natural language as "seven ate nine," our amusement would not be as sudden or as intense. There is a natural, almost mechanical progression in the way that "7, 8, 9" rolls through our minds and off of our tongues.[59] It is a common sequence that we have repeated to ourselves and out loud many, many times in the past; so common, in fact, that we hardly even think about it as it passes our lips. However, the ingenuity of the humorist who constructed this riddle forces us to think anew about its potential meaning from another perspective. The surprising novelty and the creativity of this riddle lies in the fact that it makes us think of a succession of three numerals in a strange, new way. An ambiguity that might otherwise not have been brought to light emerges clearly in this riddle and demonstrates a superficial, though amusing, point of association between numbers and words.

The type of thinking that appears to be involved in this riddle is something akin to what Koestler calls *bisociative*. However, perhaps the term "bisociation" is misleading, for it seems as though, at least in the case of humor, there may be more than two frames of reference called upon. Consider the following riddle, in some ways similar to the example from above:

According to Freud, what comes between fear and sex? Fünf.

Here, it is not only two systems of meaning that are drawn upon, but three. In this riddle, like the one above, our amusement is spurred by an ambiguity arising between the language of numbers and natural language. However in this instance, the natural languages drawn upon are two separate ones: English and German. In German, the symbols *4* and *6* are *vier* and *sechs,* which to an English speaker's ear sound very similar to the words *fear* and *sex.* The setup for this riddle, referring as it does to Sigmund Freud, primes the audience into thinking about the substance of psychological issues concerning fear and sex, as well as bringing to mind German authorship. However, the punch line redirects us, and forces our thoughts to consider the sound of the words at issue, thereby introducing us to a new perspective in which those sounds are understood in terms of a sequence of numbers: 4, 5, 6. Thus, this riddle forces us not simply to "bisociate," but to "trisociate" between the system of numbers, the system of the English language, and the system of the German language.

I see no reason why the number of systems between which amusing associations may potentially be drawn would necessarily have to be limited, and in fact, the sophistication of a piece of humor might partly be judged on the basis of the amount of background information upon which it draws. A humorist, in the construction of witticisms, demonstrates mastery of, and the ability to navigate between, a variety of perspectives. In communicating a joke, an audience is, furthermore, called upon to recognize and follow the maneuvers of the humorist as associations and relationships are drawn between those systems of thought. As a consequence, in the sharing of humorous laughter, there is also a shared familiarity based upon knowledge and intellect. This aspect of humor has, of course, never gone unnoticed. Ted Cohen, for instance, points out that the understanding of any joke requires that the audience and joke teller share some common background information, and so all jokes, he tells us are "conditional." "It is a vital feature of much joking that only a suitably qualified audience—one that can meet the condition—can receive the joke, and the audience derives an additional satisfaction from knowing this about itself."[60] I would add that it is not just the audience, but the humorist as well that derives satisfaction from the successful delivery of a joke. An understanding is formed between joke teller and audience based not only upon their joint access to a body of information and beliefs about the world, but also by their common ability to make the conceptual associations necessary to comprehend the joke. Of course, depending upon the degree of divergence between the belief systems actually endorsed by jokester and audience, an understanding does not necessarily lead to comradeship. One can "get" a joke, be offended by it, and so question the motivations of the joke teller. Jokes can drive a wedge between teller and audience no less than they can draw them closer together. But this is a topic that threatens to carry us far afield from the issues at hand.

I have speculated in this chapter that humorous amusement is related to encounters with incongruity. All incongruities produce a certain degree of tension and conflict within us, but with the humorous attitude it becomes possible to experience that dissonance as amusing. Humor allows us to confront incongruities and, instead of becoming overwhelmed by them, to understand them in an unusual and original fashion. The creative ability to step outside of routine ways of thinking about things, to adopt new and unconventional perspectives, is part and parcel of the humorous attitude. With it, we are allowed the luxury of lingering upon seeming nonsense, yet we remain unsatisfied with leaving it at that. Humor requires work, and in the confrontation with incongruity it undertakes the impossible task of making sense out of nonsense. In this activity, the humorist exercises a talent, and in so doing demonstrates to the rest of the world a creative competency, energy, and ingenuity that is relatively rare and excellent.

I wish to stress that the humorous attitude is not simply a passive reaction to the world's stimuli. It is, rather, a talent or a capacity for reinterpretation. The humorist, upon encountering an incongruity, demands of it that it make some contribution to the enjoyment of life. Such an individual refuses to rest satisfied with the unsettled and anxious feelings that some incongruity initially provokes. Rather, the humorist actively searches for ways to understand and appreciate the phenomenon, and if no ready-made framework exists, a new perspective is created from which the incongruity might appear amusing and less threatening. Humor, thus, involves not only a reaction to unthreatening incongruity, but also the capacity to *make* incongruities unthreatening and to interpret them in a manner that produces amusement. With humor, the individual engages in a directed and methodical procedure of mental processing that juggles and associates concepts with the ultimate intention of finding in them some sort of pleasing arrangement. When humorists engage their sense of humor, they do so by utilizing their own imaginative powers to conceive of things in a manner that brings them pleasure. They gain a distance from the more immediate and dangerous worries of reality by abstracting and withdrawing their attention from the perceptions that threaten them from without. Instead, they redirect their attentions inward, manipulating concepts in a manner that brings enjoyment and comic delight. This manipulation may be done playfully and without the worry that such "experiments" will have irreversible, destructive consequences. Rather, in playing with concepts, the humorist introduces us all to creative and new ways of thinking about our own powers of imagination.

Humor involves a capacity to tolerate and enjoy incongruity. The riddles that I offered above are good illustrations of how this talent figures into the humorous attitude. Appreciating these riddles depends upon one's proficiency at holding a variety of seemingly incompatible and incongruous concepts in one's head all at once. If understood unequivocally from only a single viewpoint, these riddles would lose their amusing quality. The key to our enjoyment in such cases seems to rest not so much in figuring something out, or in solving some sort of conundrum, but rather in adopting an attitude wherein we feel comfortable thinking about an incongruity and considering it from a number of differing perspectives, none of which alone really serves to provide a fully comprehensible assessment of the phenomenon. The humorous attitude is at home with this sort of ongoing contemplation. It is amiable toward both ambiguity and incongruity and finds pleasure in playing with concepts that seem incompatible with one another.

It has been claimed by Kant and a whole tradition of rationalist philosophers that the pleasure in hearing a riddle or a joke really comes at the point that we discover its solution, and that it is only in the resolution of incongruity that humans find pleasure and amusement. If this is the case, then a riddle perfectly illustrates not the enjoyment of incongruity itself, but rather the resolution of apparent incongruities. However, there are cases of sheer absurdity and nonsense that do call our attention, admit no hope for resolution, yet still provoke us toward amusement. One need only think of the absolutely absurd yet hilarious story by Nicolai Gogol titled *The Nose* in order to find an example of unresolved incongruity that motivates us to laughter and amusement. In this story, the main protagonist wakes up to discover that his nose is missing. He soon discovers that his nose has disguised itself as a State Councillor and is running about town conducting business. None of this makes any real sense no matter how many differing ways that we try to understand it. But in confronting the absurd conceptual incongruity involved here (if we have a sense of humor) we experience a sense of amusement and pleasure.[61] The pleasure may even be so intense that we laugh out loud. We form pictures in our minds, trying to understand how a nose could wear a cloak, pray at church, drive a coach, etc. We try to concoct metaphorical and allegorical explanations for the imagery. We wonder if the author was insane or on drugs, etc. In considering the incongruities of this story from all of these different viewpoints, however, our amusement is only amplified. None of these interpretations alone does justice to the richness and genius of the tale, but in racing between them and gathering them together, we engage in the exercise of our sense of humor.

The claim that only the resolution of incongruity produces amusement is, thus, probably too strong. It does seem plausible that unresolved incongruities are themselves capable of provoking us to amusement as well. What is central in the humorous attitude is not the discovery of some solution to an apparent incongruity but rather the openness involved in surveying incongruities from a variety of perspectives and taking pleasure in the process along the way. The humorous attitude is not equivalent to the attitude of the puzzle solver, though curiosity and imagination are involved with both. Humor does not necessarily involve an expectation that our interpretational exertions will lead to final answers or unambiguous outcomes. The humorous attitude is flexible and creative both in its approach to life's problems and in its demands for results. Humor is not opposed to seriousness but it rounds off our more serious states of mind by reminding us that our own way of looking at things is only one among a potentially infinite number of ways. Humor puts us, and everything that seems ultimately important to us, in its place. In this respect, it is perhaps, as I shall claim in the conclusion that follows, the best lens through which to view the problem of nihilism.

Conclusion

Humor as a Response to Nihilism

... for in laughter all that is evil comes together, but is pronounced holy and absolved by its own bliss; and if this is my alpha and omega, that all that is heavy and grave should become light; all that is body, dancer; all that is spirit bird—and verily, that is my alpha and omega: Oh how should I not lust after eternity and after the nuptial ring of rings, the ring of recurrence?
—Friedrich Nietzsche, *Thus Spoke Zarathustra*

The basic presumptions and values that nihilists take for granted are anything but foreign to our contemporary way of thinking, and it is for this reason that the problem of nihilism has, in recent times, become an intense issue of focus. Nihilism is a syndrome that, while neither solely modern nor Western, has gained much attention in the modern West. Though the first use of the term only dates back to anti-Kantian criticisms of the eighteenth century, the problem that is at the core of these criticisms is as old as humanity itself. Keiji Nishitani, in fact, has claimed that "nihilism is a problem that transcends time and space and is rooted in the essence of human being."[1] Whether or not he is literally correct in this regard, it certainly may be admitted that at virtually all points in history there have been individuals possessing an idealistic yearning for perfection and that this desire has normally been met with frustration. Humans, it seems, quite frequently and routinely fall short of their highest ideals, and although in so doing they very often produce quite splendid accomplishments, they also expose themselves to the experience of nihilism.

Our inquiry into German, Russian, Nietzschean, world-war and, postwar nihilism in the first part of this investigation educated us to some of the themes and patterns of thought that are common among nihilistic philosophies. With nihilism we found that there develops a feeling that any human successes are relatively worthless and without intrinsic value because none of them is able to mend the ever-present rift between the "real" experience of despairing failure and the "ideal" aspiration toward perfect communion with Being, Truth, Justice, and Goodness. This rift is an incongruous, conceptual "break" that demands and holds the nihilist's attention. It focuses the nihilist's thought, calling awareness to a host of troubling questions. If all that we do is a vain struggle toward the superlative, and if this struggle must culminate in death and nothingness, why strive for anything? How is one to avoid despair when all that we are capable of producing is prone to decline and decay? What is to be done when we live in a world that refuses to grant us Truth, Goodness, Justice, or meaningful lives? Why not simply destroy everything if nothing has worth? These recurrent, nihilistic questions are lamentations of anguish as well as sincere and hopeful requests for guidance. The world of the nihilist is one in which utopias, God, and perfection are all exquisite, tempting, and yet cruelly implausible pipe dreams.

In chapter 4 we distilled out and made explicit the philosophical assumptions lying latent in the works of nihilist authors. Nihilists seem to believe three things: (1) humans are alienated from the highest, most absolute perfections; (2) this situation is not as it should be; and (3) there is nothing that can be done to change this situation. These three assumptions comprise the nihilist philosophy, and they imply a situation that I have labeled "nihilistic incongruity." Nihilistic incongruity is the circumstance faced by nihilists when they think through and face the existential consequences of their philosophical assumptions about reality. It is a situation in which nothing that is actually attainable appears to have real significance or value, since nothing that is actually attainable measures up to the permanence, timelessness, and certainty that characterize the superlative goodness of the highest ideals. The world ought not to be the way that it is, claims the nihilist, but there is nothing that can be done to change that. Humans are too puny, too stupid, too alienated from the true nature of reality to have any consequential effects. As a result of the confrontation with nihilistic incongruity, nihilists have traditionally expressed a deep sense of anxiety, pain, emptiness, and despair about life. In discovering how truly powerless they are, they become overwhelmed by feelings of distress concerning a world that is beyond their control.

To many, nihilistic incongruity seems an irretrievably bleak circumstance; one that condemns the nihilist to a life of despair and passivity, and there are undoubtably many nihilists who fall into a black pit of depression, never to climb out, and never to fight against the meaninglessness of the universe. This motivates us to wonder, why don't nihilists follow the lead of skeptical pragmatists or postmodernists and work to move "beyond nihilism"? In chapter 5 we probed the nature of the nihilist's commitment to the premises of nihilism and discovered the answer to this question. Lying behind the experience of nihilistic failure and frustration is a sort of sublime respect for the idea of "the absolute," or "the infinite," and though there is a recognition that such an ideal can never be made real, the nihilist cannot abandon the desire for its perfect actualization. Both Kant and Freud have given attention to this desire, and both were led to the conclusion that since it can lead nowhere except to despair, it is an irrational yearning. But as Kierkegaard astutely points out, there is an ambiguity involved in the usage of the term *despair*. On the one hand, it may be used to suggest a purely negative state of psychological despondency and dejection. On the other, it may be used without negative connotations simply to describe a situation in which hope for a valued outcome evaporates. It is in this second sense that nihilism necessarily leads to despair, not the first sense.

Though the nihilist must despair of attaining the absolute, this is not an unequivocally negative situation. In finding every *actual* thing to be worthless and without value, the nihilist still retains an *ideal* notion of what would constitute value. Thus, it is not quite correct to claim that nihilism is a doctrine holding that everything is worthless. It is, rather, a doctrine holding that everything that *actually exists* is relatively worthless in comparison to the highest ideas of perfection. At the same time that it indicates a falling away from those things that are of the highest value, the experience of nihilism makes its casualties aware of their highest idealistic aspirations. Nihilism directs attention toward all that is of inferior worth only by way of contrast with all that is considered to be of superlative value, and in so doing it activates a sense of longing and desire emphasizing not only the puniness of actual human capacities, but the potential nobility of the highest human aspirations.

In chapter 6, we attempted to use this insight in order to cast new light on the phenomenon of nihilistic incongruity itself. If it is true that nihilists find the superlative ideals of absolute Being, Truth, Goodness, etc. to be the highest and most correct objects of value, then anything that allows the nihilist to develop a more attuned appreciation of these objects and to linger in their presence might be considered to possess a certain degree of instrumental value. Though nihilistic incongruity, on the one hand, causes frustration by separating the nihilist from all that is supremely valuable, on the other, it acts to draw that individual into a relationship with the objects of highest value. Consequently, it may be understood as no less useful than it is painful. Once this useful potential of nihilistic incongruity has been recognized, the phenomenon need no longer appear as an utterly destructive threat. Instead, it might come to be thought of as a moment of transformative possibility, a spur toward continuing reflection, activity, and unlimited growth and change.

The world view of the nihilist does not promise any hope for the end of struggle, failure, or frustration, but the manner in which individuals react to and cope with this situation need not be gloomy desperation. Contrary to the claims of Kant, Freud, and most contemporary philosophers, the phenomenon of nihilistic incongruity does not necessarily culminate in destructive despair. Among recent thinkers, it is perhaps only Heidegger who correctly observes that nihilistic incongruity, though often associated with negativity, destruction, and despair, is not in its essence a negative phenomenon. "The essence of nihilism contains nothing negative,"[2] he writes, going on to point out that the "essence" of nihilism:

> is the destiny of Being itself . . . nihilism is the promise of Being in its uncon-
> cealment in such a way that it conceals itself precisely as the promise, and in
> staying away simultaneously provides for its own omission.[3]

Enigmatic though this passage may be, it none the less, I believe, represents the most accurate philosophical articulation of nihilism extant. Being itself encompasses all that "is," and so is reflected in everything that exists, including the failures and frustrations of life, claims Heidegger. Though this reflection often goes unrecognized, it still offers a potential point of orientation and focus for continuing philosophical exploration and inquiry. In promoting distance and separation from the absolute, nihilistic incongruity "conceals" Being as a whole from the nihilist. Yet in this concealment, the nihilist detects the "promise" of something "more." Being "withdraws" from the nihilist each time that the nihilist advances, but in its withdrawal, it still mesmerizes, tempting and attracting the nihilist. The incongruity between what nihilists have at any particular point and what they wish to have may promote feelings of discord and tension, but if they allow themselves to linger in the contemplation of this incongruity, they may become enraptured by the "enigma" that is the unrealizable "promise" and the "mystery" of Being itself.

Desire and longing for the full "unconcealment" of Being is thus encouraged by the experience of nihilism, according to Heidegger. The nihilist "cares" about Being itself, and is not able to abandon devotion to it simply because it withdraws with every advance. My only complaint concerning Heidegger's formulation of nihilism is that he tends to overemphasize the ontological elements of the phenomenon. As we have already discovered in Part One, nihilistic incongruity may also manifest itself in epistemological, existential, political, and ethical fashions. In fact, nihilistic incongruity is implied at any time that there is an irreconcilable disunity between the real-life abilities of human beings and their most dearly valued final ends. Consequently, I see no reason why the list of nihilisms could not be extended to include such things as aesthetic nihilism (the vain desire for absolute Beauty), anarchistic nihilism (the vain desire for absolute freedom), pacifist nihilism (the vain desire for absolute peace), liberal nihilism (the vain desire for the needs of all human beings to be met), etc. The list of "nihilisms" might extend to encompass any type of thinking that aims toward, and desires the perfect consummation of, an ideal.

In chapter 6 we explored just some of the perspectives from which nihilistic incongruity might be viewed in terms of its positive and useful functions. The perpetuation of creative activity, the pursuit of higher and higher levels of excellence, and the retention of a relationship to the only things that are considered intrinsically valuable, are all "goods" that may potentially be extracted from the experience of vainly striving toward unattainable ideals. Though despair and frustration are ever-present dangers for the nihilist, by holding true to very ambitious goals this individual also retains an orientation that may encourage ceaseless activity, hard work, and high levels of attainment. In light of the highest ideals of nihilism itself, then, nihilistic incongruity might possess some degree of instrumental value. Not only might it be thought of as a potentially useful vehicle for the incremental betterment of collectives and the individuals that comprise them, but it might be conceived of as a tether that binds the nihilist fast in a continuing relationship to that which is truly valuable in and of itself.

I would like to emphasize that the discussions undertaken in the fifth and sixth chapters of this work are not necessarily intended as recommendations of the nihilist's system of thought. They are, instead, intended only as an exploration of some of the ways that nihilism might be situated within human experience and viewed in terms of its instrumental value. If we allow ourselves to think along with nihilists, concerning ourselves not with trying to undermine and argue against their world view, but with drawing out the potentially positive and constructive implications of it, both nihilists, and we ourselves, may learn some interesting and important lessons. It is possible to conceive of nihilism as a phenomenon that contributes to the richness and fullness of human life if we only allow ourselves to imagine the larger purposes it might serve. Insofar as it necessarily implies an existential confrontation with failure and frustration, nihilism certainly cannot completely be separated from despair. However, neither must nihilistic incongruity be encountered as an irretrievably destructive threat to the full and committed pursuit of life. It might, in fact, be appraised of in such a manner that it appears as an ally in the struggle toward all that is most passionately desired.

To become reconciled with the necessary failures and frustrations of life, seeing them as the flip side of moderate and limited human successes, allows the nihilist to cultivate a modesty of character that might help to enrich life rather than detracting from its meaningfulness. Though nihilism has been relentlessly criticized for overemphasizing the dark side of human experience, it might be equally true that this overemphasis represents a needed counterbalance to shallow optimism and arrogant confidence in human power. Nihilism reminds us that humans are not gods, and that despite all of the accomplishments and wonders of civilization, humans cannot alter the fact that they possess only a finite amount of mastery and control over their own destinies.

This aspect of nihilism has not been emphasized nearly enough in the literature that deals with such subjects. The spirit of seriousness and gravity that has surrounded most discussions concerning nihilism focuses predominately on the dysfunctional aspects of this experience. It has most often been likened to a "cancer," "sickness," or a "disease," suggesting that it is nothing more than a destructive danger. However, if what I have claimed in this book has any plausibility, then the incongruity lying at the heart of nihilism might be conceived of as a potentially useful spur for both human activity and reflection. This being the case, nihilism may not be an unqualified evil at all. Instead, it might be thought of as a kind of good. If this is so, then it makes sense to adopt an attitude toward nihilism different from that suggested in the past by most others. Rather than rejecting nihilism as something to be "overcome," perhaps it should be embraced. Perhaps it is not nihilistic incongruity that needs to be altered, but our attitude toward it.

Once attention has been drawn to the conceptual incongruity between the actual and the ideal that lies at the root of nihilism, a response is called for. Since the nihilistic situation first beckons by way of a conceptual incongruity, an appropriate response to its recognition should be in those terms. In chapter 7 we found that incongruity in general is a phenomenon that tends to produce feelings of tension. It makes itself known through the discord and dissonance that emerges from a confrontation between two or more incompatible things. Negative affective states often accompany our encounters with dangerous and threatening incongruities. Such feelings motivate us to take a practical, and serious, concern in eliminating or resolving incongruity, doing away with dissonance and making the world a less uneasy place to live in.

However, contrary to what Kant and a whole tradition of rationalism claims, incongruities are not always, or even usually, responded to with feelings of negativity. Just as they may sometimes strike us as threatening, so may incongruities sometimes be encountered as unthreatening. Though all incongruities are characterized by dissonance and discord, the humorous attitude is able to appropriate that conflict, and to understand it in terms of amusement. Humor is a creative and transformative talent that encourages one not only to linger on incongruity, but to understand incongruous dissonance as something that is comically pleasing. This feat is accomplished, at least in large part, by means of shifting one's viewpoint and imagining alternative perspectives from which the incongruity in question might appear in a more pleasing and unthreatening light. Sometimes this process may lead to the resolution of the incongruity in question, producing a denouement that makes a joke out of the phenomenon. However, the process involved in humor is not overwhelmingly concerned with problem solving. Rather, its essence lies in the ability to play with concepts and thereby to conceive of new and different ways of thinking about things. While the realities and incongruities of the world may never change, humor allows us the opportunity to shift our way of viewing them, and in so doing to conceive of all our experiences, be they good or evil, as constructive opportunities for affirmative enjoyment.

In good humor we are able to see things from more than a single, rigid, and narrow-minded viewpoint. Humor allows us to change our perspective in order to comprehend how it is that all things in the world might fit into a grander structure of hidden, conceptual associations. This attitude has the potential to make even our own suffering bearable by giving it a place within that structure. To take our own sufferings, frustrations, and insecurities too seriously is a vain exercise in egotism. To approach them with a humorous manner, on the other hand, does justice to both our pain and the world in which that pain takes place. With humor we recognize that distressing feelings occur, yet we are able to transform them into occasions for enjoyment. In so doing we affirm the world and take an elevated kind of pleasure from what would otherwise be simply agonizing. This is perhaps the major service humor may perform in the confrontation with nihilism. While despair and frustration are undeniable aspects associated with nihilistic phenomena, the nihilist need not ultimately surrender to these feelings. With humor, even the problem of nihilism may appear within its appropriate context as a painful yet ultimately valuable phenomenon in the history of our world.

The humorous response to nihilism consists in adopting an attitude that allows the nihilist to break the tyrannical grip of overly serious thought. In thinking that is overly serious, one becomes inappropriately invested in a single way of deliberating about a subject. An overly serious thinker becomes so immersed in a topic that its importance becomes magnified out of all proportion to its surrounding context. As the subjective importance of the topic of inquiry grows, the importance of other things around it diminishes. When we are too serious, we concern ourselves only with reaching solutions and final understandings of things. We become invested in unraveling some mystery, or in solving some problem at the cost of other equally important commitments. For example, Raskolnikov, in Dostoyevsky's *Crime and Punishment*, was overly serious about testing the limits of his own power and cleverness. In the process he destroyed and injured not only those around him, but himself as well.[4]

Seriousness is committed, earnest, and somber. The humorous attitude, on the other hand, moderates our seriousness, reminding us that in the grand scheme of things, nothing is really that important. It encourages us to investigate a wide variety of alternative perspectives and to even indulge those ways of looking at things that are false, absurd, or just plain silly. Rather than encouraging a single-minded devotion to solving life's mysteries, humor encourages ceaseless playfulness. It takes delight in surprising and clever leaps of the imagination and it considers dead ends and setbacks not so much as failures, but as enriching aspects of Being that might be productively explored and experienced.

Of course, just as a person can be overly serious, so too may a person be insufficiently serious. A person incapable of seriousness is just a buffoon who refuses to think things through or to deliberate over consequences and implications. However, a humorous attitude is not the same as an attitude lacking in seriousness. It is, rather, an ability to see things within the context of multiple perspectives. Humor, as Bakhtin has pointed out, in its fullest sense "purifies and completes"[5] our seriousness rather than denying it. It is an attitude that revises an incomplete, fragmented, and one-sided view of reality into a more well-rounded and masterful understanding.

A humorist possesses a precious and praiseworthy talent. It is a talent with which civilized societies have at times been uneasy, however. In making the world comedic and a matter for joking, the humorist has been called not only a fool, but also a dangerous influence upon the masses. Plato may have been the first to warn against the humorist's talents, but this basic critique has remained the same for thousands of years. Comedy, jokes, and humor are potentially subversive tools that, in their power to make the dangers of the world look small, also have the power to overthrow and destroy the serious spirit of reverence that tradition and authority have bestowed upon our leaders and social institutions. It was for these reasons that Bakhtin, in a very un-Platonic manner, heaped praise upon laughter and humor. Its power to bring all that is serious and threatening down to earth makes it both the perfect weapon against arrogance and the perfect tonic for the oppressed. In its fullest, richest sense, humor rounds off and complements the sad and grieving emotions that we usually associate with loss, devastation and decline. It interprets these emotions by placing them within some grander context, thereby transforming them into occasions for appreciation and understanding. The seriousness of certain emotions may at times become overwhelming and may threaten to destroy us unless we are able to gain some sort of distance from them and ourselves. The humorous attitude allows for this sort of distance.

The humorous attitude does not eradicate or do away with all negativity or sadness. What it does, rather, is to encourage individuals to become comfortable holding within their minds a variety of contrasting and incongruous assessments of a situation all at once. Humorous thinking, for instance, allows the nihilist to entertain feelings of personal frustration while also understanding at another level of conception that such frustration might be instrumental in the pursuit of collective progress and for the overall enrichment of the individual soul. Humor tolerates such ambivalent states of mind and in fact finds pleasure and amusement in them. On the other hand, humor is intolerant of the single-mindedness that so often consumes and destroys the overly serious person. To the person in good humor, an overly serious person is just like someone who is unable to understand a really clever joke. It does not matter how intricately you explain and elaborate upon the cleverness and enjoyable nature of a joke. If someone is unwilling to understand and delight in the ambiguities and incongruities that jokes thrive on, then there is no hope for the production of amusement in that person. Such an individual is exasperating and is, insofar as they are just unwilling to engage in humorous thought, considered to be quite deficient. Over-seriousness is a symptom of rigidity and a lack of imagination. It represents a kind of orientation that refuses to see things in new, unusual, different or creative ways.

The heavy air of gloom and despair that permeates most discussions of nihilism is the result of an overly serious and single-minded emphasis on the hurtful and negative aspects of failure, despair, and frustration. However, there is a vast constellation of possible alternative perspectives that might be entertained allowing nihilistic incongruity to be viewed not simply as an occasion for dejection and depression, but as an opportunity for unending, creative, and vital activity. With a humorous attitude the nihilist is encouraged to imagine the ways in which nihilistic incongruity might be considered good and productive of pleasure. During the course of the present inquiry I have attempted to elucidate a number of these perspectives, and to demonstrate that a single-minded emphasis on the grim and unpleasant aspects of nihilism is too unbalanced an orientation to be philosophically satisfying.

I propose that we try to imagine a new type of creature: The humorous nihilist. Part of the talent exercised by a humorous nihilist would be the ability to place the experience of nihilism within a context that encloses and makes sense of its vicissitudes. Understood as a means rather than as an end in itself, nihilism might then become bearable. With the creative ability to conceive of new and unthreatening ways to view the phenomenon, a humorous nihilist could defuse the all too common overemphasis on despair and negativity that has generally come to be associated with nihilism. In learning to conceive of nihilistic incongruity from perspectives that accentuate its beneficial and positive aspects, the humorous nihilist would promote lightheartedness and laughter, transforming an otherwise threatening phenomenon into an occasion for amusement. After all, as Freud has pointed out:

> The principal thing is the intention which humor fulfills, whether it concerns the subject's self or other people. Its meaning is: "Look here! This is all that this seemingly dangerous world amounts to. Child's play—the very thing to jest about!"[6]

... and indeed the intention of the humorous response to nihilism is to uplift human souls and to conquer the attitude of despairing seriousness that is traditionally associated with nihilism.

The nihilistic world view does not necessarily imply destructive negativity. It rests upon certain premises that, when clearly understood, imply an incongruity that might be exploited for the purposes of constructive activity. There is a vast abyss, a cleft, between human beings and the world that can never be healed, claims the nihilist. Ontologically we are separated from Being; epistemologically we are incapable of certainty; existentially we are alienated from the Good life; politically and ethically we are unable to achieve Justice. This all may sound terrible and negative, but that is only because it is not uncommon for people to possess certain values holding that the highest perfection would consist in direct commerce with Being, absolutely certain knowledge, a life of satisfaction, and the fulfillment of Justice. The descriptive picture that nihilists paint conflicts with the way that they themselves desire the world to be, and for this reason nihilism leads to dissatisfaction and unease. Further, it is because dissatisfaction and unease are experienced as negative and unpleasant that it is often a natural and automatic response to dismiss nihilism as a philosophy of negativity. The use of the term *nihilism* as a weapon, I think, often is rooted in this sort of notion. Since nihilism emphasizes the hopelessness of finally achieving some heaven-like state of final satisfaction with the world, it is often equated with despair and pessimism. People, especially those who are used to being rewarded for their efforts at work, school, or at home, want to believe that all of life's efforts will likewise be rewarded. The thought that reality is indifferent, and in fact resolutely resistant to our advances, is interpreted as tragic.

But, as Walter Kaufman has quite correctly pointed out, "The difference between tragedy and comedy is not in essence one of subject matter, but depends upon our point of view."[7] The same material that serves as the building blocks for a serious and tragic interpretation of nihilism may also serve as the foundation for a more lighthearted and good humored interpretation of the phenomenon. Both comedy and tragedy are sprouts off of a common root, but the flowers that they produce look quite different from one another. Tragedy looks like despair and anxiety. It interprets the contrast between human effort and the necessities of nature as a terrifying and fearful vulnerability to the cosmos. Tragedy sees humankind as helplessly struggling in the presence of fate, locked in a battle that it is bound to lose. Comedy, on the other hand, looks amused and stimulated. It views the incongruity between human desire and ability as absurd or ludicrous, as an opportunity for amusement.

What the humorous attitude has to offer those caught within the grip of nihilistic incongruity is an opportunity to temper and augment their one-sidedness with a "comic vision" of life. Humor invites the nihilist to understand the world in a more well-balanced and philosophically enriching way than this individual may be used to. With humor the nihilist is goaded into conceiving of different ways of thinking about the troubling rift that exists between the finite and the infinite. With these conceptions, the humorous nihilist accomplishes a mighty and creative task, bringing into existence new viewpoints and aspects of understanding. The more of these viewpoints that the nihilist is able to construct, the more well-rounded and complex becomes the individual's orientation toward nihilistic incongruity. The good humored nihilist ultimately may eventually become unable to take any single perspective on nihilism too seriously. In allowing themselves to become exposed to many differing and incompatible perspectives on nihilism, good humored nihilists might never be able to retreat into narrow and single-minded ignorance again. Once nihilism has been conceived of from more than a single, serious-minded perspective, there's no going back to an unambiguously gloomy and pessimistic outlook.

Erasmus, in singing the praises of folly, professed a bit of wisdom that needs to be rediscovered by the nihilist: "But methinks I hear the philosophers saying 'tis a miserable thing for a man to be foolish, to err, mistake, and know nothing truly. Nay rather, this is to be a man."[8] If the nihilist is correct, then there is nothing to be done about our situation, and it is in the very nature of human beings to be imperfect, yet to strive for perfection. But perhaps it is not only an occasion for sadness to understand that our highest ideals are mere pipe-dreams that will never be made real. Rather, perhaps it is also an occasion for wondrous amusement. To adopt a humorous attitude is not to deny that human life is full of suffering, despair and failure. However it refuses to be dominated or crushed by this reality. With humor, the dangers of life become smaller, and the humorist, in laughing at the world, laughs at him or herself as a part of that world.

The world view of the nihilist suggests that we must despair of ever attaining ultimate and final satisfaction with ourselves or our place in the world. Life is a vain and unending struggle culminating in nothing, and all that seems beautiful and worthy is mere illusion, subject to decline and decay. The pain of longing for what will be is chronically replaced by the pain of mourning for what was, and our lives are lived in a tense and unsettled state of unending desire for the ideal, which does not, and never will, exist in our here and now reality. The nihilist desires perfection but realizes that perfection is beyond reach. This incongruity between what is desired and what is actually possible lies at the heart of the problem of nihilism. Because it emphasizes frustration, pain, the vanity of struggle, and the hopelessness of attaining perfection, the philosophy of nihilism has traditionally been criticized as a doctrine advocating despair and depression.

However, there is more than one way to view nihilistic incongruity. In the past most have opted for a dark and gloomy picture of the phenomenon, but with this investigation I think that I have perhaps suggested some new and more constructive perspectives on the problem. I hope that some of the speculations and reasonings contained in this work will act as a kind of provocation to others, encouraging them to imagine ways in which nihilistic incongruity might be conceived of as useful. The more perspectives that we are able to bring into orbit around nihilistic incongruity, the more likely that the phenomenon will appear not as a threat, but as an amusing and thought provoking focus for continuing philosophical meditation.

The message that I hope has successfully been delivered through this book is that failure and frustration, even when experienced in the pursuit of that which is supremely important to us, are not the worst things in the world. In fact, they may serve a purpose in making us, and the world we live in, richer and more profound. Human dignity, it seems to me, is not so much a matter of what we accomplish successfully, but of our willingness to continue striving toward what we think is good and worthy. In remaining dissatisfied and discontented with the world as it is, the nihilist retains a strange sort of rebellious, heroic, and admirable dignity.

POSTSCRIPT

Before closing, I would like to offer a few scattered and brief observations about the relationship of a humorous nihilism to philosophy, education, and to recent terrorist activities in the United States. These remarks are not intended to be exhaustive, or even very extensive. Rather, they are areas of inquiry that I think may warrant further meditation and investigation in the future.

I contend that a humorous attitude toward nihilism is eminently "philosophical." Philosophy, or the "love of wisdom," involves a kind of thinking that requires an attitude of curiosity and care for what is True, Good, and lasting. When Pythagoras, who first coined the term, was asked if he thought himself wise, he reportedly responded that he was not wise, but that he *loved* wisdom. Rather than consisting in a closed body of knowledge, or a collection of logical tools and methods, philosophy, in this sense, involves an attitude of enthusiasm for questioning and investigation into the world. It is a pursuit and a process that never ends and is never satisfied. Unlike certain other fields or disciplines, philosophy is especially friendly to constant questioning, speculation, and reflection. It doesn't claim to offer final answers, and it delights in the constant and unceasing probing of the world. For philosophy, there are always more questions to ask and more things to explore. If philosophy is considered in this sense, as an *attitude* of openness and enthusiasm for ceaseless inquiry, then we might begin to suspect that it bears an uncanny resemblance to humorous nihilism.

The humorous nihilist would be an individual who, like Socrates, constantly aspired toward the ideal without ever resting in the arrogantly complacent belief that it had been reached. As a nihilist, such an individual would love and care about Truth, Being, Goodness, etc., yet would find them constantly out of reach. As a humorist, this individual would understand this circumstance as amusing and worthy of continued attention. Humor and nihilism, when combined with one another, would produce a sort of balance in which a serious devotion to the ideal is tempered by a lightheartedness and amusement that encourages continued striving and creative activity. The humorous nihilist is an individual who, though committed to the pursuit of wisdom, is able to conceive of, and be amused by, the ultimate absurdity of such a pursuit.

Educators, as well as philosophers, must concern themselves with the pursuit of ideals such as wisdom, and so the problem of nihilism is of potential concern to them as well. Some of our insights into nihilism's useful functions have ramifications for teachers who, as is quite common today, encounter students caught in the grip of nihilism. Working with a traditional, negative understanding of nihilism, an educator has little leverage with which to persuade and motivate a nihilistic student toward the completion of a program of study. At their worst, such encounters might quickly deteriorate into a battle of world views, with the educator attempting to convince nihilistic students that their way of looking at the world is all wrong, and vice versa. What our present inquiry suggests, however, is that such a tactic is unnecessary. A teacher with the proper amount of patience may be able to help students to draw out the positive implications of their nihilism, and in so doing motivate them to engage in the ongoing, yet perhaps vain, pursuit of Knowledge, Truth, and Wisdom. Treating nihilistic students as individuals with an unusual amount of integrity, rather than treating them as individuals who have given up on life and learning, is the first step that a teacher can take in defusing the negativity in despair. By encouraging a humorous attitude toward nihilism, a teacher may be instrumental in fostering a creative capacity and a renewed dignity that might lead to great accomplishments. The complaints of contemporary American authors, such as Alan Bloom, who lament the nihilism of American college students miss this exciting opportunity by lingering on an overly negative interpretation of the phenomenon.

Part and parcel of understanding nihilism in a humorous fashion involves becoming adept at interpreting the experiences of failure and frustration within a larger context in which they serve a functional and positive role. While the language of failure and success is undeniably entrenched in schools and their evaluation systems, unfortunately shame is all too often attached to failure, and it is common for failing students to be dismissed as unmotivated underachievers. A more humorous attitude toward failure and frustration in the classroom, however, might help to encourage students to take chances with their thinking. It might encourage them to attempt the formulation of a wider variety of interesting and creative perspectives on the issues under scrutiny, and in so doing come to an understanding of others and the ways that they think about things. Taking a humorous attitude toward failure, seeing it as something unthreatening, may make both students and teachers more willing to open up to one another, encouraging them to experiment with different ways of thinking about issues, and thus provoking them to be more open-minded and less complacent with their own "answers" to the problems of the world.

Open-mindedness to different ways of thinking about the world is part and parcel of the humorous attitude. As we have seen, such an attitude takes work and rarely comes naturally. Especially when confronted by phenomena that are threatening to us, either physically or conceptually, it is difficult to break free from our usual ways of viewing things and to regard them from new perspectives. Difficult as it might be, there are reasons why we should at least attempt to cultivate this talent in ourselves, however. By adopting a humorous attitude toward threatening phenomena, we challenge ourselves to confront our fears and to gain a richer and more multifaceted understanding of reality. Rather than limiting ourselves to a narrow, flat, and fragmentary view of the world, with humor, we strive toward a more rich, full, and well-rounded vision. When it comes to relations with our fellow human beings, this sort of openness has the potential to facilitate dialogue between groups and individuals who are not used to listening to one another very closely. Such dialogue may act as a means by which acrimony might be vented and tensions dissipated. In allowing ourselves to linger humorously in the presence of one another's conflicting and incongruous perspectives concerning the world, we might, through philosophy, accomplish what is all too often accomplished through violence.

America has, in recent years, experienced some of the horrific consequences that can result when the desperation of some citizens finds no positive means of expression other than destruction and violence. The Unabomber, the shootings at Columbine High School, and the bombing in Oklahoma City are all examples of domestic forms of terror exhibiting characteristics of the sort of frustrated nihilistic idealism elaborated upon throughout this book. Though it might be comforting for us to think that the individuals involved in these incidents were simply insane misfits or sadists who craved nothing more than to inflict pain on others, the evidence seems to suggest that this is far from the truth. In each of these cases, the perpetrators apparently harbored a deep and brooding sense of hopelessness about the world and their abilities to change the order of things in accordance with their highest hopes and ideals. As with many of the nihilists we have encountered throughout this book, these individuals lashed out at the world in a final and desperate attempt to express a frustrated longing for perfection. Understanding this motivation is, perhaps, a necessary step toward authentically addressing the problem of terrorism in our contemporary world.[1]

We can see the signs of nihilistic longing expressed in the manifesto written by the Unabomber, Ted Kaczynski. He, in fact, draws an explicit parallel between his own goals and those of nineteenth-century Russian nihilists:

> In the Russian case, revolutionaries were actively working to undermine the old order. Then, when the old system was put under sufficient additional stress . . . it was swept away by revolution. What we propose is something along these lines. . . . Our goal is only to destroy the existing form of society.[2]

These lines should remind us of those written by Sergei Nechayev more than 130 years ago in his *Catechism of the Revolutionary*. Like Nechayev, Kaczynski feels that the present system is corrupt and should be destroyed. It is technology, according to Kaczynski, that is at the root of this corruption. Due to the power of technology, life in modern society has become unfulfilling, people have suffered psychologically and physically, and the environment has been decimated. The best option is to wipe the slate clean and to dismantle the entire technological/economic order that has led to human degradation and environmental ruin. Though much suffering will accompany the dismantling of the present order, "It would be better to dump the whole stinking system and take the consequences."[3]

A similar disgust for the system, coupled with a frustrated desire for Justice, has been expressed by Timothy McVeigh, the person held responsible for the bombing of the federal building in Oklahoma City. McVeigh's act of destruction and violence seems to have been motivated by his frustration over the government's handling of the Branch Davidian crisis in Waco, Texas. McVeigh saw himself as a sort of avenging force that, even though it would ultimately lead to his own destruction, could strike a blow against the U.S. government, which he saw as the world's biggest bully. Here we once again encounter an individual who sees personal annihilation as the most favorable option in an imperfect world.

The shooters at Columbine High School likewise destroyed themselves and many of those around them, in this instance out of a frustrating sense of their own social impotence. Their case has raised the subject of schoolyard bullying to the level of a national issue, and if anything positive can be said to have come out of the deaths of schoolchildren, it is the recognition that the nihilism of many of today's youths is more than just dramatic posturing. If we wish to avoid the potentially violent and devastating consequences of that nihilism, we should learn to understand the dynamics of nihilistic thinking and demonstrate its positive potential for the promotion of life over death and creation over destruction.

The stakes are especially high today. As the events of September 11 have shown, the threat of nihilistic terrorism does not originate only from within the Western world. Nihilistic thinking knows no national or geographic boundaries, and when coupled with an attitude of absolute negativity and the will to destruction, the potential lies open for worldwide catastrophe. All too commonly, there is a tendency to dismiss the rage, frustration, and despondency of those who engage in nihilistic acts of terror because their sense of despair exhibits itself in a destructive manner. Citizens and public officials often react with an outright dismissal of the concerns of such individuals, shutting off dialogue, becoming entrenched in their own ways of thinking, and, sadly, retaliating with violence in kind. However, it is my own feeling that such reactions only exacerbate the situation. An unwillingness to think along with others and to entertain their complaints and concerns only furthers the sense of isolation, powerlessness, and negativity that fuels terrorism.

It may be difficult for us to think humorously about nihilistic terror in the present social climate, and it may even strike some readers as a completely distasteful suggestion. Humor, like philosophy, requires distance, and perhaps we are presently too close to the problem of terrorism to regard it in the manner that I am suggesting. However, I still feel it is important to highlight the fact that we need to think more broadly about the sorts of incongruities and frustrations that motivate fellow human beings to destroy themselves and others in the vain pursuit of ultimate ideals. Doing so may allow us to understand these acts of violence from a new perspective, and in learning something about the way terrorists think, we may learn how to manipulate that thinking for positive ends.

There are many more concrete lessons and inferences to be drawn from the insights articulated in this work. However, this is not the place for them. These few, final remarks on philosophy, education, and terrorism are just some cursory observations that certainly warrant further investigation and development. They rest, however, on the insight that lies at the center of this entire investigation. A humorous attitude makes nihilism less of a threat and more of a motivation for inquiry and meditation. In defusing the negative and gloomy overtones of nihilism, the door is opened to utilizing it as a tool for the betterment and enrichment of humankind.

NOTES

INTRODUCTION

1. De Sousa points out, "Determinism and fatalism are often confused, perhaps because both seem to entail the impossibility of freedom.... Yet they are logically antithetical. . . . The central idea of determinism is that every event depends on its antecedents. Fatalism, on the contrary, views some particular event ... as inevitable no matter what the antecedents turn out to be. The point is that determinism is a causal notion, whereas fatalism is a teleological one." Ronald de Sousa, *The Rationality of Emotion* (Cambridge: The MIT Press, 1997), pp. 85–86.

2. Originally published in Dutch in 1960. The English translation was published in 1980. Johan Goudsblom, *Nihilism and Culture* (New Jersey: Rowan and Littlefield, 1980).

3. Ibid., p. x.

4. Ibid., p. 69.

5. Ibid., p. 109.

6. Ibid., p. 190.

7. Ibid., p. x.

8. Ibid., p. 177.

9. Michael Allen Gillespie, *Nihilism before Nietzsche* (Chicago: The University of Chicago Press, 1995), p. 255.

10. Stanley Rosen, *Nihilism: A Philosophical Essay* (New Haven and London: Yale University Press, 1969), p. 206.

11. Throughout this book Rosen uses terms such as *speech, reason,* and *rationality* almost interchangeably. I believe this is so because he has in mind the Ancient Greek notion of "Logos," the meaning of which encompasses all of the following: "reason, word, speech, discourse, definition, principle, or ratio." W. L. Reese, *Dictionary of Philosophy and Religion* (New Jersey: Humanities Press, 1980).

12. Rosen. p. 212.

13. Ibid., p. 213.

14. Ibid., p. 216.

15. Ibid., p. 136.

16. See Keiji Nishitani, *The Self-Overcoming of Nihilism*, trans. Graham Parkes with Setsuko Aihara (Albany: State University of New York Press, 1990); Martin E. Marty, *Varieties of Unbelief* (New York: Anchor Books, 1966); Michael Novak, *The Experience of Nothingness* (New York: Harper Torchbooks, 1970); Michael Novak, *Awakening from Nihilism* (n.p.: Crisis Books, 1995); Cornel West, *Race Matters* (Boston: Beacon Press, 1993).

17. Karen Carr, *The Banalization of Nihilism* (Albany: State University of New York Press, 1992), p. 7.

18. Ibid., pp. 17–18.

19. Ibid., p. 7.

CHAPTER 1. GERMAN AND RUSSIAN NIHILISM

1. Friedrich Nietzsche, *The Will to Power*, ed. Walter Kaufman, trans. Walter Kaufman and R. J. Hollingdale (New York: Vintage Books, 1967), p. 17.

2. Gillespie, p. vii.

3. Goudsblom, p. 14.

4. Goudsblom claims to have been unable to locate purported references to the term *nihilism* in the writings of Augustine. Cho recognizes "relatively obscure occurrences of the term in Latin and French sources." Stephen Wagner Cho, "Before Nietzsche: Nihilism as a Critique of German Idealism," *Graduate Faculty Philosophy Journal* 18, no. 1 (1995): p. 205. Gillespie specifically cites F. L. Goetzius's 1733 work *De nonismo et nihilismo in theologia* as the first place where the term *nihilism* appears in print, though this work was "relatively unknown and apparently played no role in the later reappearance and development of the concept." Gillespie, p. 65.

5. "For we are brought to the conclusion that we can never transcend the limits of possible experience, though that is precisely what this science is concerned, above all else, to achieve. This situation yields, however, just the very experiment by which, indirectly, we are enabled to prove the truth of this first estimate of our *a priori* knowledge of reason, namely, that such knowledge has to do only with appearances, and must leave the thing in itself as indeed real *per se*, but not known by us." Immanuel Kant, *Critique of Pure Reason*, trans. Norman Kemp Smith (New York: St. Martin's Press, 1965), p. 24.

6. Cho, p. 207.

7. Goudsblom quotes the words of Heinrich von Kleist who reacted with despair upon reading Kant's *Critique of Pure Reason:* "I recently became acquainted with Kant-

ian philosophy—and now I must quote you a thought from it, though I do not imagine that it will shake you as deeply or as painfully as it did me. We cannot decide whether that which we call truth is real truth or whether it only seems so. . . . My sole, my highest goal has foundered and I no longer have an aim." Goudsblom, pp. 36–37. I have found even today, in teaching introductory philosophy courses, that students often react in a very disturbed and unsettled manner when introduced to Kant's Transcendental philosophy for the first time.

8. Cho, p. 206.

9. See Friedrich Heinrich Jacobi, "Jacobi to Fichte," in *The Main Philosophical Writings and the Novel Allwill* (Montreal & Kingston, London, Buffalo: McGill-Queens University Press, 1994), pp. 497–536. See especially p. 519: "Since outside the mechanism of nature I encounter nothing but wonders, mysteries, and signs; and I feel a terrible horror before the *nothing, the absolutely indeterminate, the utterly void* . . . I have nothing confronting me, after all, except nothingness; and even chimeras are a good match for that. . . . Truly my dear Fichte, I would not be vexed if you, or anyone else, were to call Chimerism the view I oppose to the Idealism that I chide for *Nihilism.*"

10. Gillespie is an exception. He claims that because the Russian intellectual critics of Left Hegelianism were aware of Jacobi's writings, "The Russian debate over nihilism is . . . an extension of the German controversy." Gillespie, p. 138. Though this may be so, the character and temper of Russian nihilism is sufficiently unique to warrant making a distinction between it and the German variant.

11. For instance: Reese, *Dictionary of Philosophy and Religion;* Geddes MacGregor, *Dictionary of Religion and Philosophy* (New York: Paragon House, 1989); Ted Honderich, ed., *Oxford Companion to Philosophy* (New York: Oxford University Press, 1995). Gillespie attributes this mistake to the fact that Hegelian philosophy for a time seemed to solve the problem, and so the term *nihilism* temporarily "disappeared so completely that many later scholars came to believe . . . that Turgenev had invented the term." Gillespie, p. 110.

12. Ivan Turgenev, *Fathers and Sons* (1862), trans. George Reavy (New York: Signet Books, n.d.), p. 55.

13. Alan Hodge, "Foreword," in ibid., p. vii.

14. Nikolai Chernyshevsky, *What is to Be Done?* [1863], trans. Michael R. Katz (Ithaca and London: Cornell University Press, 1996). Not to be confused with Lenin's nonfiction work of the same name. The title is a tribute to Chernyshevsky's influence on Lenin. It is also a phrase that seems to recur quite often throughout nihilist oriented literature.

15. Stephen Lovell, "Nihilism, Russian," in *Routledge Encyclopedia of Philosophy* (New York: Routledge, 1998).

16. Ernest J. Simmons, "Introduction," in *Notes from Underground, Poor People, The Friend of the Family,* trans. Constance Garnett (New York: Dell Publishing Co., 1960), p. 15.

17. This rumor has been thrown into suspicion by the discovery of a letter written by Bakunin to Nechayev in which Bakunin angrily denounces Nechayev's secret scheming and threatening behavior. Bakunin promises to break off all relations with the young nihilist unless, among other conditions, he drops "the absurd idea that revolution can be made outside the people and without its participation. . . ." See Mikhail Bakunin, *Bakunin on Violence: Letter to Nechayev* (1870) (New York: Anarchist Switchboard, n.d.), p. 46.

18. The circumstances surrounding Nechayev's death are unclear. The Peter and Paul Fortress was reserved for those prisoners considered to be among the most dangerous in Russia. These inmates had little if any contact with the outside world or with each other. Once imprisoned it was expected that they would never be released. Prisoners were referred to by number rather than name. The official records show that the inmate believed to occupy Nechayev's cell was found dead on November 21, 1881. The cause of death was reported as "dropsy complicated by scurvy." See Robert Payne, *The Terrorists* (New York: Funk and Wagnalls, 1957), p. 128.

19. Sergei Nechayev, *Catechism of the Revolutionary* (1869) (London: Violette Nozieres Press and AK Press, 1989), p. 4.

20. Ibid., pp. 4–5.

21. Albert Camus, *The Rebel*, trans. Anthony Bower (New York: Vintage Books, 1956), pp. 149–150.

22. In his 1904 defense of the Russian nihilist Sazonov, who used a bomb to assassinate Count Von Plehve, the Russian minister of the interior, the lawyer Kazorinov stated, "The bomb was loaded not with dynamite but with the tears and sufferings of the people." See Payne, *The Terrorists*, p. 251.

23. Nietzsche, it should be noted, was a big fan of Dostoyevsky, but Turgenev is, as Walter Kaufman writes, "never mentioned in Nietzsche's books." Walter Kaufman, ed., *The Will to Power*, by Friedrich Nietzsche, p. 51 n. 45.

24. Goudsblom, p. 13.

25. Gillespie, p. vii.

26. Carr, p. 15.

27. Camus, *The Rebel*, p. 65.

CHAPTER 2. NIETZSCHEAN NIHILISM

1. Nietzsche, *The Will to Power*, p. 17.

2. Ibid., p. 9.

3. Ibid., p. 3. He also here claims to have "lived through the whole of nihilism, to the end, leaving it behind, outside himself." This suggests that he has overcome nihilism. In my interpretation of Nietzsche's philosophy, as will become apparent, I do not believe this to be the case. To be fair, much of Nietzsche's treatment of nihilism occurs in *The Will To Power*, which is not a finished, polished, or complete work. It is,

rather, a compilation of notes, selected and edited first by his sister, and since then by a long line of editors and commentators, all of whom have been criticized in one way or another for distorting Nietzsche's philosophy. In any case, the problems with *WTP* are enormous, though it is important for our present purposes since it contains Nietzsche's most extended discussion of nihilism.

4. Ibid.

5. I would like to stress at this point that what follows is my own interpretation of Nietzsche's take on nihilism, constructed from my reading of a number of his texts. The topic of Nietzsche's nihilism is a controversial subject, and as is the case with most material of this type, no absolutely authoritative interpretation has been produced.

6. Nietzsche, *The Antichrist,* in *The Portable Nietzsche,* ed. and trans. Walter Kaufman (New York: Penguin Books, 1984), p. 592.

7. Ibid., p. 597.

8. Ibid., p. 602.

9. Ironically, Richard Wagner did not share this opinion. He had nothing but praise for the "greatness of spirit" possessed by Mikhail Bakunin, the Russian anarchist who was in competition with Karl Marx for control of the Worker's International and who was close friends with Sergei Nechayev. (See chapter 1.)

10. Nietzsche, *Twilight of the Idols,* in *The Portable Nietzsche,* p. 534.

11. Ibid. "The Problem of Socrates," pp. 473–479. "Socrates' decadence is suggested not only by the admitted wantonness and anarchy of his instincts, but also by the hypertrophy of the logical faculty and that *sarcasm of the rachitic* which distinguishes him." p. 475. Though the Socratic legacy is traditionally thought to lie with Plato and Aristotle, we should not forget that his influence is also exhibited in the more "decadent" schools of Greek thought—Cynicism, Stoicism, Epicureanism, and Skepticism.

12. Ibid., p. 478.

13. Nietzsche, *The Birth of Tragedy,* trans. Clifton P. Fadiman (New York: Dover Publications, 1995), p. 168.

14. Nietzsche, *The Gay Science,* trans. Walter Kaufman (New York: Vintage Books, 1974), p. 168.

15. Ibid., p. 336.

16. In *Birth of Tragedy* Nietzsche conceptually separates these two impulses very distinctly from one another. However, in his later works he seems to modify this distinction, absorbing elements of one into the other. Especially in *Twilight of the Idols,* pp. 519–520, he conceives both impulses as "kinds of frenzy." For this reason, Kaufman has written that Nietzsche starts his philosophic career as a dualist and ends it as a monist. See Walter Kaufman, *Nietzsche: Philosopher, Psychologist, Anitchrist* (Princeton: Princeton University Press, 1974).

17. Nietzsche, *Birth of Tragedy,* p. 56.

18. Nietzsche, "Notes," in *The Portable Nietzsche,* p. 39.

19. Nietzsche, *The Antichrist,* p. 647.

20. Ibid., p. 646.

21. Ibid.

22. Ibid.

23. Hans-Georg Gadamer, "The Drama of Zarathustra," in *Nietzsche's New Seas,* ed. Michael Allen Gillespie and Tracy Strong. (Chicago: The University of Chicago Press, 1988), pp. 220–231.

24. Nietzsche, *Thus Spoke Zarathustra,* in *The Portable Nietzsche,* p. 324.

25. Ibid., pp. 340–343.

26. Ibid., p. 332.

27. Nietzsche, *The Will to Power,* pp. 35–36.

28. Nietzsche, *Twilight of the Idols,* p. 467.

29. Keith Ansell-Pearson, *An Introduction to Nietzsche as Political Thinker: The Perfect Nihilist* (New York: Cambridge University Press, 1994), p. 205.

30. This claim was, he says, made in his doctoral dissertation. He is now less adamant about it. See David Farrell Krell, trans., "Analysis," in Martin Heidegger, *Nietzsche, Volume One: The Will To Power as Art* (San Francisco: HarperCollins, 1991), p. 247.

31. Martin Heidegger, *Nietzsche, Volume Four: Nihilism,* ed. David Farrell Krell (San Francisco: HarperCollins, 1991), p. 204.

32. Martin Heidegger, *Being and Time,* trans. Joan Stambaugh (Albany: State University of New York Press, 1996), p. 40.

33. Ibid., p. 42.

34. Ibid.

35. Martin Heidegger, "What is Metaphysics?" in *Basic Writings,* ed. David Farrell Krell (New York: Harper Collins, 1993), p. 101.

36. Ibid., p. 103.

37. Heidegger, "The End of Philosophy and the Task of Thinking," in *Basic Writings,* p. 432.

38. Heidegger, *Nietzsche, Volume One,* p. 61.

39. Ibid., p. 19.

40. Martin Heidegger, *Nietzsche, Volume Two: The Eternal Recurrence of the Same,* trans. David Farrell Krell (San Francisco: HarperCollins, 1991), p. 205.

41. Heidegger, *Nietzsche, Volume Four,* p. 203.

42. Heidegger, *Nietzsche, Volume One,* p. 9.

43. Heidegger, *Nietzsche, Volume Four,* p. 240.

44. Nietzsche, *Ecce Homo,* in *Basic Writings of Nietzsche,* trans. and ed. Walter Kaufman. (New York: The Modern Library, 1968), p. 687.

45. Heidegger, "Letter on Humanism," in *Basic Writings*, p. 264.

46. Karl Löwith, *Martin Heidegger and European Nihilism* (New York: Columbia University Press, 1995), p. 38.

47. "Behold the Man." Pilate's words to Jesus.

48. Walter Kaufman, trans. and ed., introduction to *Ecce Homo*, in *Basic Writings of Nietzsche*, p. 658.

CHAPTER 3. WORLD-WAR AND POSTWAR NIHILISM

1. John McKay, Bennet Hill, John Buckler, *A History of World Societies* (Boston: Houghton Mifflin, 1996), p. 1026.

2. Kaufman, *Nietzsche: Philosopher, Psychologist, Antichrist*, p. 8.

3. After Nietzsche's collapse into mental illness in 1889, his sister took charge of the editorship of his writings and took care of him until his death ten years later. Under her leadership, the Nietzsche Archives became a kind of intellectual shrine for the emerging Nazi movement. Elisabeth Förster-Nietzsche became active in promoting her brother's legacy as the intellectual foundation for Nazism. This was only possible through the distortion of his texts, which quite often lash out at anti-Semites while praising the strength of the Jewish people's character. Because of this perverse political use of the institution, Oswald Spengler withdrew his membership in the Nietzsche Archives. Others, such as Heidegger, became ever more enthusiastic supporters of its mission.

Elisabeth had also previously been involved in a failed attempt to establish an "Aryan" colony in Paraguay with her husband, Bernhard Förster. Correspondence between Friedrich N. and his sister demonstrate that Friedrich N. disapproved of this venture. "This accursed anti-Semitism . . . is the cause of a radical breach between me and my sister." See Ben Macintyre, *Forgotten Fatherland: The Search For Elisabeth Nietzsche* (New York: Farrar Straus Giroux, 1992), p. 115.

4. William Barrett, *Irrational Man* (New York: Doubleday Books, 1962), p. 34.

5. Keiji Nishitani, *The Self-Overcoming of Nihilism*, p. 178.

6. Hermann Rauschning, *The Revolution of Nihilism: Warning to the West* (New York: Alliance Book Corporation, 1939), p. 90.

7. Ibid., p. 59.

8. He even makes the curious observation that the Nazi emphasis on marching was calculated to involve people in thoughtless action that would engulf them in this "dynamism."

9. Ibid., p. 90.

10. Goudsblom, p. 17. Rauschning is not the only author to see in the Nazis a kind of nihilism. Albert Camus, Martin Marty, and Yukio Mishima also refer to the Nazis as nihilists. The popular college history textbook, *A History of World Societies*, also refers to National Socialism in this way.

11. Walter Kaufman, ed., *Existentialism from Dostoevsky to Sartre* (New York: Meridian Books, 1975), p. 11.

12. Albert Camus, "An Absurd Reasoning," in *The Myth of Sisyphus and Other Essays,* trans. Justin O'Brien (New York: Vintage Books, 1955), p. 18.

13. Ibid., p. 23.

14. Ibid., "The Myth of Sisyphus," p. 90.

15. Ibid., p. 91

16. Literally, "arguments by the stick," otherwise known as the appeal to force.

17. Camus, *The Rebel,* p. 7.

18. Ibid., p. 13.

19. Jean-Paul Sartre, "Existentialism Is a Humanism," in *Existentialism From Dostoevsky to Sartre,* p. 362.

20. Camus, *The Rebel,* p. 22.

21. Camus, *The Myth of Sisyphus,* p. v.

22. Van Meter Ames, "Existentialism: Irrational, Nihilistic," *The Humanist,* no. 1 (1950): pp. 15–22.

23. Alan R. Pratt, ed., *The Dark Side: Thoughts on the Futility of Life from the Ancient Greeks to the Present* (New York: Citadel Press, 1994), p. xviii.

24. Roy Starrs, *Deadly Dialectics* (Honolulu: University of Hawaii Press, 1994), p. 173.

25. Yukio Mishima, *Confessions of a Mask,* trans. Meredith Weatherby (New York: New Directions, 1958), p. 21.

26. Ibid., p. 183.

27. Yukio Mishima, *Sun and Steel,* trans. John Bester (Tokyo, New York, San Francisco: Kodansha International, 1982), p. 7.

28. Ibid., p. 8.

29. Ibid., p. 9. In a review dealing with Georges Bataille's *Madame Edwarda and My Mother,* Mishima remarks on the vain attempt involved in trying to capture reality through words: "What is certain, nevertheless, is that, being aware that the sacred quality hidden in the experience of eroticism is something impossible for language to reach (this is also due to the impossibility of re-experiencing anything through language), Bataille still expresses it in words. It is the verbalization of a silence called God, and it is also certain that a novelist's greatest ambition could not lie anywhere else but here." Yukio Mishima, introduction to *My Mother, Madame Edwarda, The Dead Man,* by Georges Bataille (New York: Marion Boyars, 1995), p. 12.

30. One of Mishima's biographers and translators, John Nathan, explains that he turned down the opportunity, after his success with *The Sailor Who Fell from Grace with the Sea,* to translate *Silk and Insight* into English. "[T]he writing was jugular, a gorgeous example of what Japanese critics were calling 'Mishima-beauty.' To render it in English would have been an enormous labor; even before I had finished the first read-

ing I knew I would never find the enthusiasm I would need to sustain me through the translation." John Nathan, *Mishima: A Biography* (Boston: Little Brown and Company, 1974), p. 204. The term *Mishima-beauty* came to refer to Mishima's rich and unrealistic style, characterized by his delight in the lyrical play of language. In this he sought to retain, in his own words, the "purity of words." *Sun and Steel,* p. 10. The novel *Silk and Insight* has, incidentally, just recently been translated into English.

31. Mishima, *Sun and Steel,* p. 17.

32. Mishima, *Confessions of a Mask,* p. 30.

33. Mishima was sued for libel by a prominent politician because of the resemblance that the politician bore to a character in *After the Banquet.* Mishima was also threatened with violence by right-wing reactionaries as well as by left-wing reactionaries. He has been called a fascist, coward, pervert, loser, homosexual, and a decadent. I guess you can't please everyone!

34. Mishima, *Sun and Steel,* p. 44. Good advice for Heidegger.

35. Ibid., p. 41.

36. Tsunetomo Yamamoto, *Hagakure: The Book of the Samurai,* trans. William Scott Wilson. (New York: Avon Books, 1979), p. 17.

37. Yukio Mishima, *The Way of the Samurai,* trans. Kathryn Sparling (New York: Pedigree Books, 1983), p. 52.

38. Yukio Mishima, *The Voices of the Heroic Dead* (1966), quoted in Marguerite Yourcenar, *Mishima: A Vision of the Void,* trans. Alberto Manguel (New York: Farrar, Straus and Giroux, 1986), p. 113.

39. Mishima, *The Way of the Samurai,* p. 18. Roy Starrs also uses the concept of "feminization," as adopted from Adler's psychology, to analyze Mishima's work.

40. Ibid., p. 52.

41. Quoted in Henry Scott-Stokes, *The Life and Death of Yukio Mishima* (New York: Dell Publishing Co., 1975), pp. 53, 309.

42. Quoted in Yourcenar, p. 149.

43. Alan Bloom, *The Closing of the American Mind* (New York: Simon and Schuster, 1987), p. 139.

44. Bloom is concerned not with all college students, but with "the good students in the better colleges and universities" (p. 49). There are, apparently, twenty-five such schools.

45. Ibid., p. 25.

46. Ibid., p. 61.

47. Ibid., p. 147.

48. Charles Taylor, *The Ethics of Authenticity* (Cambridge: Harvard University Press, 1991), p. 10.

49. Ibid., p. 68.

50. Ibid., p. 60.

51. Ibid., p. 120.

52. Other recipients of this prize include: Mother Teresa, Billy Graham, Alexander Solzhenitsyn, and Desmond Tutu (among others).

53. Novak, *Awakening From Nihilism*, p. 51.

54. Novak, *The Experience of Nothingness*, p. 12.

55. Ibid., p. 115.

56. Ibid., p. 10.

57. Novak, *Awakening From Nihilism*, p. 54.

58. Ibid., p. 55.

59. Novak, *The Experience of Nothingness*, p. 119.

CHAPTER 4. NIHILISTIC INCONGRUITY

1. Crane Brinton, *Nietzsche* (New York: Harper Torchbooks, 1965), pp. 211–212. Kaufman, while praising Brinton as a fine historian, criticizes his use of "composite quotations which consist of lines picked from different contexts and put together in a manner that suggests a semblance of continuity." Kaufman, *Nietzsche: Philosopher, Psychologist, Antichrist*, p. 291 n. 7. This, though, only reinforces Brinton's own point that the ambiguity of Nietzsche's texts plays a major role in their appropriation by the Nazis.

2. Huston Smith, *The World's Religions* (New York: HarperCollins, 1991), p. 101.

3. Arthur Danto, *Nietzsche as Philosopher* (New York: Columbia University Press, 1980), p. 28.

4. See Roy Starrs, *Deadly Dialectics*.

5. Mishima did, at times, refer approvingly to the Nazis. He also wrote a play with the title "My Friend Hitler."

6. Charles Kielkopf, "The Logic of Nihilism," *The New Scholasticism* 49, no. 2 (Spring 1975): p. 164. Kielkopf's concern in this paper is rather unusual. He attempts to construct a definition of nihilism in terms of modal logic. His formulation "everything is possibly possible" (p. 168) is modeled on the statement "Everything is permitted," and is intended to capture the sense of meaninglessness that nihilism is thought to imply. I think it is a highly questionable starting point.

7. Victor E. Frankl, *Man's Search for Meaning: An Introduction to Logotherapy* (Boston: Beacon Press, 1992), p. 152.

8. Alan White, "Nietzschean Nihilism: A Typology," *International Studies in Philosophy* 19 (Summer 1987): p. 34.

9. Ibid.

10. Ibid., p. 35. He doesn't tell us what these senses are.

11. A. A. Long, *Hellenistic Philosophy* (Berkeley and Los Angeles: University of California Press, 1986), pp. 86–87.

12. There is a story told about Pyrrho claiming that when his teacher fell into a bog and yelled for assistance, Pyrrho refused to help on the basis that "he had no reason to suppose that being saved would benefit him." Wallace I. Matson, *A New History of Philosophy: Volume I* (New York: Harcourt Brace Jovanovich, 1987), p. 171.

13. Max Stirner, *The Ego and Its Own: The Case of the Individual against Authority*, trans. Steven Byington (London: Rebel Press, 1993), p. 24.

14. Ibid., p. 5.

15. Ibid., p. 366.

16. Ibid., p. 319.

17. Before publishing *The Ego and Its Own*, Stirner explored the implications of his ideas for the philosophy of education. In *The False Principle of Our Education, or Humanism and Realism*, Stirner argues that education should serve the free growth and development of students as individuals rather than being focused on the cultivation of a particular type of human being (as in humanism) or on specific, useful technical skills (as in realism). The presupposition that education must serve some ideal is education's "false principle." Stirner himself was a teacher at a private girl's school and so, presumably, had the opportunity to practice what he preached. See Max Stirner, *The False Principle of Our Education, or Humanism and Realism*, trans. Robert Beebe, ed. James J. Martin. (Colorado Springs: Ralf Myles Publisher, Inc., 1967).

18. See for example the entry for epistemological nihilism in W. L. Reese, *Dictionary of Philosophy and Religion*. For an extended treatment of Stirner as a nihilist see R. W. K. Patterson, *The Nihilistic Egoist, Max Stirner* (London, Oxford, and New York: Oxford University Press, 1971).

19. Patterson was correct, then, to title his book on Max Stirner not *The Egoistic Nihilist*, but rather *The Nihilistic Egoist*. Karen L. Carr, on the other hand, is incorrect to call Stirner's book "the most frankly nihilistic work ever written" (p. 164 n. 6). Carr cites the German title of Stirner's book as *Das Ich und Sein Eigenes* rather than, correctly, as *Der Einzige und sein Eigentum*. I'm not sure where she gets the former title, but it looks like a literal retranslation of the most popular English-language title back into German. The title of Stirner's book has been interpreted in a number of ways since the words *Einzige* and *Eigentum* have no exact translation into English. "Der Einzige" means something like "the only one," or "the unique one." "Eigentum" means something like "ownness." "Sein" is a possessive pronoun that could mean "his" or "its." In consequence, the title has appeared in English as: *The Unique One and Its Owness, The Unique One and Its Property, The Ego and His Own, The Ego and Its Own*.

20. Richard Rorty, *Contingency, Irony, and Solidarity* (New York: Cambridge University Press, 1999), p. 73.

21. Ibid., p. 115.

22. Ibid., p. 84.

23. The fact that he cannot offer any kind of justification against competing "stories" about the world means that Rorty cannot offer any arguments against those who do not share his "final vocabulary." It does seem to cause Rorty some distress, however, that in the picture he has constructed, there is no reason, other than the contingencies of socialization, for a person to prefer or choose fascism over liberalism. Although, as he has pointed out, there is nothing in his "ironism" that necessarily leads to elitism or absolutism, there is nothing that necessarily leads to liberalism.

24. Carr, p. 113.

25. Rorty, p. 44.

26. This may be the reason why there is so much controversy concerning Nietzsche's nihilism.

27. For similar suggestions on how to deal with the "threat" of nihilism see Kent Bach, *Exit Existentialism: A Philosophy of Self-Awareness* (Belmont: Wadsworth Publishing Co., 1973). When I was a graduate student at San Francisco State University, I took a number of Bach's classes, which had a predominantly analytic emphasis. While visiting with him during his office hours the topic of nihilism came up and he told me that he had written a book on nihilism. He then gave me a copy of *Exit Existentialism*. At the time I was quite surprised that a philosopher with such an analytic and pragmatic bent would be interested in this topic. However, I now see how pragmatism can be a reaction to the problem of nihilism.

28. Keiji Nishitani, *The Self-Overcoming of Nihilism*, p. 1.

29. Nietzsche, *Will To Power*, p. 23.

30. E. M. Cioran, *On the Heights of Despair*, trans. Ilinca Zarifopol-Johnston (Chicago and London: The University of Chicago Press, 1992), p. x.

31. Ibid., p. 81.

32. Ralph Harper expresses this sentiment when he writes, "Today one reads with uneasiness even Socrates' exhortation to pursue truth, and we would feel slightly ridiculous if our teachers expected us to talk this way in the street. The very word 'truth' seems to have lost its right to be capitalized. We do not believe in absolutes anymore." Ralph Harper, *The Seventh Solitude* (Baltimore: John Hopkins Press, 1967), p. 128.

CHAPTER 5. DECLINE, DECAY, AND FALLING AWAY

1. In a recent article in the *Atlantic Monthly*, Alston Chase calls the student atmosphere of Harvard University in the 1950s a "culture of despair" largely due to the conflicting values communicated through its general education program. On the one hand, students were encouraged to pursue value-free, scientific, academic inquiry. On the other, they were introduced to nihilist authors such as Nietzsche and Oswald Spengler who suggest that such inquiry "threatens civilization." "From the humanists we learned that science threatens civilization. From the scientists we learned that science cannot be stopped. Taken together they implied that there was no hope. Gen Ed had created at Harvard a culture of despair." This culture, Chase suggests, bred the

modern-day nihilist terrorist, Ted Kaczynski, who became known as the Unabomber because his bombing attacks targeted universities and airports. See Alston Chase, "Harvard and the Making of the Unabomber," *The Atlantic Monthly* 285, no. 6 (June 2000): pp. 41–65.

2. David Farrell Krell agrees when he writes, "[N]ihilism remains bewildering and hazardous. It has therefore been a painful embarrassment for me to read a number of contemporary monographs and essays on nihilism by professional philosophers for whom the matter is ultimately quite simple. Such essays boil down to the remonstrance, 'If you people would only put away such dangerous and destructive writers as Nietzsche and Heidegger, and go back to the truly inspirational philosophers of our tradition, embracing the timeless wisdom of their texts (as elucidated in my own modest commentaries), all of this nihilism business would vanish like a bad dream.'" He goes on with venom, but not without a good point. See David Farrell Krell, "Analysis," in *Nietzsche Volume Four: Nihilism,* by Martin Heidegger, p. 262.

3. Nietzsche, *The Gay Science,* p. 175.

4. Nietzsche, *Will to Power,* p. 508.

5. Heidegger, *Being and Time,* p. 119.

6. Ibid., p. 166.

7. Ibid., p. 248.

8. Ibid., p. 255.

9. Mishima, *Sun and Steel,* p. 86.

10. Ibid., p. 72.

11. Gillespie, *Nihilism Before Nietzsche,* pp. 135–136. Gillespie is among those who offer a quite implausible solution to nihilism by suggesting that the nihilist should just "step back from willing" (p. xxiii).

12. Camus, *The Myth of Sisyphus and Other Essays,* p. 90.

13. Ibid., p. 89.

14. Rauschning, p. 59.

15. Mikhail Bakunin, *The Political Philosophy of Bakunin,* ed. G. P. Maximoff (New York: The Free Press, 1953), pp. 94–95. Valery A. Kuvakin writes: "A leaning towards vitalism, an exaggeration of the phenomenon of animality, and hence a danger of reductionist anthropologism is distinctly palpable here." See Valery A. Kuvakin, "Mikhail Bakunin," in *A History of Russian Philosophy: Volume I,* ed. Valery A. Kuvakin (Buffalo: Prometheus Books, 1994), p. 295.

16. See Nietzsche, *Will to Power,* p. 271. The modern art movement called Futurism was an attempt to represent and depict this inner force of motion visually. Perhaps the two most important philosophical influences on Futurism came from Nietzsche's conception of Will to Power and Henri Bergson's conception of "Elan Vital." Luigi Russolo's 1907 etching *Nietzsche and Madness* vividly illustrates this fascination with motion and energy, and its status as the core of the human life force. In it we see Nietzsche's profile surrounded by a swirling mass of sweeping lines that appear to emanate

from within his own head. The lines are evocative of a tangle of hair, and in fact terminate in a face that glares back at Nietzsche's own. Nietzsche's madness, the message seems to be, is the result of a too intimate and unmediated look into his own unsettled depths. See Richard Humphreys, *Futurism* (New York: Cambridge University Press, 1999), pp. 17–18.

17. Mishima, *Sun and Steel,* pp. 69–70.

18. Immanuel Kant, *Critique of Judgment,* trans. Werner S. Pluhar (Indianapolis: Hackett Publishing Company, 1987), p. 103.

19. Ibid., p. 107.

20. Ibid., p. 113.

21. Ibid.

22. Ibid., p. 120.

23. Ibid.

24. Ibid., p. 142.

25. Ibid., p. 135.

26. Ibid., p. 125.

27. Ibid., p. 339.

28. Ibid., p. 120.

29. Ibid.

30. Ibid. This is also at the root of the "antinomies" that Kant gives attention to in *Critique of Pure Reason*. The "psychological idea," the "cosmological idea," and the "theological idea," are all illicit and "fruitless" attempts by our reason to understand that which cannot be understood. "[A]ll such pretensions, while perhaps honestly meant, must be absolutely groundless, inasmuch as they relate to a kind of knowledge to which man can never attain" (p. 570). However, while in the case of the antinomies there is expressed a desire to know something, through the application of pure reason, about that which is beyond experience, in the case of fanaticism there is a desire to experience particular things that exhibit qualities found only in the faculties of the mind. The two "mistakes," thus, seem to be the converse of one another. For a discussion of the antinomies, see Kant, *Critique of Pure Reason,* pp. 297–570.

31. Kant, *Critique of Judgment,* p. 136.

32. Ibid.

33. It is interesting to find Kant claiming that "indignant desperation" is itself aesthetically sublime, while "despondent desperation" is not. Any of the "languid" affects he categorizes along with "the beautiful." See Kant, *Critique of Judgment,* p. 133.

34. Hospers's criteria are themselves derived from Kant's discussion in *Critique of Judgment*. See especially Kant, *Critique of Judgment,* pp. 44–53.

35. John Hospers, ed., *Introductory Readings in Aesthetics* (London: The Free Press, 1969), p. 3.

36. Smith, *The World's Religions,* pp. 22–26.

37. Ibid., p. 113.

38. Søren Kierkegaard, *The Sickness unto Death,* ed. and trans. Howard V. Hong and Edna H. Hong (Princeton: Princeton University Press, 1980).

39. Ibid., p. 26.

40. David Michael Levin, *The Body's Recollection of Being: Phenomenological Psychology and the Deconstruction of Nihilism* (London, Boston, Melbourne, and Henly: Routledge and Kegan Paul, 1985), p. 1.

41. Kierkegaard makes the observation that "the real reason men are offended by Christianity is that it is too high, because its goal is not man's goal, because it wants to make man into something so extraordinary that he cannot grasp the thought." Kierkegaard, p. 83. This sentiment is echoed by Michael Polanyi in the 13th Arthur Stanley Eddington Memorial Lecture: "Since no society can live up to Christian precepts, any society professing Christian precepts must be afflicted by an internal contradiction, and when the tension is released by rebellion its agents must tend to establish a nihilist Messianic rule." Polanyi obviously has a different feeling toward Christianity than does Kierkegaard. See Michael Polanyi, *Beyond Nihilism* (London: Cambridge University Press, 1960), p. 4.

42. Heidegger, *Being and Time,* p. 136.

CHAPTER 6. AMBITION, ASPIRATION, AND ASCENT

1. *Varieties of Unbelief,* p. 107.

2. Sigmund Freud, *Civilization and Its Discontents,* ed. and trans. James Strachey (New York: W.W. Norton & Company, Inc. 1961), p. 30.

3. Ibid.

4. Sigmund Freud, *Beyond the Pleasure Principle,* ed. and trans. James Strachey (New York: W.W. Norton & Company, Inc. 1961), p. 50.

5. Freud, *Civilization and Its Discontents,* p. 22.

6. Freud, *Beyond the Pleasure Principle,* p. 50.

7. Cioran, *On the Heights of Despair,* p. 30.

8. Heidegger, *Being and Time,* p. 99.

9. This idea is reminiscent of St. Thomas Aquinas's fourth proof of God's existence in the *Summa Theologica.* This is the argument from graduation. "Among beings there are some more and some less good, true, noble and the like. But *more* and *less* are are predicated of different things according as they resemble in their different ways something which is the maximum, as a thing is said to be hotter according as it more nearly resembles that which is hottest; so that there is something which is truest, something best, something noblest, and, consequently, something which is most being, for those things that are greatest in truth are greatest in being. . . ." See St. Thomas

Aquinas, *Summa Theologica*, in *Basic Writings of St. Thomas Aquinas*, Vol. I. (New York: Random House, 1945).

10. Plato, *Plato's Republic*, trans. G. M. A. Grube (Indianapolis: Hackett Publishing Company, 1974), especially pp. 163–166.

11. Recall the discussion concerning "fanaticism," chapter 5.

12. Harper, *The Seventh Solitude*, p. 125.

13. Socrates makes this same point in Plato's Symposium: "No god is a philosopher or seeker after wisdom. Neither do the ignorant seek after wisdom. For herein is the evil of ignorance, that he who is neither good nor wise is nevertheless satisfied: he feels no want, and has therefore no desire." Plato, *Symposium and Phaedrus* (New York: Dover Publications, 1993), p. 27.

14. "The opposition of the real and ideal is an irreconcilable one, and the one can never become the other: if the ideal became the real, it would no longer be the ideal; and if the real became the ideal, the ideal alone would be, but not at all the real. The opposition of the two is not to be vanquished otherwise than if some one annihilates both." Stirner, *The Ego and Its Own*, p. 362.

15. Harry Frankfurt, *Necessity, Volition, and Love* (New York: Cambridge University Press, 1999), p. 84.

16. John Dewey, *Reconstruction in Philosophy* (Boston: Beacon Press, 1957), p. 120.

17. Edwin Locke et al., "Goal Setting and Task Performance: 1969–1980," *Psychological Bulletin* 90, no.1 (1981): p. 131.

18. Ibid., p. 132.

19. Edwin A. Locke and Gary P. Latham, *A Theory of Goal Setting and Task Performance* (New Jersey: Prentice-Hall, 1990), p. 27.

20. Ibid., p. 241.

21. Simone de Beauvoir, *The Ethics of Ambiguity*, trans. Bernard Frechtman (Seaucus: Carol Publishing Group, 1997), p. 34.

22. Iris Murdoch, *The Sovereignty of Good* (New York: Schocken Books, 1971), p. 61.

23. Allen Wheelis, *The Listener* (New York: W.W. Norton and Company, 1999), p. 252.

CHAPTER 7. HUMOR AND INCONGRUITY

1. John Morreall, *Comedy, Tragedy, and Religion* (Albany: State University of New York Press, 1999), p. 153.

2. John Morreall, ed., "Funny Ha-Ha, Funny Strange, and Other Reactions to Incongruity," in *The Philosophy of Laughter and Humor* (Albany: State University of New York Press, 1987), p. 196.

3. Immanuel Kant, *Grounding for the Metaphysics of Morals*, trans. James W. Ellington (Indianapolis: Hackett Publishing Company, 1981), p. 8. Perhaps Kant never heard of the appendix?

4. Kant, *Critique of Pure Reason*, p. 90.

5. It was, of course, Aristotle who pointed out the importance of pity and fear in tragedy. See Aristotle, *Poetics* 9.1452a.1.

6. This example is just one version of a common gag. I remember a cartoon from *Mad Magazine* that depicted a collision between the *Titanic* and *Lusitania*. Their lifeboats had been deployed, but the lifeboats, too, had collided.

7. For an interesting discussion of the primitive "startle" response in humans see Jenefer Robinson, "Startle," *The Journal of Philosophy* 92, no. 2 (February 1995): pp. 53–74.

8. Kant, *Critique of Judgment*, pp. 203–204.

9. Ibid., p. 206.

10. Morreall, "Funny Ha-Ha . . . ," p. 201.

11. Henri Bergson, *Laughter: An Essay on the Meaning of the Comic*, trans. Cloudesley Brereton and Fred Rothwell (Kobenhavn and Los Angeles: Green Integer Books, 1999), p. 39. Arthur Koestler has pointed out that if Bergson's theory was correct, a whole host of things which are not at all laughable would appear comic: Egyptian statues, Byzantine mosaics, epileptic fits, a pulse or heartbeat, or even a corpse. Bergson's theory is, I think, implausible in its details. Despite this it represents an interesting attempt to bring together a number of elements that are exhibited in much laughter and humor. See Arthur Koestler, *The Act of Creation* (New York: The Macmillan Company, 1967), p. 47.

12. Mikhail Bakhtin claims that because of elements such as these, Bergson's theory of laughter "brings out mostly its negative functions." Bakhtin, p. 71.

13. Bergson, *Laughter*, p. 158.

14. Aristotle, *Poetics*, 5.1449a.35.

15. Roger Scruton, "Laughter," in *The Philosophy of Laughter and Humor*, p. 157.

16. A similar point is made by Bergson: "Comic absurdity is of the same nature as that of dreams." See Bergson, *Laughter: An Essay on the Meaning of the Comic*, p. 167. Like Freud, Bergson finds a special kind of logic at work in both dreams and laughing situations "which is not the logic of reason." The logic of laughing situations is, in fact, more similar to the kind of false logic studied in critical thinking courses under the heading of "fallacies." For an example of a book that fully exploits this connection between fallacious reasoning and laughter see S. Morris Engel, *With Good Reason: An Introduction to Informal Fallacies* (New York: St. Martin's Press, 1994).

17. Sigmund Freud, *Jokes and Their Relation to the Unconscious*, ed. and trans. James Strachey (New York: Penguin Books, 1976), p. 19.

18. Joey Adams, *The Joey Adams Joke Dictionary* (New York: The Citadel Press, 1962), p. 27. I have slightly modified the joke from the form in which it appears in this book.

19. Kant, *Critique of Judgment,* p. 204.

20. Freud later asserts that strictly speaking, all jokes are tendentious. He thus, perhaps, overcomplicates matters by introducing the term *innocent joke.* It may simplify matters to use the term *jest* instead.

21. Freud, *Jokes,* p. 168.

22. Kant, *Critique of Judgment,* p. 206.

23. Freud, *Jokes,* p. 234.

24. John Morreall, *Comedy, Tragedy, and Religion.* See especially "Chapter Four: The Tragic Vision Versus the Comic Vision," pp. 21–39.

25. Walter Kaufman, *Tragedy and Philosophy* (Princeton: Princeton University Press, 1968), p. 77.

26. The pop-cultural phenomenon of the "cult movie" has a certain illustrative relevance in this regard. Many of these films are older productions that were originally intended to be serious, but due to changing attitudes, social conditions, and standards of production, are now enjoyed for their comedic value instead. In this case, we might say that the comic vision originates from the audience that reinterprets the raw material, which is the movie, in terms of comedy.

27. Eric Bentley, "Tragedy and Comedy: Some Generalizations," in *Types of Drama: Plays and Essays, Fourth Edition,* ed. Sylvan Barnet, Morton Berman, and William Burto (Boston, Toronto: Little, Brown and Company, 1985), p. 526.

28. David Barrett, ed., *Aristophanes: The Wasps, The Poet and the Women, The Frogs* (New York: Penguin Books, 1964), p. 16.

29. Morreall, *Comedy, Tragedy, and Religion,* p. 13.

30. Kant, *Critique of Judgment,* p. 207.

31. Sigmund Freud, "Humor," in *Character and Culture,* ed. Phillip Rieff (New York: Collier Books, 1963), p. 264.

32. Ibid., p. 263.

33. Freud, *Jokes,* p. 290.

34. Ibid., p. 265.

35. Ibid., p. 293.

36. This is the standard psychoanalytic term used to translate the ambiguous German word *Besetzung,* which means (among other things) "occupy," "charge" (as in electrical charge), "possess." It denotes the energetic forces that are invested in mental phenomena. A cathexis urges toward the consummation of mental acts, while an anti-cathexis blocks the consummation of those same acts. Objects, too, are sometimes said to be cathected insofar as an individual invests a quantum of energy in the desire for them. In a letter to Ernest Jones, Freud suggests that the English word *interest* would provide an adequate translation of *Besetzung.* See Peter Gay, *Freud: A Life For Our Time* (New York: W.W. Norton and Company, 1988), p. 465 n.

37. Bergson, *Laughter,* p. 10.

38. Morreall, ed., "Amusement and Other Mental States," in *Philosophy of Laughter and Humor*, p. 221.

39. Ibid., p. 222.

40. Morreall thinks of humor as a relatively late evolutionary development. Practical, emotional responses come first in our history. If this is in fact the case, then it may suggest why Freud talks as though the humorous response is a kind of unexpected reaction as opposed to some of the more "natural" emotional reactions. Perhaps base, emotional responses to incongruity are the initial, unthinking response of our organisms today because they are tried and true, having served us well in the battle for survival. Humor, as a later development, may be a response still in the process of being refined. It is a less developed capacity, far from instinctual, but holding long-term promise. The rules of emotions, in other words, may be more deeply inscribed into our natures than the preliminary guidelines of humor. If such is the case, it might explain why an emotional response would appear more automatic, more "hardwired," than does a humorous response. The construction of humor still requires work. It has not as yet become an instinctual capacity.

41. Morreall, *Comedy, Tragedy, and Religion*, p. 148.

42. de Sousa, *The Rationality of Emotion*, p. 287. The label comes from combining Horace Walpole's and Henri Bergson's last names. Horace Walpole is famous for the saying, "The world is a comedy for those who think, a tragedy for those who feel." Apparently de Sousa considers the sentiment underlying this statement one that radically separates humor and emotion. I'm not so sure about that. We are, of course, creatures who both think and feel.

43. Bakhtin, p. 71.

44. Ibid., p. 81.

45. Ibid., p. 82.

46. Ibid., p. 71.

47. Ibid., p. 123.

48. Harvey Mindess, *Laughter and Liberation* (Los Angeles: Nash Publishing, 1971), p. 206.

49. Marie Collins Swabey, *Comic Laugher: A Philosophical Essay* (n.p.: Archon Books, 1970), p. 185.

50. Psychologists Herbert M. Lefcourt and Rod A. Martin conclude that the humorous attitude, specifically as delineated by Freud, is associated with a sense of personal mastery. See Herbert M. Lefcourt and Rod A. Martin, *Humor and Life Stress: Antidote to Adversity* (New York: Springer-Verlag, 1986).

51. Arthur Asa Berger, *An Anatomy of Humor* (New Brunswick: Transaction Publishers, 1993), p. 163.

52. Ibid., p. 164.

53. Ibid., pp. 164–165.

54. Mindess, p. 214.

55. William F. Fry and Melanie Allen, "Humor as a Creative Experience: The Development of a Hollywood Humorist," in *Humor and Laughter: Theory, Research, and Applications,* ed. Anthony Chapman and Hugh C. Foot (New York: John Wiley & Sons, 1976), pp. 245–247.

56. Koestler, *The Act of Creation,* p. 95.

57. See Freud, "The Moses of Michelangelo," in *Character and Culture,* pp. 80–106.

58. See Freud, *Future of an Illusion* (New York: Anchor Books, 1964).

59. Bergson comes to mind once again.

60. Ted Cohen, *Jokes* (Chicago: The University of Chicago Press, 1999), p. 12.

61. Not everyone has approached this story with a sense of humor. Gogol, in 1836, submitted *The Nose* to *The Contemporary Review.* It was rejected for being too sordid. See David Magarshack, introduction to *The Overcoat and Other Tales of Good and Evil,* by Nicolai V. Gogol (New York: W.W. Norton and Company, 1965), p. 7.

CONCLUSION

1. Nishitani, *The Self-Overcoming of Nihilism,* p. 3.

2. Heidegger, *Nietzsche Vol. Four,* p. 221.

3. Ibid., p. 226.

4. Simone de Beavoir, in fact, claims that seriousness is a form of "bad faith" that denies us the freedom at the foundation of human being. See de Beavoir, pp. 46–57. Because the serious person subordinates himself to "values that are unconditioned" (p. 46), this individual falsely and inauthetically becomes committed to absolute ends. She, quite correctly, sees in the nihilist a "disappointed seriousness" (p. 52), insofar as the nihilist comes to accept that the highest values, or ends, are beyond realization. However, she incorrectly thinks of the nihilist as one who absolutely rejects the worthiness of all values on this basis, and that in so doing the nihilist ends up with "a positive desire for destruction" (p. 57). De Beavoir, thus, along with so many others, spuriously emphasizes negativity and destructiveness as an essential part of nihilism. Furthermore, she does so in a strange way that borders on incoherence. After telling us about the dangerous fanaticism of the "serious man," she then also tells us that the nihilist, who "contests the serious world" (p. 57), is also dangerous due to a "rejection of the world and man" (p. 57). In other words, both the serious and those who lack seriousness are dangerous and deluded.

5. Bakhtin, p. 123.

6. Freud, "Humor," p. 268.

7. Kaufman, *Tragedy and Philosophy,* p. 40.

8. Erasmus, *The Praise of Folly* (1668), trans. John Wilson (Ann Arbor: The University of Michigan Press, 1958), p. 51.

POSTSCRIPT

1. It might be pointed out that Ted Kaczynski (The Unabomber) in fact suffers from mental illness. However, he also graduated from Harvard and the University of Michigan, worked as a mathematics professor at the University of California at Berkeley, and published a number of professional papers in addition to writing his manifesto *Industrial Society and Its Future*. It would be a fallacy of the ad hominem variety to dismiss all of Kaczynski's arguments and claims solely because he suffers from mental illness.

2. Ted Kaczynski, *Industrial Society and Its Future,* in Nancy Gibbs et al., *Mad Genius* (New York: Warner Books, 1996), pp. 244–245.

3. Ibid., p. 244.

Bibliography

Adams, Joey. *The Joey Adams Joke Dictionary*. New York: The Citadel Press, 1962.

Allison, David B., ed. *The New Nietzsche: Contemporary Styles of Interpretation*. New York: Delta, 1977.

Ames, Van Meter. "Existentialism: Irrational, Nihilistic." *Humanist* 1 (February 1950): pp. 15–22.

Ansell-Pearson, Keith. *An Introduction to Nietzsche as Political Thinker: The Perfect Nihilist*. New York: Cambridge University Press, 1994.

Aquinas, Thomas. *Basic Writings of St. Thomas Aquinas*, Vol. I. Edited by Anton C. Pegis. New York: Random House, 1945.

Aristotle. *The Basic Works of Aristotle*. Edited by Richard McKeon. New York: Random House, 1941.

Bach, Kent. *Exit Existentialism: A Philosophy of Self-Awareness*. Belmont, CA: Wadsworth, 1973.

Bakhtin, Mikhail. *Rabelais and His World*. Translated by Helene Iswolsky. Cambridge: MIT Press, 1968.

Bakunin, Mikhail. *The Political Philosophy of Bakunin: Scientific Anarchism*. Edited by G. P. Maximoff. New York: Free Press, 1953.

———. *God and The State*. New York: Dover, 1970.

———. *Bakunin on Violence: Letter to S. Nechayev*. New York: Anarchist Switchboard, n.d.

Barrett, David, ed. *Aristophanes: The Wasps, The Poet and the Women, The Frogs*. New York: Penguin Books, 1964.

Barrett, William. *Irrational Man*. New York: Anchor Books, 1962.

———. *Death of the Soul*. New York: Anchor Books, 1986.

Bataille, Georges. *My Mother, Madame Edwarda, The Dead Man*. New York: Marion Boyars, 1995.

Baudelaire, Charles. *The Essence of Laughter and Other Essays, Journals, and Letters.* Edited by Peter Quennell. New York: Meridian Books, 1956.

Beauvoir, Simone de. *The Ethics of Ambiguity.* Translated by Bernard Frechtman. Secaucus: Citadel Press, 1997.

Bentley, Eric. "Tragedy and Comedy: Some Generalizations." *Types of Drama: Plays and Essays, Fourth Edition.* Edited by Sylvan Barnet, Morton Berman, and William Burto. Boston, Toronto: Little, Brown, 1985.

Berger, Arthur Asa. *An Anatomy of Humor.* New Brunswick, NJ: Transaction, 1993.

Bergson, Henri. *Laughter: An Essay on the Meaning of the Comic.* Translated by Cloudesley Brereton and Fred Rothwell. Los Angeles: Green Integer Books, 1999.

The Bible. Revised Standard Edition. New York: American Bible Society, 1952.

Bloom, Alan. *The Closing of the American Mind.* New York: Simon and Schuster, 1987.

Brinton, Crane. *Nietzsche.* New York: Harper Torchbooks, 1965.

Brittan, Arthur. *Masculinity and Power.* New York: Basil Blackwell, 1989.

Buddha. *Wisdom of the Buddha: The Unabridged Dhammapada.* Translated and edited by F. Max Müller. Mineola, NY: Dover, 2000.

Burke, Edmund. *A Philosophical Enquiry Into the Origin of Our Ideas of the Sublime and Beautiful.* Edited by James T. Boulton. Notre Dame: University of Notre Dame Press, 1968.

Camus, Albert. *The Myth of Sisyphus and Other Essays.* Translated by Justin O'Brien. New York: Random House, 1955.

———. *The Rebel.* Translated by Anthony Bower. New York: Vintage Books, 1956.

———. *The Stranger.* Translated by Stuart Gilbert. New York: Vintage Books, 1946.

Carr, Karen Leslie. *The Banalization of Nihilism.* Albany: State University of New York Press, 1992.

Cartwright, Nancy. *Nature's Capacities and Their Measurement.* New York: Oxford University Press, 1989.

Chapman, Antony J., and Hugh C. Foot, eds. *Humor and Laughter: Theory, Research, and Applications.* New York: John Wiley, 1976.

Chase, Alston. "Harvard and the Making of the Unabomber." *The Atlantic Monthly* 285, no. 6 (June 2000): pp. 41–65.

Chernyshevsky, Nikolai. *What is to Be Done?* (1863). Translated by Michael R. Katz. Ithaca: Cornell University Press, 1989.

Cho, Stephen Wagner. "Before Nietzsche: Nihilism as a Critique of German Idealism." *Graduate Faculty Philosophy Journal* 18, no. 1 (1995): pp. 205–232.

Cioran, E. M. *On the Heights of Despair.* Translated by Ilinca Zarifopol-Johnston. Chicago: University of Chicago Press, 1992.

———. *A Short History of Decay.* Translated by Richard Howard. New York: Arcade, 1998.

Clark, John P. *Max Stirner's Egoism.* London: Freedom Press, 1976.

Cohen, Ted. *Jokes: Philosophical Thoughts on Joking Matters.* Chicago: University of Chicago Press, 1999.

Crankshaw, Edward. *The Shadow of the Winter Palace: The Drift to Revolution 1825–1917.* New York: Penguin Books, 1976.

Crosby, Donald A. *The Specter of the Absurd: Sources and Criticisms of Modern Nihilism.* Albany: State University of New York Press, 1988.

Crowther, Paul. *Critical Aesthetics and Postmodernism.* New York: Oxford University Press, 1996.

Danto, Arthur. *Nietzsche as Philosopher.* New York: Columbia University Press, 1980.

Dauer, Francis Wantanabe. "The Picture as the Medium of Humorous Incongruity." *American Philosophical Quarterly* 25, no. 3 (July 1988): pp. 241–251.

de Sousa, Ronald. *The Rationality of Emotion.* Cambridge: MIT Press, 1997.

Dewey, John. *Reconstruction in Philosophy.* Boston: Beacon Press, 1957.

Dostoyevsky, Fyador. *Notes from Underground, Poor People, The Friend of the Family.* Translated by Constance Garnett. New York: Dell, 1960.

———. *Crime and Punishment.* Translated by Constance Garnett. New York: Bantam Books, 1982.

Durkheim, Emile. *Suicide.* Edited by George Simpson. Translated by John A. Spaulding. New York: Free Press, 1951.

Edwards, James C. *The Plain Sense of Things: The Fate of Religion in an Age of Normal Nihilism.* University Park: Pennsylvania University Press, 1997.

Engel, S. Morris. *With Good Reason: An Introduction to Informal Fallacies.* New York: St. Martin's Press, 1994.

Erasmus. *The Praise of Folly.* Translated by John Wilson. Ann Arbor: University of Michigan Press, 1958.

Fandozzi, Phillip R. *Nihilism and Technology.* Washington, DC: University Press of America, 1982.

Fischer, Klaus P. *History and Prophecy: Oswald Spengler and the Decline of the West.* Durham, SC: Moore, 1977.

Frankfurt, Harry G. *The Importance of What We Care About: Philosophical Essays.* New York: Cambridge University Press, 1988.

———. *Necessity, Volition, and Love.* New York: Cambridge University Press, 1999.

Frankl, Viktor E. *Man's Search for Meaning: An Introduction to Logotherapy.* Boston: Beacon Press, 1992.

Freud, Sigmund. *Jokes and Their Relation to the Unconscious.* Edited and translated by James Strachey. New York: W.W. Norton, 1960.

———. *Civilization and Its Discontents.* Edited and translated by James Strachey. New York: W.W. Norton, 1961.

———. *Beyond the Pleasure Principle*. Edited and translated by James Strachey. New York, W.W. Norton, 1961.

———. *An Autobiographical Study*. Translated by James Strachey. New York: W.W. Norton, 1963.

———. *Character and Culture*. Edited by Phillip Rieff. New York: Collier Books, 1963.

———. *The Future of an Illusion*. Edited by James Strachey. Translated by W. D. Robson-Scott. Garden City, NY: Anchor Books, 1964.

———. *New Introductory Lectures on Psychoanalysis*. Edited and translated by James Strachey. New York: W.W. Norton, 1965.

———. *Introductory Lectures on Psychoanalysis*. Edited and translated by James Strachey. New York: W.W. Norton, 1977.

Gadamer, Hans-Georg. *Truth and Method*. New York: Continuum, 1997.

Gay, Peter. *Freud: A Life For Our Time*. New York: W.W. Norton, 1988.

Gibbs, Nancy et al. *Mad Genius: The Odyssey, Pursuit, and Capture of the Unabomber Suspect*. New York: Warner Books, 1996.

Gillespie, Michael Allen. *Nihilism Before Nietzsche*. Chicago: University of Chicago Press, 1995.

———, and Tracy B. Strong, eds. *Nietzsche's New Seas: Explorations in Philosophy, Aesthetics, and Politics*. Chicago: University of Chicago Press, 1988.

Gillman, Sander, ed. *Conversations With Nietzsche*. New York: Oxford University Press, 1987.

Gogol, Nicolai V. *The Overcoat and Other Tales of Good and Evil*. Translated by David Magarshack. New York: W.W. Norton, 1957.

Goudsblom, Johan. *Nihilism and Culture*. Totowa, NJ: Rowman and Littlefield, 1980.

Gurewitch, Morton. *Comedy: The Irrational Vision*. Ithaca: Cornell University Press, 1975.

Harper, Ralph. *The Seventh Solitude*. Baltimore: John Hopkins University Press, 1967.

Heidegger, Martin. *Nietzsche*. Edited and translated by David Farrell Krell. New York: HarperCollins, 1991.

———. *Basic Writings*. Edited and translated by David Farrell Krell. New York: HarperCollins, 1993.

———. *Being and Time*. Translated by Joan Stambaugh. Albany: State University of New York Press, 1996.

Honderich, Ted, ed. *Oxford Companion to Philosophy*. New York: Oxford University Press, 1995.

Hospers, John, ed. *Introductory Readings in Aesthetics*. London: Free Press, 1969.

Huges, H. Stuart. *Oswald Spengler: A Critical Estimate*. New York: Charles Scribner's Sons, 1962.

Humphreys, Richard. *Futurism*. New York: Cambridge University Press, 1999.

Jacobi, Friedrich Heinrich. *The Main Philosophical Writings and the Novel Allwill*. Buffalo: McGill-Queens University Press, 1994.

Kant, Immanuel. *Critique of Pure Reason*. Translated by Norman Kemp Smith. New York: St. Martin's Press, 1965.

———. *Grounding for the Metaphysics of Morals*. Translated by James W. Ellington. Indianapolis: Hackett, 1981.

———. *Critique of Judgment*. Translated by Werner S. Pluhar. Indianapolis: Hackett, 1987.

Kaufman, Walter. *Nietzsche: Philosopher, Psychologist, Antichrist*. Princeton: Princeton University Press, 1974.

———. *Tragedy and Philosophy*. Princeton: Princeton University Press, 1992.

———, ed. *Existentialism from Dostoevsky to Sartre*. New York: Meridian Books, 1975.

Kelly, Aileen. *Mikhail Bakunin: A Study in the Politics of Utopianism*. New Haven and London: Yale University Press, 1987.

Kielkopf, Charles F. "The Logic of Nihilism." *New Scholasticism* 49 (Spring 1975): pp. 162–176.

Kierkegaard, Søren. *The Sickness unto Death*. Edited and Translated by Howard V. Hong and Edna H. Hong. Princeton: Princeton University Press, 1980.

———. *Fear and Trembling*. Translated by Alastair Hannay. New York: Penguin Books, 1985.

Koestler, Arthur. *The Act of Creation*. New York: Macmillan, 1967.

Korsmeyer, Carolyn. "Disgust." *Aesthetics as Philosophy: Proceedings of the XIV International Congress for Aesthetics*. Edited by Alec Erjavec. Ljubljana, Slovenia, 1999.

Kutasova, I. M. "Albert Camus: Nihilist vs. Nihilism." *Soviet Studies in Philosophy* 14 (Spring 1976): pp. 72–92.

Kuvakin, Valery A., ed. *A History of Russian Philosophy: From the Tenth Through the Twentieth Centuries*. Buffalo: Prometheus Books, 1994.

Lawler, James. "Marx's Theory of Socialisms: Nihilistic and Dialectical." In *Debating Marx*. Edited by Louis Patsouras. Lewiston, N.Y.: Edwin Mellen Press, 1994.

Lefcourt, Herbert M., and Rod A. Martin. *Humor and Life Stress: Antidote to Adversity*. New York: Springer-Verlag, 1986.

Levin, David Michael. *The Body's Recollection of Being*. Boston: Routledge and Kegan Paul, 1985.

———. *The Opening of Vision: Nihilism and the Postmodern Situation*. New York: Routledge, 1988.

———, ed. *Pathologies of the Modern Self*. New York: New York University Press, 1987.

Locke, Edwin A., and Gary P. Latham. *A Theory of Goal Setting and Task Performance*. New Jersey: Prentice Hall, 1990.

Locke, Edwin A., Gary P. Latham, Lise M. Saari, and Karyll N. Shaw. "Goal Setting and Task Performance: 1969–1980." *Psychological Bulletin* 90, no. 1 (1981): pp. 125–152.

Long, A. A. *Hellenistic Philosophy*. Berkeley: University of California Press, 1986.

Lovell, Stephan. "Nihilism, Russian." In *Routledge Encyclopedia of Philosophy*. New York: Routledge, 1998.

Lowell, Robert. *Notebook*. New York: Farrar, Straus and Giroux, 1970.

Löwith, Karl. *Martin Heidegger and European Nihilism*. New York: Columbia University Press, 1995.

Lyotard, Jean-Francois. *The Postmodern Condition: A Report on Knowledge*. Minneapolis: University of Minnesota Press, 1997.

MacGreggor, Geddes. *Dictionary of Religion and Philosophy*. New York: Paragon House, 1989.

Macintyre, Ben. *Forgotten Fatherland: The Search For Elisabeth Nietzsche*. New York: Farrar, Straus and Giroux, 1992.

Marty, Martin E. *The Varieties of Unbelief*. New York: Anchor Books, 1966.

Matson, Wallace I. *A New History of Philosophy: Volumes I and II*. New York: Harcourt Brace Jovanovich, 1987.

McKay, John, Bennett Hill, and John Buckler. *A History of World Societies*. Boston: Houghton Mifflin, 1996.

McKinney, Ronald H. "Coping With Postmodernism: Christian Comedy and Tragedy." *Philosophy Today* 41, no. 4/4 (Winter 1997): pp. 520–529.

Mindess, Harvey. *Laughter and Liberation*. Los Angeles: Nash, 1971.

Mishima, Yukio. *Confessions of a Mask*. Translated by Meredith Weatherby. New York: New Directions, 1958.

——— . *Sun and Steel*. Translated by John Bester. New York: Kodansha, 1982.

——— . *The Way of the Samurai*. Translated by Kathryn Sparling. New York: Perigee Books, 1983.

Morreall, John. *Taking Laughter Seriously*. Albany: State University of New York Press, 1983.

——— . *Comedy, Tragedy, and Religion*. Albany: State University of New York Press, 1999.

——— , ed. *The Philosophy of Laughter and Humor*. Albany: State University of New York Press, 1987.

Murdoch, Iris. *The Sovereignty of Good*. New York: Schocken Books, 1971.

Nathan, John. *Mishima: A Biography*. Boston: Little Brown, 1974.

Nechayev, Sergei. *Catechism of the Revolutionary*. London: Violette Nozieres Press and AK Press, 1974.

Nietzsche, Friedrich. *The Will to Power*. Edited by Walter Kaufman. Translated by Walter Kaufman and R. J. Hollingdale. New York: Vintage Books, 1967.

————. *Basic Writings of Nietzsche*. Edited and translated by Walter Kaufman. New York: Random House, 1968.

————. *The Gay Science*. Translated by Walter Kaufman. New York: Vintage Books, 1974.

————. *The Portable Nietzsche*. Edited and translated by Walter Kaufman. New York: Penguin Books, 1984.

————. *The Birth of Tragedy*. Translated by Clifton P. Fadiman. New York: Dover, 1995.

Nishitani, Keiji. *The Self-Overcoming of Nihilism*. Translated by Graham Parkes with Setsuko Aihara. Albany: State University of New York Press, 1990.

Novak, Michael. *The Experience of Nothingness*. New York: Harper and Row, 1971.

————. *Awakening from Nihilism*. n.p.: Crisis Books, 1995.

Patterson, R. W. K. *The Nihilistic Egoist, Max Stirner*. New York: Oxford University Press, 1971.

Payne, Robert. *The Terrorists*. New York: Funk and Wagnalls, 1957.

Pervin, Lawrence A., ed. *Goal Concepts in Personality and Social Psychology*. London: Lawrence Erlbaum Associates, 1989.

Pfeifer, Karl. "Laughter, Freshness, and Titillation." *Inquiry* 40 (February 1997): pp. 307–322.

Plato. *Plato's Republic*. Translated by G. M. A. Grube. Indianapolis: Hackett, 1974.

————. *Symposium and Phaedrus*. New York: Dover, 1993.

Polanyi, Michael. *Beyond Nihilism*. New York: Cambridge University Press, 1960.

Popkin, Richard H. *The History of Scepticism From Erasmus to Descartes*. New York: Koninklijke Van Gorcum, 1960.

Pratt, Alan R., ed. *The Dark Side: Thoughts of the Futility of Life from the Ancient Greeks to the Present*. New York: Citadel Press, 1994.

Rauschning, Hermann. *The Revolution of Nihilism: Warning to the West*. New York: Alliance, 1939.

Reese, W. L. *Dictionary of Philosophy and Religion*. Atlantic Highlands, NJ: Humanities Press, 1980.

Robinson, Jenefer. "Startle." *The Journal of Philosophy* 92, no. 2 (February 1995): pp. 53–74.

Rorty, Richard. *Contingency, Irony, and Solidarity*. New York: Cambridge University Press, 1999.

Rosen, Stanley. *Nihilism: A Philosophical Essay*. New Haven: Yale University Press, 1969.

Scott-Stokes, Henry. *The Life and Death of Yukio Mishima*. New York: Dell, 1975.

Smith, Huston. *The World's Religions*. New York: HarperCollins, 1991.

Smith, James Leroy. "Nihilism and the Arts." *Journal of Aesthetics and Art Criticism*. 33 (Spring 1975): pp. 329–338.

Sogomonov, Y., and P. Landesman. *Nihilism Today*. Moscow: Progress, 1977.

Spengler, Oswald. *The Decline of the West*. Translated by Charles Francis Atkinson. New York: Alfred A. Knopf, 1937.

———. *Letters of Oswald Spengler, 1913–1936*. Edited and translated by Arthur Helps. New York: Alfred A. Knopf, 1966.

———. *Selected Essays*. Chicago: Henry Regnery, 1967.

Starrs, Roy. *Deadly Dialectics: Sex, Death, and Nihilism in the Works of Yukio Mishima*. Honolulu: University of Hawaii Press, 1994.

Stirner, Max. *The Ego and Its Own*. Translated by Steven Byington. London: Rebel Press, 1993.

———. *The False Principle of Our Education*. Edited by James J. Martin. Translated by Robert H. Beebe. Colorado Springs: Ralph Myles, 1984.

Swabey, Marie Collins. *Comic Laughter: A Philosophical Essay*. n.p.: Archon Books, 1970.

Taylor, Charles. *The Ethics of Authenticity*. Cambridge: Harvard University Press, 1991.

Thielicke, Helmut. *Nihilism: Its Origin and Nature—With a Christian Answer*. Translated by John W. Doberstein. New York: Schocken Books, 1969.

Turgenev, Ivan S. *Fathers and Sons* (1862). Translated by George Reavy. New York: Modern Library, n.d.

Vattimo, Gianni. *The End of Modernity*. Baltimore: The John Hopkins Press, 1988.

Watson, Richard A. *The Breakdown of Cartesian Metaphysics*. Atlantic Highlands, NJ: Humanities Press, 1987.

West, Cornel. *Race Matters*. Boston: Beacon Press, 1993.

Wheelis, Allen. *The Moralist*. Baltimore: Penguin Books, 1974.

———. *The Listener: A Psychoanalyst Examines His Life*. New York: W.W. Norton, 1999.

White, Alan. "Nietzschean Nihilism: A Typology." *International Studies in Philosophy* 19 (Summer 1987): pp. 29–44.

Willhoite Jr., Fred H. *Beyond Nihilism: Albert Camus's Contribution to Political Thought*. Baton Rouge: Louisiana State University, 1968.

Yamamoto, Tsunetomo. *Hagakure*. Translated by William Scott Wilson. New York: Avon Books, 1979.

Yarmolinsky, Avrahm. *The Road to Revolution: A Century of Russian Radicalism*. Princeton: Princeton University Press, 1986.

Yourcenar, Marguerite. *Mishima: A Vision of the Void*. Translated by Alberto Manguel. New York: Farrar, Straus and Giroux, 1987.

INDEX

Absurdity, 47–49, 64–65, 68, 81, 85, 95, 131, 149, 153, 168
Adler, Alfred, 105
Aesthetic thinking, 100
Alienation, 2, 8, 35, 64, 71, 84; epistemological, 69; ethical, 69–70; existential, 69; ontological, 69; political, 69–70
Allen, Melanie, 148
Ambiguity, 136, 140, 148, 150, 153
America. *See* United States
Amusement, 4, 124, 131–135, 137, 143, 145, 150, 152, 154, 164–165, 168
Anarchism, 18, 22–24, 27, 32, 34, 45, 49, 72, 94
Anger, 142
Anguish, 50, 75, 83
Anomie, 57
Ansell-Pearson, Keith, 34
The Antichrist, 40
Antinomies, 186n.30
Anxiety, 1, 5, 36, 38, 43, 64, 68, 83, 93, 94, 118, 124, 126, 132, 156, 164
Apollonian, 24–26, 31, 40–41, 48, 64
Aquinas, Saint Thomas, 187n.9
Arendt, Hannah, 41
Aristophanes, 140
Aristotle, 9, 26, 34, 115, 135, 139–140, 144
Argumenta ad Baculum, 48
Asia, 7, 50, 55, 65; China, 65; India, 65. *See also* Japan

Ataraxia, 78–79, 81
Atheism, 46, 64
Attic Tragedy, 26
Augustine, Saint, 174n.4
Authenticity, 35, 41, 56–57, 95. *See also* Inauthenticity
Awakening From Nihilism, 58

Bach, Kent, 184n.27
Bad faith, 65, 192n.4
Bakhtin, Mikhail, 146, 147, 162
Bakunin, Mikhail, 15, 19, 58, 62, 64, 73, 94–95, 176n.17, 177n.9
Barrett, William, 43–44
Bataille, Georges, 180n.29
Bazarov, 18, 29, 34, 64
Beauty, 2, 115. *See also* Ideals
Becoming, 37–38
Being, 2, 6, 24–25, 32, 35, 37–39, 52–53, 64–65, 69, 73, 105–107, 109–110, 115, 120, 156–158, 164, 167; beings, 35, 39; being-in-the-world, 35; being-toward-death, 36, 103. *See also* Ideals
Being and Time. See *Sein Und Zeit*
Bentley, Eric, 140
Berger, Arthur Asa, 148
Bergson, Henri, 134–135, 142, 147–148, 185n.16, 189n.11
Berdayev, Nicholas, 19
Besetzung, 190n.36

203